COMMON and SCIENTIFIC NAMES of FISHES from the UNITED STATES and CANADA

Fifth Edition

Funding for the publication of this book was provided by the

U.S. Fish and Wildlife Service

AMERICAN FISHERIES SOCIETY
Special Publication 20

COMMON and SCIENTIFIC NAMES of FISHES from the UNITED STATES and CANADA

Fifth Edition, 1991

C. Richard Robins, *Chairman*
Reeve M. Bailey, Carl E. Bond, James R. Brooker, Ernest A. Lachner, Robert N. Lea, and W. B. Scott

Committee on Names of Fishes

Bethesda, Maryland 1991

Library of Congress Catalog Card Number: 90-86052

ISBN 0-913235-69-5 (paper)
ISBN 0-913235-70-9 (cloth)
ISSN 0097-0638

Address orders to

American Fisheries Society
5410 Grosvenor Lane, Suite 110
Bethesda, Maryland 20814-2199, USA

CONTENTS

LIST OF FAMILIES[1]

[1] For explanatory comments on the spellings in this list see page 4.

INTRODUCTION

Each edition of the list of the names of fishes of the United States and Canada has been a major revision and enlargement of its predecessor; this fifth edition is no exception. The earlier lists, published in 1948, 1960, 1970, and 1980 as American Fisheries Society Special Publications 1, 2, 6, and 12, have been widely used and have contributed substantially toward the goal of achieving uniformity in common names and avoiding confusion in nomenclature. From 570 entries in the 1948 list, coverage increased to 1,872 species in 1960, 2,131 in 1970, and 2,268 in 1980. The present edition includes 2,428 species. In this list, as in 1980, the Committee on Names of Fishes has endeavored to include common names for all native and established exotic species in the region of coverage. The number of exotic species found in our waters continues to rise. For many, however, there is no evidence that breeding populations have become established. Others are established in very limited waters and some, including species seemingly well entrenched, have been eliminated by unfavorable environmental conditions or by direct action of fishery managers. The exotic species included on our list and in Appendix 2, Table 1, are those that seem to be permanently and widely established. Other exotic species that are not included in the main list but are treated in Appendix 2 are species that have been collected in the field but have no known breeding populations (Table 2), species that have disappeared after having bred successfully or otherwise survived for substantial periods in our waters (Table 3), and exotic species established only in Hawaii (Table 4). In this edition, we also provide common names for those few hybrid fishes that are important in fishery management or in the sport or commercial fisheries. These hybrid combinations are given in Appendix 3.

Many of the additions to this fifth edition have resulted from more thorough surveys of mid- and outer-shelf areas along the Carolinas and of the Florida "Middle Grounds" in the eastern Gulf of Mexico, the Flower Garden reefs off Texas, and the Bering Sea. New species continue to be described from our fresh waters. More thorough systematic studies both have led to the recognition of species previously thought to be synonyms and, conversely, have demonstrated that some species on previous lists are synonyms and are thus to be removed from the list.

Comprehensive listing of all species in the area of coverage is attempted with the following exceptions. Many species that occur beyond our bathymetric (200 m) and geographical limits have early life history stages that have been caught in our shelf waters. These species are excluded from this list as are many mesopelagic species that may occur over the outer shelf off Florida, the west coast of the United States, and other areas where deep waters occur very close to shore. We have not tried to limit the list otherwise. All species, even if small, secretive, or rare, are of real or potential importance as laboratory experimental animals, in public or private aquaria, for bait, or (most often), simply as objects of natural history inquiry or aesthetic appeal. Some species once disdained as "trash fish" are commercially harvested and highly valued today. Considerable attention is being focused on using the by-catch of fisheries and, as a result, species formerly discarded are now entering the market place. An increased environmental consciousness has focused attention on native fishes as indicators of the condition of freshwater streams. Endangered species are written about in newspapers and popular magazines. Thus, comprehensive listing is fully justified. The book's plan of organization and indexing is such that comprehensiveness will not interfere with use of this list by those with special interests.

Area of Coverage

The present list purports to include all species of fishes known from the fresh waters of the continental United States and Canada, and those marine species inhabiting contiguous shore waters on or above the continental shelf, to a depth of 200 m (656 feet). In the Atlantic Ocean, the shore fishes from Greenland, eastern Canada and United States, and the northern Gulf of Mexico to the Rio Grande are included, but those from Iceland, Bermuda, the Bahamas, Cuba and the other West Indian islands, and Mexico are excluded unless they occur also in the region covered. In the Pacific, the area treated includes that part of the continental shelf from the Mexican–United States boundary to Bering Strait. The

Arctic shore waters of Alaska and Canada are included. Hawaii, with a large and strikingly different Indo-Pacific fish fauna, is excluded except that species introduced into Hawaiian waters are included in Appendix 2, Table 4. Deep-sea fishes, whether benthic or mesopelagic, are excluded unless adults appear in our shelf waters. In practice, this line of distinction is difficult to apply and becomes arbitrary, especially if the eggs and larval stages are considered. Pelagic fishes that enter waters over the continental shelf are included.

The list provides a general guide to occurrence: "A" denotes Atlantic Ocean and includes the Arctic Ocean east of the Boothia Peninsula (i.e., 95°W longitude); "P" refers to the Pacific Ocean and includes the western Arctic; and "F" indicates occurrence in fresh water. A bracketed "[I]" follows the indication of occurrence for any exotic (introduced) species established within our area of coverage; this symbol is not used for expanded distribution of a species within our areas. For example, shad and striped bass were successfully introduced into Pacific drainages from the Atlantic; on our list, their occurrence is indicated by A–F–P without [I]. An "[X]" indicates that the species is considered to be extinct (see the fourth edition, Appendix 4).

Some users of the list have suggested refinement of our occurrence notation to indicate major watersheds for the freshwater species. This need has been met by publication of the Atlas of North American Freshwater Fishes, by D. S. Lee et al., 1980, North Carolina State Museum of Natural History. Also, the transportation of species across watersheds, diversion of waterways, and other factors make refinement a difficult task. Thus, we have retained the simple guide to occurrence described above.

Synopsis of Families

Family names are important in information identification and retrieval. They are widely used in fishery literature, popular books on fishes, and dictionaries and encyclopedias. Changes in family names promote confusion and are to be avoided wherever possible.

Considerable disagreement exists concerning the spelling of many scientific names of families. For some, traditional spelling is demonstrably incorrect in a classical sense; for others the proper spelling is not so clearly derived. Traditional spellings, according to the International Commission on Zoological Nomenclature, are to be maintained, yet the Commission has amended traditional spellings in petitions submitted for other purposes. Thus, Echeneidae was changed to Echeneididae and the latter was placed on the Official List of Family-Group Names in Zoology. Such changes are deplored by this Committee. Adjectival variations of the family name are used by scientists in literature discussing such fishes; to our view echeneid and Echeneidae are more felicitous than echeneidid and Echeneididae. The Commission's views appear to have changed in this regard. It recently conserved Cobitidae (over the classically correct Cobitididae) and published remarks by the Commissioners included very strong statements deploring the past practice of the Commission. More cases involving family name spellings are pending.

The following families are those the spellings of which are in question or vary in current literature. The bold entry in each pair is the one judged to be grammatically correct. When neither entry is bold, available information is equivocal. Anarhichadidae (Anarhichantidae), Anoplopomidae (**Anoplopomatidae**), Dasyatidae (**Dasyatididae**), Echeneidae (**Echeneididae**). Eleotridae (**Eleotrididae**), Engraulidae (Engraulididae), Ephippidae (**Ephippididae**), Grammicolepidae (**Grammicolepididae**), Grammidae (**Grammatidae**). **Lampridae** (LampridAfter), Myliobatidae (**Myliobatididae**), Nettastomidae (**Nettastomatidae**), Odontaspidae (**Odontaspididae**), Paralepidae (**Paralepididae**), Pempheridae (**Pempherididae**), **Percophidae** (Percophididae), Pholidae (Pholididae), **Rhinobatidae** (Rhinobatididae), **Stomiidae** (Stomiatidae), Synodidae (**Synodontidae**). Our use follows prevailing recent practice. Thus we use Anoplopomatidae but Eleotridae and Engraulidae.

Some recent uses (e.g., Ostraciontidae for Ostraciidae, Carapodidae for Carapidae) are simply incorrect. These we have not attempted to identify here. Three families, the spelling of whose names were in contention, have now been ruled on by the International Commission; Cobitidae, Petromyzontidae, and Rhincodontidae, previously used by our Committee, are now officially correct.

For more extensive comment on this problem see G. C. Steyskal, 1980, "The Grammar of Family-Group Names as Exemplified by Those of Fishes," Proc. Biol. Soc. Wash. 93(1):168.

The Law of Priority now applies to family-group names (Article 23 of the International Code of Zoological Nomenclature) yet few ichthyological works include synonymies of such names. For some families, the name in use is not the earliest available (e.g., Pomadasyidae versus Haemulidae; Xenocongridae versus Chlopsidae). Determination of priority in family-group names is not easily resolved. Subsequent Latinization of a non-Latinized name published prior to 1900 is to be considered available from the original date of publication of the non-Latinized name (Article 11e). Until recently there has been little search of such matters. We have followed tradition except where clear cases have been made in the literature.

Ichthyologists vary widely in their interpretation of family limits. Cladists, particularly, have fragmented many families, sometimes in the face of conflicting data. Frequently, the clarification of one lineage only serves to destabilize other lines for which no solutions are proposed. Mayr, 1989, Auk 106:511, remonstrated that "no classification should be abandoned until it is definitely falsified. Otherwise we would have an incessant turmoil in our information retrieval systems." We agree. Generally we have interpreted family limits broadly, preferring to treat many groups at the subfamilial or tribal level.

Common Names

The Committee aims to develop a body of common names—a single common name for each species—that reflects broad current usage; to create a richer, more meaningful, and colorful vernacular nomenclature; and to promote mechanisms that will add to the stability and universality of names applied to U.S. and Canadian fishes. Common names of fishes as used in this list are applied to individual species. These names sometimes are employed as market names as well as for other purposes. However, market names often apply to several species or differ for various reasons from the names adopted in this list, and they have not been incorporated into this work. A summary of market names, as they apply to fishes marketed in the United States, is available in "The Fish List, FDA [Food and Drug Administration] Guide to Acceptable Market Names for Food Fish Sold in Interstate Commerce 1988," U.S. Government Printing Office.

The common name as here employed is viewed as a formal, usually anglicized appellation to be used in lieu of the Latinized scientific name of a species. Past history confirms that common names are more stable than scientific names. Generic names in particular are subject to interpretation and vacillation and will remain so. Common names are more readily adaptable to lay uses than scientific names. There is clear need for standardization and uniformity in vernacular names not only for sport and commercial fishes, but as trade names, for aquarium fishes, in legal terminology, and as substitutes for scientific names in popular or scientific writing. The Committee believes that it is desirable to establish a common name for each species of fish occurring naturally or through successful introduction in the waters of Canada and the United States.

Agreement on many names may be arrived at quickly, but others are attended by complications and marked disagreement develops. This disagreement is especially true of fish known by market names that differ from names that are more familiar to anglers, biologists, or others. The existence of different names in various parts of a species' geographic range creates difficulties that seem soluble only through arbitration. Conversely, a given name may be employed in several places for diverse species. Although Committee action on such situations may not be expected to change local use quickly, it seems plainly improper to sanction use of one name for two or more different species.

After struggling with common names for many years, the Committee on Names of Fishes realized the importance of establishing a set of guiding principles to be employed in the determination of names. Such a code permits a more objective appraisal of the relative merits among several names than if selection were based primarily on personal experience and preference. Consideration of many vernacular names of fishes makes it apparent that few principles can be established for which there will be no exceptions. Many exceptions exist because at the time the Committee began to function, a majority of our larger and more abundant, hence important, species had such firmly established common names that it would have been unrealistic to reject them just to conform to a principle. The name for a species may often be decided by weighing the pros and cons among the possible choices and selecting the one that best fits the aggregate of guiding criteria. The criteria that the Committee regards as appropriate to the selection of common names of fishes are repeated below from previous lists with some amplification.

Principles Governing Selection of Common Names

1. *A single vernacular name shall be accepted for each species or taxonomic unit included.* In the present list only one fish has two approved names: cisco and lake herring for *Coregonus artedi.*

2. *No two species on the list shall have the same approved name.* Commonly used names of extralimital species should be avoided wherever possible.

3. *The expression "common" as part of a fish's name shall be avoided wherever possible.*

4. *Simplicity in names is favored.* Hyphens, suffixes, and apostrophes shall be omitted (e.g., smallmouth bass) except when they are orthographically essential (e.g., three-eye flounder), have a special meaning (e.g., C-O sole), are necessary to avoid possible misunderstanding (e.g., cusk-eel), or join two fish names, neither of which represents the fish in question, into a single name (e.g., the trout-perch, which is neither a trout nor a perch). Compounded modifying words, including paired structures, should usually be treated as singular nouns in apposition with a group name (e.g., spottail shiner, soupfin shark), but a plural modifier should usually be placed in adjectival form (e.g., blackbanded sunfish, spotted hake) unless its plural nature is obvious (e.g., fourspot flounder). Preference shall be given to names that are short and euphonious.

The compounding of brief, familiar words into a single name, written without a hyphen, may in some cases promote clarity and simplicity (e.g., tomcod, goldfish, mudminnow), but the habitual practice of combining words, especially those that are lengthy, awkward, or unfamilar, shall be avoided.

5. *Common names shall not be capitalized in text use except for those elements that are proper names.* (e.g., rainbow trout, but Sacramento perch).

6. *Names intended to honor persons (e.g., Allison's tuna, Julia's darter) are discouraged in that they are without descriptive value.* In some large groups, identical specific patronyms in the scientific names (sometimes honoring different persons) exist in related genera, and use of a patronym in the common name is confusing. In a few instances, patronyms have become so incorporated into the vernacular that they are not treated or recognized as such. These names are accepted and not capitalized (e.g., guppy, lane snapper).

7. *Only clearly defined and well-marked taxonomic entities* (usually species) *shall be assigned common names.* Most subspecies are not suitable subjects for common names, but forms that are so different in appearance (not just in geographic distribution) as to be distinguished readily by anglers, commercial fishermen, or laypersons, or for which a common name constitutes an important aid in communication, may merit separate names. There is a wide divergence of opinion concerning the criteria for recognition of subspecies. We have not named subspecies except for *Esox americanus*, the ranges of two subpecies of which overlap in the St. Lawrence watershed in an open-circle type of distribution. Subspecies have importance in evolutionary inquiry but are rarely of significance to laypersons or to biological endeavors in which common names are of concern. The common name for the species should apply to all subspecies of a taxon and may be appropriately modified by those treating subspecies. The practice of adding geographic modifiers to designate regional populations makes for a cumbersome terminology.

Hybrids are usually not named, but those important in fish management and which have established common names are treated in Appendix 3. Cultured varieties, phases, and morphological variants are not named even though they are important in commercial trade and culture of aquarium fish (e.g., the many varieties of goldfish and common carp).

8. *The common name shall not be intimately tied to the scientific name.* Thus, the vagaries of scientific nomenclature do not entail constant changing of common names. The practice of applying a name to each genus, a modifying name for each species, and still another modifier for each subspecies, while appealing in its simplicity, has the defect of inflexibility. It is simply an attempt to recreate in the vernacular name the scientific nomenclature. If a fish is transferred from genus to genus, or shifted from species to subspecies or vice versa, the common name should nevertheless remain unaffected. It is not a primary function of common names to indicate relationship. When two or more taxonomic groups (e.g., nominal species) are found to be identical, one name shall be adopted for the combined group.

9. *Names shall not violate the tenets of good taste.*

The preceding principles are largely in the nature of procedural dicta. Those given below are criteria that are regarded as aids in the selection of suitable names.

10. *Colorful, romantic, fanciful, metaphorical, and otherwise distinctive and original names are especially appropriate.* Such terminology adds to the richness and breadth of the nomenclature and yields a harvest of satisfaction to the user. Examples of such names include Dolly Varden, madtom, hogchoker, garibaldi, pumpkinseed, flier, angelfish, midshipman, and chilipepper.

11. *American Indian or any other native names are welcome for adoption as common names.* Indian names in current use include muskellunge, eulachon, mummichog, chinook, tautog, menhaden, and cisco.

12. *Regardless of origin, truly vernacular names that are widespread and in common use by the public are to be retained wherever possible.* In addition to aboriginal names, many now well-known names of North American fishes have originated with non-English-speaking fishermen: barracuda, cero, grouper, pompano, sierra (Spanish); bocaccio (Italian); capelin, inconnu (French); mako (Maori). Although too little genuine originality is evident, many excellent names have been developed by North American immigrants. Most of these conform to principles 14 and 15 below. Care should be taken to avoid words that mean the same thing in related languages but differ slightly in spelling (e.g., sierra in Spanish and serra in Portuguese).

13. *Commonly employed names adopted from traditional English usage* (e.g., cod, pike, sole, flounder, bass, perch, chub, minnow) *are given considerable latitude in taxonomic placement.* Adherence to customary English practice is to be preferred if this does not conflict with the broad general usage of another name. Many English names, however, have been applied to similar but often distantly related fishes in North America. We find "perch" in use for representatives of at least nine families of spiny-rayed fishes. "Chub" appears in such unrelated groups as the Salmonidae, Cyprinidae, and Kyphosidae. The ocean whitefish (*Caulolatilus princeps*) is not a salmonid and the Pacific pompano (*Peprilus simillimus*) is not a carangid, yet each is best known to fishermen throughout its range by the name indicated. For widely known species, the Committee believes it preferable to recognize general use than to adopt bookish or pedantic substitutes. Thus, established practice should outweigh consistency with original English usage. This is not well understood by some ichthyologists who continue to write the Committee to suggest that perch should not be used for an embiotocid or blenny and eel for certain stichaeids. Some problems have been avoided or minimized by combining names to create new words (e.g., seatrout for sea trout, mudsucker for mud sucker, surfperch for surf perch); such combinations have gained wide acceptance since they were adopted by the Committee in its earlier lists.

14. *Structural attributes, color, and color pattern are desirable sources of names and are commonly so used.* Sailfin, flathead, slippery, giant, mottled, copper, tripletail, and a multitude of other descriptors decorate fish names. Efforts should be made to select terms that are descriptively accurate, and to hold repetition of those most frequently employed (e.g., white, black, spotted, banded) to a minimum.

Following tradition in North American ichthyology and herpetology, we have attempted to restrict use of "line" or "stripe" to mean longitudinal marks that parallel the body axis and "bar" or "band" to mean vertical or transverse marks.

15. *Ecological characteristics are useful in making good names.* Such terms should be properly descriptive. Modifiers such as reef, coral, sand, rock, lake, riffle, freshwater, and mountain are well known in fish names.

16. *Geographic distribution provides suitable adjectival modifiers.* Poorly descriptive or misleading geographic characterizations (e.g., Kentucky bass for a wide-ranging species) should be corrected unless they are too deeply entrenched in current usage. In the interest of brevity, it is usually possible to delete words such as lake, river, or ocean in the names of species (e.g., Colorado squawfish, not Colorado River squawfish).

17. *Generic names may be employed as common names outright* (e.g., remora, tilapia) *or in modified form* (e.g., molly, from *Mollienesia*). Once adopted, such names should be maintained even if the generic name is changed. These vernaculars should be written in Roman and without

capitalization. Brevity and euphony are of especial importance for names of this type, which will probably be adopted most often for aquarium fishes or other smaller and little-known fishes that do not already have a well-established vernacular nomenclature.

18. *The duplication of common names for fishes and other organisms should be avoided if possible, but names in wide general use need not be rejected on this basis alone*. The name dolphin is commonly applied to certain cetaceans and to *Coryphaena hippurus*. Similarly, buffalo is employed for various artiodactyls and for suckers of the genus *Ictiobus*. On the basis of prevailing use, these names are admissible as fish names without modification.

Scientific Names

The primary purpose of this list is to recommend a common name for each species of fish in our area; it is not to impose scientific names. Common names, we believe, can be stabilized by general agreement. Scientific names, on the other hand, cannot be fixed by democratic means; the limits of some taxonomic categories will inevitably shift with advancing knowledge and in accordance with the views of specialists. Scientific names are included here in order to designate the species for which a common name is recommended. The Committee realizes, however, that many users of this list are incompletely aware of the literature or are not interested in systematics or nomenclature, but simply seek a guide to technical names. To this end the scientific nomenclature involved has been edited carefully with regard to spelling, authorities, and—for the first time—dates of original proposal. With regard to usage, the nomenclature reflects the majority opinion of the Committee.

The third edition of the "International Code of Zoological Nomenclature" was published in 1985. Bailey and Robins, 1988, Bull. Zool. Nomencl. 45(2):92–103, reviewed the new code with reference to its effect on North American fish names and listed all changes resulting from changes in the Code. The Committee also has carefully considered subsequent commentaries by others in that and other journals (e.g., H. A. Dundee and H. M. Smith, 1989, Syst. Zool. 38(3):279–283). Obviously, the Code continues to evolve and there are differences of interpretation to be resolved. We follow Bailey and Robins (op. cit.), whose manuscript was reviewed by the Committee on Names of Fishes.

In this edition we include dates of publication with each scientific name. The Committee has uncovered many incorrect uses of dates in the scientific literature and accordingly has corrected them. Some important references for determining publication dates are given in Appendix 4. Users are encouraged to contact the Committee when disagreements about dates arise.

Plan of List

The list is presented as a natural or phyletic sequence of families of fishes. Arrangement of the orders and families follows that of J. S. Nelson, 1984, "Fishes of the World," Wiley-Interscience. The classes of Recent fishes and the orders are indicated. For the latter, the ordinal names of the Goodrich system (-iformes endings) are used. Both common and technical names of families (-idae endings) are given. We have attempted to have a single common name for each family. Thus, the family Salmonidae is the trout family even though it includes trouts, salmons, whitefishes, and graylings.

Within families, genera and species are listed alphabetically; the occasional disadvantage of separating closely related forms within a family is regarded as more than offset by the greater ease in use. We follow the precedent of the fourth edition in placing the scientific names in the left-hand column and common names on the right. This makes locating an alphabetized scientific name easier, and it also clearly indicates which common names are to be capitalized.

In this edition we add the date of the original published proposal of the scientific name following the authority. Authorities and dates are commonly needed by persons who may not have ready access to the original references. Determination of the authority and the date of publication sometimes is complicated, especially for names proposed before 1900. Errors made in the fourth edition are corrected in this list and explained in Appendix 1. Our justifications for the spellings of Delaroche, Forsskål, Lacepède, and Lesueur were explained in the third (page 5) and fourth (page 8) editions. The attribution of names proposed in the M. E. Blochii Systema Ichthyologicae, 1801, by J. G. Schneider was explained in the fourth edition (page 8).

Use of the authority's name(s) reflects current interpretation of the International Code of Zoological Nomenclature. In line with those rules, the author's name(s) follows the specific name directly and without punctuation if the species, when originally described, was assigned to the same genus in which it appears here; if the species was described in another genus, the author's name(s) appears in parentheses. The date of publication is separated from the authority by a comma and is included within the parentheses where parentheses are called for. For example, Mitchill originally named the brook trout *Salmo fontinalis* in a work published in 1814; it appears here as *Salvelinus fontinalis* (Mitchill, 1814).

Previous editions of the list have received widespread use and endorsement. Many users have sent suggested changes to the Committee, and each suggestion received consideration as we prepared this edition. Stability in common names was given highest priority, and changes have been made only for substantial reason. Scientific knowledge of fishes advanced rapidly in the 1980s. Many new species have been described, many additional species were recorded within our boundaries, and numerous taxonomic revisions have been completed. Addition of species has forced modifications or changes in some common names, and the revisions have resulted in widespread change in scientific nomenclature. In some families, notably the Cyprinidae, the changes are ongoing, incomplete, and in some instances conflicting. The Committee has chosen to be conservative in adopting changes in the hope that reversals or vacillation can be avoided or minimized in future editions.

All new entries and all entries that depart in any way (common name, occurrence, scientific name, or authority) from the 1980 edition are preceded by an asterisk (*). Information describing and explaining the change is given for each such entry in Appendix 1, coded by the page on which the name appears in the main list. Information given in Appendix 1 of the 1970 and 1980 lists (pages 65–87 and 68–92, respectively), documenting the changes between editions 2 and 3 and between 3 and 4, is not repeated in this edition.

A plus sign (+) before an entry indicates that, although the entry is unchanged, a comment will be found in Appendix 1 under that name.

As before, decisions have been made by majority opinion of the Committee. Thus, no committee member subscribes to all decisions reached. In many places, information available to the Committee exceeds that in the current literature. The Committee has struggled to reach decisions regarding inclusion of such information and has been cautious about adopting changes.

The synopsis of families on pages 1 and 2 serves also as a Table of Contents. The main list, Part I, appears on pages 11–70. The appendices follow in Part II, pages 71–110. Part III, the index, begins on page 111.

Index

The single index incorporates both common and scientific names. Page references are given for approved common names of classes, orders, families, and species. A single entry is included for each species; for example brook trout is entered only under "trout, brook." In addition to approved names, the index contains also other names that are in common use, often regionally, followed by the equivalent approved name and the page reference (e.g., see bass, channel). There are a great many vernacular names of North American fishes, and extensive search would be necessary to assemble even a large fraction of them, some of which have not been used for many decades and are of historical interest only. This the Committee has not attempted to do, but most of the more widely used names are included.

Page references are given for the scientific names here entered for classes, orders, families, genera, and species. Each species is entered only under its specific name. For example, *Sciaenops ocellatus* may be located only under "*ocellatus, Sciaenops*," although an entry for *Sciaenops* directs the reader to the page on which entries for the genus begin. Scientific names of species that are not accepted in this list are excluded except for those that appeared in the fourth edition and have since been placed in synonymy as explained in Appendix 1.

Acknowledgments

This list is the result of contributions made over nearly 60 years by the many past and present members of the Committee on Names of Fishes. To all of the former members we are greatly indebted. Some have continued to contribute to the Committee's endeavors, and in this regard we thank C. C. Lindsey and Alex E. Peden. Lasting contributions were made also by many specialists leading up to the second, third, and fourth editions, where their help was acknowledged. In preparing materials for this edition we have received assistance, large and small, from so many individuals that it is impractical to attempt to list them all. Some, however, have been so continuously interested and constructively helpful in our task as to merit special mention: Kenneth W. Able; M. James Allen; William D. Anderson, Jr.; James W. Atz; Frederick M. Bayer; Robert J. Behnke; Eugenia B. Böhlke; Stephen A. Bortone; Marvin A. Braasch; John Clay Bruner; George H. Burgess; Brooks M. Burr; H. Donald Cameron; Robert C. Cashner; Ted M. Cavender; Miles M. Coburn; Daniel M. Cohen; Patrick Colgan; Bruce B. Collette; Walter R. Courtenay, Jr.; E. J. Crossman; C. E. Dawson; James K. Dooley; Lillian J. Dempster; George E. Drewry; Alan R. Emery; William N. Eschmeyer; David A. Etnier; William L. Fink, W. I. Follett; the late Robert H. Gibbs, Jr.; Carter R. Gilbert; R. Grant Gilmore; William A. Gosline, David W. Greenfield; P. H. Greenwood; Karsten E. Hartel; Phillip C. Heemstra; W. M. Howell; Clark Hubbs; Tomio Iwamoto; Robert E. Jenkins; Dawn P. Jennings; Susan S. Jewett; Witold L. Klawe; James K. Langhammer; Robert J. Lavenberg; the late Vianney Legendre; James J. Long; Richard L. Mayden; Don E. McAllister; James A. McCann; John E. McCosker; Robert Rush Miller; W. L. Minckley, Jr.; John A. Musick; Douglas W. Nelson; Joseph N. Nelson; Lawrence M. Page; William L. Pflieger; Edwin P. Pister; John E. Randall; G. Carleton Ray; William J. Richards; Catherine H. Robins; Henry W. Robison; Fred C. Rohde; Richard H. Rosenblatt; Jeffrey A. Seigel; Robert L. Shipp; C. Lavett Smith; David G. Smith; Gerald R. Smith; Michael L. Smith; William F. Smith-Vaniz; Franklin F. Snelson, Jr.; Victor G. Springer; Lynn B. Starnes; Wayne C. Starnes; Ralph F. Stearley; David L. Stein; George C. Steyskal; Camm C. Swift; William Ralph Taylor; James C. Tyler; H. J. Walker; Melvin L. Warren, Jr.; Stanley H. Weitzman; Vidar G. Wespestad; James D. Williams; Ralph W. Yerger; and Cheryl Zello.

The preparation, by W. N. Eschmeyer, of a "Catalog of the Genera of Recent Fishes," has paralleled this edition of our names list. He has brought many nomenclatural changes and problems to light, and we have exchanged data continually. We especially appreciate his efforts on our behalf.

Travel funds for committee members to attend several work sessions were provided by the American Fisheries Society. We also wish to thank our home institutions for subsidizing our efforts on this project; for travel funds, secretarial help, duplicating facilities, mail services; and for providing work space for the Committee. The staff of the American Fisheries Society's International Headquarters has helped in many ways, particularly the late Carl R. Sullivan, Executive Director; Robert L. Kendall, Managing Editor; Sally Kendall; Mary R. Frye; Catherine W. Richardson; and Beth D. McAleer. The various presidents of the American Fisheries Society have been continuously encouraging to the Committee. We also thank the Ichthyological Division of the U.S. National Museum of Natural History for providing space and library facilities for our Committee.

Appendix 2 of this edition is separately authored as indicated. We thank those authors for their contribution.

PART I

Scientific Name, Occurrence, and Accepted Common Name

SCIENTIFIC NAME	OCCURRENCE[1]	COMMON NAME
CLASS MYXINI—HAGFISHES		
ORDER MYXINIFORMES		
Myxinidae—hagfishes		
Eptatretus deani (Evermann & Goldsborough, 1907)	P	black hagfish
Eptatretus stouti (Lockington, 1878)	P	Pacific hagfish
Myxine glutinosa Linnaeus, 1758	A	Atlantic hagfish
CLASS CEPHALASPIDOMORPHI—LAMPREYS		
+ORDER PETROMYZONTIFORMES		
+Petromyzontidae—lampreys		
Ichthyomyzon bdellium (Jordan, 1885)	F	Ohio lamprey
Ichthyomyzon castaneus Girard, 1858	F	chestnut lamprey
Ichthyomyzon fossor Reighard & Cummins, 1916	F	northern brook lamprey
Ichthyomyzon gagei Hubbs & Trautman, 1937	F	southern brook lamprey
Ichthyomyzon greeleyi Hubbs & Trautman, 1937	F	mountain brook lamprey
Ichthyomyzon unicuspis Hubbs & Trautman, 1937	F	silver lamprey
Lampetra aepyptera (Abbott, 1860)	F	least brook lamprey
Lampetra appendix (DeKay, 1842)	F	American brook lamprey
Lampetra ayresi (Günther, 1870)	F-P	river lamprey
Lampetra hubbsi (Vladykov & Kott, 1976)	F	Kern brook lamprey
Lampetra japonica (Martens, 1868)	F-P	Arctic lamprey
Lampetra lethophaga Hubbs, 1971	F	Pit-Klamath brook lamprey
* *Lampetra macrostoma* Beamish, 1982	F	Vancouver lamprey
Lampetra minima Bond & Kan, 1973	F[X]	Miller Lake lamprey
+*Lampetra richardsoni* Vladykov & Follett, 1965	F	western brook lamprey
* *Lampetra similis* (Vladykov & Kott, 1979)	F	Klamath lamprey
Lampetra tridentata (Gairdner, 1836)	F-P	Pacific lamprey
Petromyzon marinus Linnaeus, 1758	A-F	sea lamprey
CLASS ELASMOBRANCHIOMORPHI (CHONDRICHTHYES + HOLOCEPHALI)—CARTILAGINOUS FISHES		
ORDER CHIMAERIFORMES		
Chimaeridae—chimaeras		
Hydrolagus colliei (Lay & Bennett, 1839)	P	spotted ratfish

[1] A = Atlantic; F = Freshwater; P = Pacific; [I] = Introduced and established in our waters; [X] = extinct.
+Comment in Appendix 1.
*Change from 1980 list; see Appendix 1.

SCIENTIFIC NAME	OCCURRENCE	COMMON NAME
ORDER HEXANCHIFORMES		
Chlamydoselachidae—frill sharks		
Chlamydoselachus anguineus Garman, 1884	P	frill shark
Hexanchidae—cow sharks		
Hexanchus griseus (Bonnaterre, 1788)	A-P	sixgill shark
* *Notorynchus cepedianus* (Peron, 1807)	P	sevengill shark
ORDER HETERODONTIFORMES		
Heterodontidae—bullhead sharks		
Heterodontus francisci (Girard, 1854)	P	horn shark
***ORDER LAMNIFORMES**		
*Rhincodontidae—carpet sharks		
Ginglymostoma cirratum (Bonnaterre, 1788)	A	nurse shark
+*Rhincodon typus* Smith, 1828	A-P	whale shark
Odontaspididae—sand tigers		
Odontaspis ferox (Risso, 1810)	P	ragged-tooth shark
* *Odontaspis noronhai* (Maul, 1955)	A	bigeye sand tiger
Odontaspis taurus (Rafinesque, 1810)	A	sand tiger
Alopiidae—thresher sharks		
Alopias superciliosus (Lowe, 1841)	A-P	bigeye thresher
Alopias vulpinus (Bonnaterre, 1788)	A-P	thresher shark
*Cetorhinidae—basking sharks		
Cetorhinus maximus (Gunnerus, 1765)	A-P	basking shark
* *Megachasma pelagios* Taylor, Compagno & Struhsaker, 1983	P	megamouth shark
Lamnidae—mackerel sharks		
Carcharodon carcharias (Linnaeus, 1758)	A-P	white shark
Isurus oxyrinchus Rafinesque, 1810	A-P	shortfin mako
Isurus paucus Guitart Manday, 1966	A	longfin mako
Lamna ditropis Hubbs & Follett, 1947	P	salmon shark
Lamna nasus (Bonnaterre, 1788)	A	porbeagle
Scyliorhinidae—cat sharks		
Apristurus brunneus (Gilbert, 1892)	P	brown cat shark
Cephaloscyllium ventriosum (Garman, 1880)	P	swell shark
Parmaturus xaniurus (Gilbert, 1892)	P	filetail cat shark
Pseudotriakis microdon Brito Capello, 1868	A	false cat shark
Scyliorhinus retifer (Garman, 1881)	A	chain dogfish
Carcharhinidae—requiem sharks		
Carcharhinus acronotus (Poey, 1860)	A	blacknose shark

SCIENTIFIC NAME	OCCURRENCE	COMMON NAME
Carcharhinus altimus (Springer, 1950)	A	bignose shark
Carcharhinus brachyurus (Günther, 1870)	P	narrowtooth shark
Carcharhinus brevipinna (Müller & Henle, 1841)	A	spinner shark
Carcharhinus falciformis (Bibron, 1841)	A	silky shark
Carcharhinus isodon (Valenciennes, 1839)	A	finetooth shark
Carcharhinus leucas (Valenciennes, 1841)	A-F-P	bull shark
Carcharhinus limbatus (Valenciennes, 1841)	A	blacktip shark
+*Carcharhinus longimanus* (Poey, 1861)	A-P	oceanic whitetip shark
Carcharhinus obscurus (Lesueur, 1817)	A-P	dusky shark
Carcharhinus perezi (Poey, 1876)	A	reef shark
Carcharhinus plumbeus (Nardo, 1827)	A	sandbar shark
Carcharhinus porosus (Ranzani, 1840)	A	smalltail shark
Carcharhinus signatus (Poey, 1868)	A	night shark
* *Galeocerdo cuvier* (Peron & Lesueur, 1822)	A-P	tiger shark
+*Galeorhinus zyopterus* Jordan & Gilbert, 1883	P	soupfin shark
Mustelus californicus Gill, 1864	P	gray smoothhound
Mustelus canis (Mitchill, 1815)	A	smooth dogfish
Mustelus henlei (Gill, 1862)	P	brown smoothhound
Mustelus lunulatus Jordan & Gilbert, 1882	P	sicklefin smoothhound
Mustelus norrisi Springer, 1940	A	Florida smoothhound
Negaprion brevirostris (Poey, 1868)	A	lemon shark
Prionace glauca (Linnaeus, 1758)	A-P	blue shark
Rhizoprionodon longurio (Jordan & Gilbert, 1882)	P	Pacific sharpnose shark
Rhizoprionodon terraenovae (Richardson, 1836)	A	Atlantic sharpnose shark
Triakis semifasciata Girard, 1854	P	leopard shark

Sphyrnidae—hammerhead sharks

SCIENTIFIC NAME	OCCURRENCE	COMMON NAME
Sphyrna lewini (Griffith & Smith, 1834)	A-P	scalloped hammerhead
Sphyrna mokarran (Rüppell, 1837)	A	great hammerhead
Sphyrna tiburo (Linnaeus, 1758)	A-P	bonnethead
Sphyrna zygaena (Linnaeus, 1758)	A-P	smooth hammerhead

+ORDER SQUALIFORMES

Squalidae—dogfish sharks

SCIENTIFIC NAME	OCCURRENCE	COMMON NAME
Centroscyllium fabricii (Reinhardt, 1825)	A	black dogfish
Centroscymnus coelolepis (Bocage & Brito Capello, 1864)	A	Portuguese shark
Dalatias licha (Bonnaterre, 1788)	A	kitefin shark
Echinorhinus brucus (Bonnaterre, 1788)	A	bramble shark
Echinorhinus cookei Pietschmann, 1928	P	prickly shark
Etmopterus gracilispinis Krefft, 1968	A	broadband dogfish
Somniosus microcephalus (Bloch & Schneider, 1801)	A	Greenland shark
Somniosus pacificus Bigelow & Schroeder, 1944	P	Pacific sleeper shark
Squalus acanthias Linnaeus, 1758	A-P	spiny dogfish
* *Squalus asper* Merrett, 1973	A	roughskin dogfish
Squalus cubensis Howell Rivero, 1936	A	Cuban dogfish

SCIENTIFIC NAME	OCCURRENCE	COMMON NAME
	Squatinidae—angel sharks	
Squatina californica Ayres, 1859	P	angel shark
* *Squatina dumeril* Lesueur, 1818	A	Atlantic angel shark
	ORDER RAJIFORMES	
	Pristidae—sawfishes	
Pristis pectinata Latham, 1794	A	smalltooth sawfish
* *Pristis pristis* Linnaeus, 1758	A	largetooth sawfish
	Torpedinidae—electric rays	
Narcine brasiliensis (Olfers, 1831)	A	lesser electric ray
Torpedo californica Ayres, 1855	P	Pacific electric ray
Torpedo nobiliana Bonaparte, 1835	A	Atlantic torpedo
	Rhinobatidae—guitarfishes	
Platyrhinoidis triseriata (Jordan & Gilbert, 1880)	P	thornback
Rhinobatos lentiginosus (Garman, 1880)	A	Atlantic guitarfish
Rhinobatos productus (Ayres, 1854)	P	shovelnose guitarfish
Zapteryx exasperata (Jordan & Gilbert, 1880)	P	banded guitarfish
	Rajidae—skates	
* *Bathyraja aleutica* (Gilbert, 1896)	P	Aleutian skate
* *Bathyraja hubbsi* Ishihara & Ishiyama, 1985	P	mud skate
* *Bathyraja interrupta* (Gill & Townsend, 1897)	P	sandpaper skate
* *Bathyraja parmifera* (Bean, 1881)	P	Alaska skate
* *Bathyraja rosispinis* (Gill & Townsend, 1897)	P	flathead skate
* *Bathyraja trachura* (Gilbert, 1892)	P	roughtail skate
Raja ackleyi Garman, 1881	A	ocellate skate
Raja binoculata Girard, 1854	P	big skate
Raja eglanteria Bosc, 1802	A	clearnose skate
* *Raja erinacea* (Mitchill, 1825)	A	little skate
Raja garmani Whitley, 1939	A	rosette skate
Raja inornata Jordan & Gilbert, 1881	P	California skate
Raja laevis Mitchill, 1817	A	barndoor skate
Raja ocellata Mitchill, 1814	A	winter skate
Raja olseni Bigelow & Schroeder, 1951	A	spreadfin skate
Raja radiata Donovan, 1807	A	thorny skate
* *Raja rhina* (Jordan & Gilbert, 1880)	P	longnose skate
Raja senta Garman, 1885	A	smooth skate
Raja spinicauda Jensen, 1914	A	spinytail skate
* *Raja stellulata* (Jordan & Gilbert, 1880)	P	starry skate
Raja texana Chandler, 1921	A	roundel skate
	Dasyatidae—stingrays	
Dasyatis americana Hildebrand & Schroeder, 1928	A	southern stingray
Dasyatis centroura (Mitchill, 1815)	A	roughtail stingray
Dasyatis dipterura (Jordan & Gilbert, 1880)	P	diamond stingray
Dasyatis sabina (Lesueur, 1824)	A-F	Atlantic stingray
* *Dasyatis say* (Lesueur, 1817)	A	bluntnose stingray

SCIENTIFIC NAME	OCCURRENCE	COMMON NAME
Dasyatis violacea (Bonaparte, 1832)	A-P	pelagic stingray
Gymnura altavela (Linnaeus, 1758)	A	spiny butterfly ray
Gymnura marmorata (Cooper, 1864)	P	California butterfly ray
Gymnura micrura (Schneider, 1801)	A	smooth butterfly ray
	*Urolophidae—round stingrays	
Urolophus halleri Cooper, 1863	P	round stingray
Urolophus jamaicensis (Cuvier, 1816)	A	yellow stingray
	Myliobatidae—eagle rays	
Aetobatis narinari (Euphrasen, 1790)	A	spotted eagle ray
Myliobatis californica Gill, 1865	P	bat ray
Myliobatis freminvillei Lesueur, 1824	A	bullnose ray
Myliobatis goodei Garman, 1885	A	southern eagle ray
Rhinoptera bonasus (Mitchill, 1815)	A	cownose ray
	Mobulidae—mantas	
* *Manta birostris* (Walbaum, 1792)	A-P	manta
Mobula hypostoma (Bancroft, 1831)	A	devil ray
Mobula japanica (Müller & Henle, 1841)	P	spinetail mobula
* *Mobula thurstoni* (Lloyd, 1908)	P	smoothtail mobula

CLASS OSTEICHTHYES—BONY FISHES
ORDER ACIPENSERIFORMES

SCIENTIFIC NAME	OCCURRENCE	COMMON NAME
	Acipenseridae—sturgeons	
Acipenser brevirostrum Lesueur, 1818	A-F	shortnose sturgeon
Acipenser fulvescens Rafinesque, 1817	F	lake sturgeon
Acipenser medirostris Ayres, 1854	F-P	green sturgeon
Acipenser oxyrhynchus Mitchill, 1814	A-F	Atlantic sturgeon
Acipenser transmontanus Richardson, 1836	F-P	white sturgeon
Scaphirhynchus albus (Forbes & Richardson, 1905)	F	pallid sturgeon
Scaphirhynchus platorynchus (Rafinesque, 1820)	F	shovelnose sturgeon
	Polyodontidae—paddlefishes	
Polyodon spathula (Walbaum, 1792)	F	paddlefish

*ORDER LEPISOSTEIFORMES

SCIENTIFIC NAME	OCCURRENCE	COMMON NAME
	Lepisosteidae—gars	
Lepisosteus oculatus (Winchell, 1864)	F	spotted gar
Lepisosteus osseus (Linnaeus, 1758)	F	longnose gar
Lepisosteus platostomus Rafinesque, 1820	F	shortnose gar
Lepisosteus platyrhincus DeKay, 1842	F	Florida gar
Lepisosteus spatula Lacepède, 1803	F	alligator gar

ORDER AMIIFORMES

SCIENTIFIC NAME	OCCURRENCE	COMMON NAME
	Amiidae—bowfins	
Amia calva Linnaeus, 1766	F	bowfin

SCIENTIFIC NAME	OCCURRENCE	COMMON NAME
ORDER OSTEOGLOSSIFORMES		
Hiodontidae—mooneyes		
Hiodon alosoides (Rafinesque, 1819)	F	goldeye
Hiodon tergisus Lesueur, 1818	F	mooneye
ORDER ELOPIFORMES		
Elopidae—tarpons		
Elops affinis Regan, 1909	F-P	machete
Elops saurus Linnaeus, 1766	A-F	ladyfish
Megalops atlanticus Valenciennes, 1847	A-F	tarpon
***ORDER ALBULIFORMES**		
Albulidae—bonefishes		
Albula vulpes (Linnaeus, 1758)	A-P	bonefish
Notacanthidae—spiny eels		
Notacanthus chemnitzi Bloch, 1787	A	spiny eel
ORDER ANGUILLIFORMES		
Anguillidae—freshwater eels		
Anguilla rostrata (Lesueur, 1817)	A-F	American eel
Moringuidae—spaghetti eels		
Moringua edwardsi (Jordan & Bollman, 1889)	A	spaghetti eel
Neoconger mucronatus Girard, 1858	A	ridged eel
*Chlopsidae—false morays		
Chilorhinus suensoni Lütken, 1852	A	seagrass eel
Chlopsis bicolor Rafinesque, 1810	A	bicolor eel
Kaupichthys hyoproroides (Strömann, 1896)	A	false moray
Kaupichthys nuchalis Böhlke, 1967	A	collared eel
Muraenidae—morays		
* *Anarchias similis* (Lea, 1913)	A	pygmy moray
Echidna catenata (Bloch, 1795)	A	chain moray
Enchelycore carychroa Böhlke & Böhlke, 1976	A	chestnut moray
Enchelycore nigricans (Bonnaterre, 1788)	A	viper moray
* *Gymnothorax conspersus* Poey, 1867	A	saddled moray
Gymnothorax funebris Ranzani, 1839	A	green moray
Gymnothorax hubbsi Böhlke & Böhlke, 1977.	A	lichen moray
* *Gymnothorax kolpos* Böhlke & Böhlke, 1980	A	blacktail moray
* *Gymnothorax madeirensis* (Johnson, 1862)	A	sharktooth moray
* *Gymnothorax miliaris* (Kaup, 1856)	A	goldentail moray
Gymnothorax mordax (Ayres, 1859)	P	California moray
Gymnothorax moringa (Cuvier, 1829)	A	spotted moray
Gymnothorax nigromarginatus (Girard, 1859)	A	blackedge moray

SCIENTIFIC NAME	OCCURRENCE	COMMON NAME
* *Gymnothorax polygonius* Poey, 1875	A	polygon moray
* *Gymnothorax saxicola* Jordan & Davis, 1891	A	honeycomb moray
Gymnothorax vicinus (Castelnau, 1855)	A	purplemouth moray
Muraena retifera Goode & Bean, 1882	A	reticulate moray
* *Muraena robusta* Osorio, 1909	A	stout moray
* *Uropterygius macularius* (Lesueur, 1825)	A	marbled moray
	Synaphobranchidae—cutthroat eels	
Dysomma anguillare Barnard, 1923	A	shortbelly eel
* *Synaphobranchus kaupi* Johnson, 1862	A	northern cutthroat eel
	Ophichthidae—snake eels	
Ahlia egmontis (Jordan, 1884)	A	key worm eel
* *Aplatophis chauliodus* Böhlke, 1956	A	tusky eel
Aprognathodon platyventris Böhlke, 1967	A	stripe eel
Apterichtus ansp (Böhlke, 1968)	A	academy eel
Apterichtus kendalli (Gilbert, 1891)	A	finless eel
Bascanichthys bascanium (Jordan, 1884)	A	sooty eel
Bascanichthys scuticaris (Goode & Bean, 1880)	A	whip eel
* *Callechelys guiniensis* (Osorio, 1894)	A	shorttail snake eel
Callechelys muraena Jordan & Evermann, 1896	A	blotched snake eel
Callechelys springeri (Ginsburg, 1951)	A	ridgefin eel
Caralophia loxochila Böhlke, 1955	A	slantlip eel
Echiophis intertinctus (Richardson, 1848)	A	spotted spoon-nose eel
* *Echiophis punctifer* (Kaup, 1860)	A	snapper eel
* *Ethadophis akkistikos* McCosker & Böhlke, 1984	A	indifferent eel
* *Gordiichthys ergodes* McCosker, 1989	A	irksome eel
Gordiichthys irretitus Jordan & Davis, 1891	A	horsehair eel
* *Gordiichthys leibyi* McCosker & Böhlke, 1984	A	string eel
Ichthyapus ophioneus (Evermann & Marsh, 1900)	A	surf eel
Letharchus velifer Goode & Bean, 1882	A	sailfin eel
* *Lethogaleos andersoni* McCosker & Böhlke, 1982	A	forgetful snake eel
* *Myrichthys breviceps* (Richardson, 1845)	A	sharptail eel
Myrichthys maculosus (Cuvier, 1816)	P	tiger snake eel
* *Myrichthys ocellatus* (Lesueur, 1825)	A	goldspotted eel
Myrophis punctatus Lütken, 1851	A	speckled worm eel
Myrophis vafer Jordan & Gilbert, 1883	P	Pacific worm eel
Ophichthus cruentifer (Goode & Bean, 1896).	A	margined snake eel
Ophichthus gomesi (Castelnau, 1855)	A	shrimp eel
* *Ophichthus hyposagmatus* McCosker & Böhlke, 1984	A	faintsaddled snake eel
Ophichthus melanoporus Kanazawa, 1963	A	blackpored eel
* *Ophichthus omorgmus* McCosker & Böhlke, 1984	A	dottedline snake eel
Ophichthus ophis (Linnaeus, 1758)	A	spotted snake eel
* *Ophichthus puncticeps* (Kaup, 1860)	A	palespotted eel
* *Ophichthus rex* Böhlke & Caruso, 1980	A	king snake eel
Ophichthus triserialis (Kaup, 1856)	P	Pacific snake eel
Ophichthus zophochir (Jordan & Gilbert, 1882)	P	yellow snake eel
* *Pseudomyrophis fugesae* McCosker, Böhlke & Böhlke, 1982	A	diminutive worm eel

SCIENTIFIC NAME	OCCURRENCE	COMMON NAME
Nemichthyidae—snipe eels		
Nemichthys scolopaceus Richardson, 1848	A-P	slender snipe eel
Nettastomatidae—duckbill eels		
Facciolella gilberti (Garman, 1899)	P	dogface witch-eel
Hoplunnis diomedianus Goode & Bean, 1896	A	blacktail pike-conger
Hoplunnis macrurus Ginsburg, 1951	A	freckled pike-conger
Hoplunnis tenuis Ginsburg, 1951	A	spotted pike-conger
* *Saurenchelys cognita* Smith, 1989	A	longface eel
Congridae—conger eels		
Ariosoma anale (Poey, 1860)	A	longtrunk conger
Ariosoma balearicum (Delaroche, 1809)	A	bandtooth conger
Conger oceanicus (Mitchill, 1814)	A	conger eel
Conger triporiceps Kanazawa, 1958	A	manytooth conger
Gnathophis bathytopos Smith & Kanazawa, 1977	A	blackgut conger
Gnathophis bracheatopos Smith & Kanazawa, 1977	A	longeye conger
Gnathophis catalinensis (Wade, 1946)	P	Catalina conger
* *Heteroconger halis* (Böhlke, 1957)	A	brown garden eel
* *Heteroconger luteolus* Smith, 1989	A	yellow garden eel
Hildebrandia flava (Goode & Bean, 1896)	A	yellow conger
Hildebrandia gracilior (Ginsburg, 1951)	A	whiptail conger
Paraconger caudilimbatus (Poey, 1867)	A	margintail conger
Uroconger syringinus Ginsburg, 1954	A	threadtail conger
* *Xenomystax congroides* Smith & Kanazawa, 1989	A	bristletooth conger
ORDER CLUPEIFORMES		
Clupeidae—herrings		
Alosa aestivalis (Mitchill, 1814)	A-F	blueback herring
Alosa alabamae Jordan & Evermann, 1896	A-F	Alabama shad
Alosa chrysochloris (Rafinesque, 1820)	A-F	skipjack herring
Alosa mediocris (Mitchill, 1814)	A-F	hickory shad
Alosa pseudoharengus (Wilson, 1811)	A-F	alewife
Alosa sapidissima (Wilson, 1811)	A-F-P	American shad
Brevoortia gunteri Hildebrand, 1948	A	finescale menhaden
Brevoortia patronus Goode, 1878	A	gulf menhaden
Brevoortia smithi Hildebrand, 1941	A	yellowfin menhaden
Brevoortia tyrannus (Latrobe, 1802)	A	Atlantic menhaden
* *Clupea harengus* Linnaeus, 1758	A	Atlantic herring
* *Clupea pallasi* Valenciennes, 1847	P	Pacific herring
Dorosoma cepedianum (Lesueur, 1818)	A-F	gizzard shad
Dorosoma petenense (Günther, 1867)	A-F-P	threadfin shad
Etrumeus teres (DeKay, 1842)	A-P	round herring
Harengula clupeola (Cuvier, 1829)	A	false pilchard
Harengula humeralis (Cuvier, 1829)	A	redear sardine
Harengula jaguana Poey, 1865	A-F	scaled sardine
Harengula thrissina (Jordan & Gilbert, 1882)	P	flatiron herring
Jenkinsia lamprotaenia (Gosse, 1851)	A	dwarf herring
Jenkinsia majua Whitehead, 1963	A	little-eye herring

SCIENTIFIC NAME	OCCURRENCE	COMMON NAME
Jenkinsia stolifera (Jordan & Gilbert, 1884)	A	shortband herring
* *Opisthonema libertate* (Günther, 1867)	P	deepbody thread herring
Opisthonema medirastre Berry & Barrett, 1963	P	middling thread herring
Opisthonema oglinum (Lesueur, 1817)	A-F	Atlantic thread herring
Sardinella aurita Valenciennes, 1847	A	Spanish sardine
Sardinella brasiliensis (Steindachner, 1875)	A	orangespot sardine
Sardinops sagax (Jenyns, 1842)	P	Pacific sardine

+Engraulidae—anchovies

SCIENTIFIC NAME	OCCURRENCE	COMMON NAME
Anchoa cayorum (Fowler, 1906)	A	key anchovy
Anchoa compressa (Girard, 1858)	P	deepbody anchovy
Anchoa cubana (Poey, 1868)	A	Cuban anchovy
Anchoa delicatissima (Girard, 1854)	P	slough anchovy
Anchoa hepsetus (Linnaeus, 1758)	A	striped anchovy
Anchoa lamprotaenia Hildebrand, 1943	A	bigeye anchovy
Anchoa lyolepis (Evermann & Marsh, 1900)	A	dusky anchovy
Anchoa mitchilli (Valenciennes, 1848)	A-F	bay anchovy
Anchoa nasuta Hildebrand & Carvalho, 1948	A	longnose anchovy
Anchoviella perfasciata (Poey, 1860)	A	flat anchovy
Cetengraulis mysticetus (Günther, 1867)	P	anchoveta
Engraulis eurystole (Swain & Meek, 1885)	A	silver anchovy
Engraulis mordax Girard, 1854	P	northern anchovy

*ORDER GONORYNCHIFORMES

*Chanidae—milkfishes

SCIENTIFIC NAME	OCCURRENCE	COMMON NAME
* *Chanos chanos* (Forsskål, 1775)	P	milkfish

ORDER CYPRINIFORMES

+Cyprinidae—carps and minnows

SCIENTIFIC NAME	OCCURRENCE	COMMON NAME
Acrocheilus alutaceus Agassiz & Pickering, 1855	F	chiselmouth
Agosia chrysogaster Girard, 1856	F	longfin dace
Campostoma anomalum (Rafinesque, 1820)	F	central stoneroller
Campostoma oligolepis Hubbs & Greene, 1935	F	largescale stoneroller
Campostoma ornatum Girard, 1856	F	Mexican stoneroller
* *Campostoma pauciradii* Burr & Cashner, 1983	F	bluefin stoneroller
Carassius auratus (Linnaeus, 1758)	F[I]	goldfish
Clinostomus elongatus (Kirtland, 1838)	F	redside dace
Clinostomus funduloides Girard, 1856	F	rosyside dace
Couesius plumbeus (Agassiz, 1850)	F	lake chub
Ctenopharyngodon idella (Valenciennes, 1844)	F[I]	grass carp
* *Cyprinella analostana* Girard, 1859	F	satinfin shiner
* *Cyprinella caerulea* (Jordan, 1877)	F	blue shiner
* *Cyprinella callisema* (Jordan, 1877)	F	Ocmulgee shiner
* *Cyprinella callistia* (Jordan, 1877)	F	Alabama shiner
* *Cyprinella callitaenia* (Bailey & Gibbs, 1956)	F	bluestripe shiner
* *Cyprinella camura* (Jordan & Meek, 1884)	F	bluntface shiner
* *Cyprinella chloristia* (Jordan & Brayton, 1878)	F	greenfin shiner
* *Cyprinella formosa* (Girard, 1856)	F	beautiful shiner

SCIENTIFIC NAME	OCCURRENCE	COMMON NAME
* *Cyprinella galactura* (Cope, 1868)	F	whitetail shiner
* *Cyprinella gibbsi* (Howell & Williams, 1971)	F	Tallapoosa shiner
* *Cyprinella labrosa* (Cope, 1870)	F	thicklip chub
* *Cyprinella leedsi* (Fowler, 1942)	F	bannerfin shiner
* *Cyprinella lepida* Girard, 1856	F	plateau shiner
* *Cyprinella lutrensis* (Baird & Girard, 1853)	F	red shiner
* *Cyprinella monacha* (Cope, 1868)	F	spotfin chub
* *Cyprinella nivea* (Cope, 1870)	F	whitefin shiner
* *Cyprinella proserpina* (Girard, 1856)	F	proserpine shiner
* *Cyprinella pyrrhomelas* (Cope, 1870)	F	fieryblack shiner
* *Cyprinella spiloptera* (Cope, 1868)	F	spotfin shiner
* *Cyprinella trichroistia* (Jordan & Gilbert, 1878)	F	tricolor shiner
* *Cyprinella venusta* Girard, 1856	F	blacktail shiner
* *Cyprinella whipplei* Girard, 1856	F	steelcolor shiner
* *Cyprinella xaenura* (Jordan, 1877)	F	Altamaha shiner
* *Cyprinella zanema* (Jordan & Brayton, 1878)	F	Santee chub
Cyprinus carpio Linnaeus, 1758	F[I]	common carp
Dionda diaboli Hubbs & Brown, 1957	F	Devils River minnow
Dionda episcopa Girard, 1856	F	roundnose minnow
Eremichthys acros Hubbs & Miller, 1948	F	desert dace
* *Erimystax cahni* (Hubbs & Crowe, 1956)	F	slender chub
* *Erimystax dissimilis* (Kirtland, 1840)	F	streamline chub
* *Erimystax harryi* (Hubbs & Crowe, 1956)	F	Ozark chub
* *Erimystax insignis* (Hubbs & Crowe, 1956)	F	blotched chub
* *Erimystax x-punctatus* (Hubbs & Crowe, 1956)	F	gravel chub
Exoglossum laurae (Hubbs, 1931)	F	tonguetied minnow
Exoglossum maxillingua (Lesueur, 1817)	F	cutlips minnow
Gila alvordensis Hubbs & Miller, 1972	F	Alvord chub
Gila atraria (Girard, 1856)	F	Utah chub
Gila bicolor (Girard, 1856)	F	tui chub
Gila boraxobius Williams & Bond, 1980	F	Borax Lake chub
Gila coerulea (Girard, 1856)	F	blue chub
Gila copei (Jordan & Gilbert, 1881)	F	leatherside chub
Gila crassicauda (Baird & Girard, 1854)	F[X]	thicktail chub
Gila cypha Miller, 1945	F	humpback chub
Gila ditaenia Miller, 1945	F	Sonora chub
Gila elegans Baird & Girard, 1853	F	bonytail
* *Gila intermedia* (Girard, 1856)	F	Gila chub
Gila nigrescens (Girard, 1856)	F	Chihuahua chub
Gila orcutti (Eigenmann & Eigenmann, 1890)	F	arroyo chub
Gila pandora (Cope, 1872)	F	Rio Grande chub
Gila purpurea (Girard, 1856)	F	Yaqui chub
Gila robusta Baird & Girard, 1853	F	roundtail chub
Hemitremia flammea (Jordan & Gilbert, 1878)	F	flame chub
+*Hesperoleucus symmetricus* (Baird & Girard, 1854)	F	California roach
* *Hybognathus amarus* (Girard, 1856)	F	Rio Grande silvery minnow
Hybognathus argyritis Girard, 1856	F	western silvery minnow
Hybognathus hankinsoni Hubbs, 1929	F	brassy minnow
Hybognathus hayi Jordan, 1885	F	cypress minnow
Hybognathus nuchalis Agassiz, 1855	F	Mississippi silvery minnow

SCIENTIFIC NAME	OCCURRENCE	COMMON NAME
Hybognathus placitus Girard, 1856	F	plains minnow
Hybognathus regius Girard, 1856	F	eastern silvery minnow
* *Hypophthalmichthys molitrix* (Valenciennes, 1844)	F[I]	silver carp
* *Hypophthalmichthys nobilis* (Richardson, 1845)	F[I]	bighead carp
Iotichthys phlegethontis (Cope, 1874)	F	least chub
+*Lavinia exilicauda* Baird & Girard, 1854	F	hitch
Lepidomeda albivallis Miller & Hubbs, 1960	F	White River spinedace
Lepidomeda altivelis Miller & Hubbs, 1960	F[X]	Pahranagat spinedace
Lepidomeda mollispinis Miller & Hubbs, 1960	F	Virgin spinedace
Lepidomeda vittata Cope, 1874	F	Little Colorado spinedace
Leuciscus idus (Linnaeus, 1758)	F[I]	ide
* *Luxilus albeolus* (Jordan, 1889)	F	white shiner
* *Luxilus cardinalis* (Mayden, 1988)	F	cardinal shiner
* *Luxilus cerasinus* (Cope, 1868)	F	crescent shiner
* *Luxilus chrysocephalus* Rafinesque, 1820	F	striped shiner
* *Luxilus coccogenis* (Cope, 1868)	F	warpaint shiner
* *Luxilus cornutus* (Mitchill, 1817)	F	common shiner
* *Luxilus pilsbryi* (Fowler, 1904)	F	duskystripe shiner
* *Luxilus zonatus* (Putnam, 1863)	F	bleeding shiner
* *Luxilus zonistius* Jordan, 1880	F	bandfin shiner
* *Lythrurus ardens* (Cope, 1868)	F	rosefin shiner
* *Lythrurus atrapiculus* (Snelson, 1972)	F	blacktip shiner
* *Lythrurus bellus* (Hay, 1881)	F	pretty shiner
* *Lythrurus fumeus* (Evermann, 1892)	F	ribbon shiner
* *Lythrurus lirus* (Jordan, 1877)	F	mountain shiner
* *Lythrurus roseipinnis* (Hay, 1885)	F	cherryfin shiner
* *Lythrurus snelsoni* (Robison, 1985)	F	Ouachita shiner
* *Lythrurus umbratilis* (Girard, 1856)	F	redfin shiner
* *Macrhybopsis aestivalis* (Girard, 1856)	F	speckled chub
* *Macrhybopsis gelida* (Girard, 1856)	F	sturgeon chub
* *Macrhybopsis meeki* (Jordan & Evermann, 1896)	F	sicklefin chub
* *Macrhybopsis storeriana* (Kirtland, 1847)	F	silver chub
* *Margariscus margarita* Cope, 1868	F	pearl dace
Meda fulgida Girard, 1856	F	spikedace
Moapa coriacea Hubbs & Miller, 1948	F	Moapa dace
Mylocheilus caurinus (Richardson, 1836)	F	peamouth
Mylopharodon conocephalus (Baird & Girard, 1854)	F	hardhead
Nocomis asper Lachner & Jenkins, 1971	F	redspot chub
Nocomis biguttatus (Kirtland, 1840)	F	hornyhead chub
Nocomis effusus Lachner & Jenkins, 1967	F	redtail chub
Nocomis leptocephalus (Girard, 1856)	F	bluehead chub
Nocomis micropogon (Cope, 1865)	F	river chub
Nocomis platyrhynchus Lachner & Jenkins, 1971	F	bigmouth chub
Nocomis raneyi Lachner & Jenkins, 1971	F	bull chub
Notemigonus crysoleucas (Mitchill, 1814)	F	golden shiner
Notropis alborus Hubbs & Raney, 1947	F	whitemouth shiner
Notropis altipinnis (Cope, 1870)	F	highfin shiner
Notropis amabilis (Girard, 1856)	F	Texas shiner
* *Notropis amblops* (Rafinesque, 1820)	F	bigeye chub
* *Notropis ammophilus* Suttkus & Boschung, 1990	F	orangefin shiner

SCIENTIFIC NAME	OCCURRENCE	COMMON NAME
+*Notropis amnis* Hubbs & Greene, 1951	F	pallid shiner
Notropis amoenus (Abbott, 1874)	F	comely shiner
Notropis anogenus Forbes, 1885	F	pugnose shiner
Notropis ariommus (Cope, 1868)	F	popeye shiner
Notropis asperifrons Suttkus & Raney, 1955	F	burrhead shiner
Notropis atherinoides Rafinesque, 1818	F	emerald shiner
Notropis atrocaudalis Evermann, 1892	F	blackspot shiner
Notropis baileyi Suttkus & Raney, 1955	F	rough shiner
Notropis bairdi Hubbs & Ortenburger, 1929	F	Red River shiner
Notropis bifrenatus (Cope, 1869)	F	bridle shiner
Notropis blennius (Girard, 1856)	F	river shiner
Notropis boops Gilbert, 1884	F	bigeye shiner
Notropis braytoni Jordan & Evermann, 1896	F	Tamaulipas shiner
* *Notropis buccatus* (Cope, 1865)	F	silverjaw minnow
Notropis buccula Cross, 1953	F	smalleye shiner
Notropis buchanani Meek, 1896	F	ghost shiner
* *Notropis cahabae* Mayden & Kuhajda, 1989	F	Cahaba shiner
Notropis candidus Suttkus, 1980	F	silverside shiner
Notropis chalybaeus (Cope, 1869)	F	ironcolor shiner
Notropis chihuahua Woolman, 1892	F	Chihuahua shiner
Notropis chiliticus (Cope, 1870)	F	redlip shiner
Notropis chlorocephalus (Cope, 1870)	F	greenhead shiner
Notropis chrosomus (Jordan, 1877)	F	rainbow shiner
Notropis cummingsae Myers, 1925	F	dusky shiner
Notropis dorsalis (Agassiz, 1854)	F	bigmouth shiner
Notropis edwardraneyi Suttkus & Clemmer, 1968	F	fluvial shiner
Notropis euryzonus Suttkus, 1955	F	broadstripe shiner
Notropis girardi Hubbs & Ortenburger, 1929	F	Arkansas River shiner
Notropis greenei Hubbs & Ortenburger, 1929	F	wedgespot shiner
Notropis harperi Fowler, 1941	F	redeye chub
Notropis heterodon (Cope, 1865)	F	blackchin shiner
Notropis heterolepis Eigenmann & Eigenmann, 1893	F	blacknose shiner
Notropis hubbsi Bailey & Robison, 1978	F	bluehead shiner
Notropis hudsonius (Clinton, 1824)	F	spottail shiner
Notropis hypselopterus (Günther, 1868)	F	sailfin shiner
Notropis hypsilepis Suttkus & Raney, 1955	F	highscale shiner
* *Notropis hypsinotus* (Cope, 1870)	F	highback chub
Notropis jemezanus (Cope, 1875)	F	Rio Grande shiner
Notropis leuciodus (Cope, 1868)	F	Tennessee shiner
* *Notropis lineapunctatus* (Clemmer & Suttkus, 1971)	F	lined chub
Notropis longirostris (Hay, 1881)	F	longnose shiner
Notropis lutipinnis (Jordan & Brayton, 1878)	F	yellowfin shiner
Notropis maculatus (Hay, 1881)	F	taillight shiner
Notropis mekistocholas Snelson, 1971	F	Cape Fear shiner
* *Notropis melanostomus* Bortone, 1989	F	blackmouth shiner
Notropis nubilus (Forbes, 1878)	F	Ozark minnow
* *Notropis orca* Woolman, 1894	F[X]	phantom shiner
Notropis ortenburgeri Hubbs, 1927	F	Kiamichi shiner
Notropis oxyrhynchus Hubbs & Bonham, 1951	F	sharpnose shiner
Notropis ozarcanus Meek, 1891	F	Ozark shiner

SCIENTIFIC NAME	OCCURRENCE	COMMON NAME
Notropis perpallidus Hubbs & Black, 1940	F	peppered shiner
Notropis petersoni Fowler, 1942	F	coastal shiner
Notropis photogenis (Cope, 1865)	F	silver shiner
Notropis potteri Hubbs & Bonham, 1951	F	chub shiner
Notropis procne (Cope, 1865)	F	swallowtail shiner
Notropis rubellus (Agassiz, 1850)	F	rosyface shiner
* *Notropis rubescens* Bailey, 1991	F	rosyface chub
Notropis rubricroceus (Cope, 1868)	F	saffron shiner
* *Notropis rupestris* Page, 1987	F	bedrock shiner
Notropis sabinae Jordan & Gilbert, 1886	F	Sabine shiner
Notropis scabriceps (Cope, 1868)	F	New River shiner
Notropis scepticus (Jordan & Gilbert, 1883)	F	sandbar shiner
Notropis semperasper Gilbert, 1961	F	roughhead shiner
Notropis shumardi (Girard, 1856)	F	silverband shiner
Notropis signipinnis Bailey & Suttkus, 1952	F	flagfin shiner
Notropis simus (Cope, 1875)	F	bluntnose shiner
Notropis spectrunculus (Cope, 1868)	F	mirror shiner
Notropis stilbius (Jordan, 1877)	F	silverstripe shiner
+*Notropis stramineus* (Cope, 1865)	F	sand shiner
Notropis telescopus (Cope, 1868)	F	telescope shiner
Notropis texanus (Girard, 1856)	F	weed shiner
+*Notropis topeka* (Gilbert, 1884)	F	Topeka shiner
Notropis uranoscopus Suttkus, 1959	F	skygazer shiner
Notropis volucellus (Cope, 1865)	F	mimic shiner
Notropis welaka Evermann & Kendall, 1898	F	bluenose shiner
* *Notropis wickliffi* Trautman, 1931	F	channel shiner
* *Notropis winchelli* (Girard, 1856)	F	clear chub
Notropis xaenocephalus (Jordan, 1877)	F	Coosa shiner
* *Opsopoeodus emiliae* Hay, 1881	F	pugnose minnow
* *Oregonichthys crameri* (Snyder, 1908)	F	Oregon chub
Orthodon microlepidotus (Ayres, 1854)	F	Sacramento blackfish
Phenacobius catostomus Jordan, 1877	F	riffle minnow
Phenacobius crassilabrum Minckley & Craddock, 1962	F	fatlips minnow
Phenacobius mirabilis (Girard, 1856)	F	suckermouth minnow
Phenacobius teretulus Cope, 1867	F	Kanawha minnow
Phenacobius uranops Cope, 1867	F	stargazing minnow
Phoxinus cumberlandensis Starnes & Starnes, 1978	F	blackside dace
Phoxinus eos (Cope, 1862)	F	northern redbelly dace
Phoxinus erythrogaster (Rafinesque, 1820)	F	southern redbelly dace
Phoxinus neogaeus Cope, 1868	F	finescale dace
Phoxinus oreas (Cope, 1868)	F	mountain redbelly dace
* *Phoxinus tennesseensis* Starnes & Jenkins, 1988	F	Tennessee dace
Pimephales notatus (Rafinesque, 1820)	F	bluntnose minnow
Pimephales promelas Rafinesque, 1820	F	fathead minnow
Pimephales tenellus (Girard, 1856)	F	slim minnow
Pimephales vigilax (Baird & Girard, 1853)	F	bullhead minnow
Plagopterus argentissimus Cope, 1874	F	woundfin
* *Platygobio gracilis* (Richardson, 1836)	F	flathead chub
+*Pogonichthys ciscoides* Hopkirk, 1974	F[X]	Clear Lake splittail

SCIENTIFIC NAME	OCCURRENCE	COMMON NAME
Pogonichthys macrolepidotus (Ayres, 1854)	F	splittail
Ptychocheilus grandis (Ayres, 1854)	F	Sacramento squawfish
Ptychocheilus lucius Girard, 1856	F	Colorado squawfish
Ptychocheilus oregonensis (Richardson, 1836)	F	northern squawfish
Ptychocheilus umpquae Snyder, 1908	F	Umpqua squawfish
Relictus solitarius Hubbs & Miller, 1972	F	relict dace
Rhinichthys atratulus (Hermann, 1804)	F	blacknose dace
Rhinichthys cataractae (Valenciennes, 1842)	F	longnose dace
* *Rhinichthys cobitis* (Girard, 1856)	F	loach minnow
* *Rhinichthys deaconi* Miller, 1984	F[X]	Las Vegas dace
Rhinichthys evermanni Snyder, 1908	F	Umpqua dace
Rhinichthys falcatus (Eigenmann & Eigenmann, 1893)	F	leopard dace
+*Rhinichthys osculus* (Girard, 1856)	F	speckled dace
Rhodeus sericeus (Pallas, 1776)	F[I]	bitterling
Richardsonius balteatus (Richardson, 1836)	F	redside shiner
Richardsonius egregius (Girard, 1858)	F	Lahontan redside
Scardinius erythrophthalmus (Linnaeus, 1758)	F[I]	rudd
Semotilus atromaculatus (Mitchill, 1818)	F	creek chub
Semotilus corporalis (Mitchill, 1817)	F	fallfish
Semotilus lumbee Snelson & Suttkus, 1978	F	sandhills chub
* *Semotilus thoreauianus* Jordan, 1877	F	Dixie chub
Tinca tinca (Linnaeus, 1758)	F[I]	tench

+Cobitidae—loaches

SCIENTIFIC NAME	OCCURRENCE	COMMON NAME
Misgurnus anguillicaudatus (Cantor, 1842)	F[I]	oriental weatherfish

+Catostomidae—suckers

SCIENTIFIC NAME	OCCURRENCE	COMMON NAME
Carpiodes carpio (Rafinesque, 1820)	F	river carpsucker
Carpiodes cyprinus (Lesueur, 1817)	F	quillback
Carpiodes velifer (Rafinesque, 1820)	F	highfin carpsucker
Catostomus ardens Jordan & Gilbert, 1881	F	Utah sucker
Catostomus bernardini Girard, 1856	F	Yaqui sucker
Catostomus catostomus (Forster, 1773)	F	longnose sucker
Catostomus clarki Baird & Girard, 1854	F	desert sucker
Catostomus columbianus (Eigenmann & Eigenmann, 1893)	F	bridgelip sucker
Catostomus commersoni (Lacepède, 1803)	F	white sucker
Catostomus discobolus Cope, 1872	F	bluehead sucker
Catostomus fumeiventris Miller, 1973	F	Owens sucker
Catostomus insignis Baird & Girard, 1854	F	Sonora sucker
Catostomus latipinnis Baird & Girard, 1853	F	flannelmouth sucker
Catostomus macrocheilus Girard, 1856	F	largescale sucker
Catostomus microps Rutter, 1908	F	Modoc sucker
Catostomus occidentalis Ayres, 1854	F	Sacramento sucker
Catostomus platyrhynchus (Cope, 1874)	F	mountain sucker
Catostomus plebeius Baird & Girard, 1854	F	Rio Grande sucker
Catostomus rimiculus Gilbert & Snyder, 1898	F	Klamath smallscale sucker
Catostomus santaanae (Snyder, 1908)	F	Santa Ana sucker
Catostomus snyderi Gilbert, 1898	F	Klamath largescale sucker

SCIENTIFIC NAME	OCCURRENCE	COMMON NAME
Catostomus tahoensis Gill & Jordan, 1878	F	Tahoe sucker
Catostomus warnerensis Snyder, 1908	F	Warner sucker
Chasmistes brevirostris Cope, 1879	F	shortnose sucker
Chasmistes cujus Cope, 1883	F	cui-ui[2]
Chasmistes liorus Jordan, 1878	F	June sucker
* *Chasmistes muriei* Miller & Smith, 1981	F[X]	Snake River sucker
Cycleptus elongatus (Lesueur, 1817)	F	blue sucker
* *Deltistes luxatus* (Cope, 1879)	F	Lost River sucker
Erimyzon oblongus (Mitchill, 1814)	F	creek chubsucker
Erimyzon sucetta (Lacepède, 1803)	F	lake chubsucker
Erimyzon tenuis (Agassiz, 1855)	F	sharpfin chubsucker
Hypentelium etowanum (Jordan, 1877)	F	Alabama hog sucker
Hypentelium nigricans (Lesueur, 1817)	F	northern hog sucker
Hypentelium roanokense Raney & Lachner, 1947	F	Roanoke hog sucker
Ictiobus bubalus (Rafinesque, 1818)	F	smallmouth buffalo
Ictiobus cyprinellus (Valenciennes, 1844)	F	bigmouth buffalo
Ictiobus niger (Rafinesque, 1819)	F	black buffalo
Lagochila lacera Jordan & Brayton, 1877	F[X]	harelip sucker
Minytrema melanops (Rafinesque, 1820)	F	spotted sucker
Moxostoma anisurum (Rafinesque, 1820)	F	silver redhorse
Moxostoma ariommum Robins & Raney, 1956	F	bigeye jumprock
Moxostoma atripinne Bailey, 1959	F	blackfin sucker
* *Moxostoma austrinum* (Bean, 1880)	F	west Mexican redhorse
Moxostoma carinatum (Cope, 1870)	F	river redhorse
Moxostoma cervinum (Cope, 1868)	F	black jumprock
Moxostoma congestum (Baird & Girard, 1854)	F	gray redhorse
Moxostoma duquesnei (Lesueur, 1817)	F	black redhorse
Moxostoma erythrurum (Rafinesque, 1818)	F	golden redhorse
Moxostoma hamiltoni (Raney & Lachner, 1946)	F	rustyside sucker
Moxostoma hubbsi Legendre, 1952	F	copper redhorse
Moxostoma lachneri Robins & Raney, 1956	F	greater jumprock
Moxostoma macrolepidotum (Lesueur, 1817)	F	shorthead redhorse
* *Moxostoma pappillosum* (Cope, 1870)	F	V-lip redhorse
Moxostoma poecilurum (Jordan, 1877)	F	blacktail redhorse
Moxostoma rhothoecum (Thoburn, 1896)	F	torrent sucker
Moxostoma robustum (Cope, 1870)	F	smallfin redhorse
Moxostoma rupiscartes Jordan & Jenkins, 1889	F	striped jumprock
Moxostoma valenciennesi Jordan, 1885	F	greater redhorse
Xyrauchen texanus (Abbott, 1861)	F	razorback sucker

*ORDER CHARACIFORMES

Characidae—characins

SCIENTIFIC NAME	OCCURRENCE	COMMON NAME
Astyanax mexicanus (Filippi, 1853)	F	Mexican tetra

[2] Pronounced kweé-wee.

SCIENTIFIC NAME	OCCURRENCE	COMMON NAME

ORDER SILURIFORMES

Ictaluridae—bullhead catfishes

* *Ameiurus brunneus* (Jordan, 1877)	F	snail bullhead
* *Ameiurus catus* (Linnaeus, 1758)	F	white catfish
* *Ameiurus melas* (Rafinesque, 1820)	F	black bullhead
* *Ameiurus natalis* (Lesueur, 1819)	F	yellow bullhead
* *Ameiurus nebulosus* (Lesueur, 1819)	F	brown bullhead
* *Ameiurus platycephalus* (Girard, 1859)	F	flat bullhead
* *Ameiurus serracanthus* (Yerger & Relyea, 1968)	F	spotted bullhead
Ictalurus furcatus (Lesueur, 1840)	F	blue catfish
Ictalurus lupus (Girard, 1858)	F	headwater catfish
Ictalurus pricei (Rutter, 1896)	F	Yaqui catfish
Ictalurus punctatus (Rafinesque, 1818)	F	channel catfish
Noturus albater Taylor, 1969	F	Ozark madtom
Noturus baileyi Taylor, 1969	F	smoky madtom
Noturus elegans Taylor, 1969	F	elegant madtom
Noturus eleutherus Jordan, 1877	F	mountain madtom
Noturus exilis Nelson, 1876	F	slender madtom
Noturus flavater Taylor, 1969	F	checkered madtom
Noturus flavipinnis Taylor, 1969	F	yellowfin madtom
Noturus flavus Rafinesque, 1818	F	stonecat
Noturus funebris Gilbert & Swain, 1891	F	black madtom
Noturus furiosus Jordan & Meek, 1889	F	Carolina madtom
Noturus gilberti Jordan & Evermann, 1889	F	orangefin madtom
Noturus gyrinus (Mitchill, 1817)	F	tadpole madtom
Noturus hildebrandi (Bailey & Taylor, 1950)	F	least madtom
Noturus insignis (Richardson, 1836)	F	margined madtom
Noturus lachneri Taylor, 1969	F	Ouachita madtom
Noturus leptacanthus Jordan, 1877	F	speckled madtom
Noturus miurus Jordan, 1877	F	brindled madtom
Noturus munitus Suttkus & Taylor, 1965	F	frecklebelly madtom
Noturus nocturnus Jordan & Gilbert, 1886	F	freckled madtom
Noturus phaeus Taylor, 1969	F	brown madtom
Noturus placidus Taylor, 1969	F	Neosho madtom
Noturus stanauli Etnier & Jenkins, 1980	F	pygmy madtom
Noturus stigmosus Taylor, 1969	F	northern madtom
Noturus taylori Douglas, 1972	F	Caddo madtom
Noturus trautmani Taylor, 1969	F	Scioto madtom
Pylodictis olivaris (Rafinesque, 1818)	F	flathead catfish
Satan eurystomus Hubbs & Bailey, 1947	F	widemouth blindcat
Trogloglanis pattersoni Eigenmann, 1919	F	toothless blindcat

Clariidae—labyrinth catfishes

Clarias batrachus (Linnaeus, 1758)	F[I]	walking catfish

Ariidae—sea catfishes

Arius felis (Linnaeus, 1766)	A-F	hardhead catfish
Bagre marinus (Mitchill, 1815)	A	gafftopsail catfish
Bagre panamensis (Gill, 1863)	P	chihuil

SCIENTIFIC NAME	OCCURRENCE	COMMON NAME
	*Loricariidae—suckermouth catfishes	
Hypostomus plecostomus (Linnaeus, 1766)	F[I]	suckermouth catfish
* *Pterygoplichthys multiradiatus* (Hancock, 1828)	F[I]	sailfin catfish
	ORDER SALMONIFORMES	
	Esocidae—pikes	
Esox americanus americanus Gmelin, 1788	F	redfin pickerel
Esox americanus vermiculatus Lesueur, 1846	F	grass pickerel
+*Esox lucius* Linnaeus, 1758	F	northern pike
Esox masquinongy Mitchill, 1824	F	muskellunge
Esox niger Lesueur, 1818	F	chain pickerel
	Umbridae—mudminnows	
Dallia pectoralis Bean, 1880	F	Alaska blackfish
Novumbra hubbsi Schultz, 1929	F	Olympic mudminnow
Umbra limi (Kirtland, 1840)	F	central mudminnow
Umbra pygmaea (DeKay, 1842)	F	eastern mudminnow
	Argentinidae—argentines	
Argentina sialis Gilbert, 1890	P	Pacific argentine
Argentina silus Ascanius, 1775	A	Atlantic argentine
Argentina striata Goode & Bean, 1895	A	striated argentine
Glossanodon pygmaeus Cohen, 1958	A	pygmy argentine
	Bathylagidae—deepsea smelts	
* *Leuroglossus schmidti* Rass, 1955	P	northern smoothtongue
* *Leuroglossus stilbius* Gilbert, 1890	P	California smoothtongue
	Opisthoproctidae—spookfishes	
Macropinna microstoma Chapman, 1939	P	barreleye
	Osmeridae—smelts	
Allosmerus elongatus (Ayres, 1854)	P	whitebait smelt
Hypomesus nipponensis McAllister, 1963	F[I]	wakasagi
Hypomesus olidus (Pallas, 1814)	F	pond smelt
Hypomesus pretiosus (Girard, 1855)	F-P	surf smelt
Hypomesus transpacificus McAllister, 1963	F-P	delta smelt
Mallotus villosus (Müller, 1776)	A-F-P	capelin
+*Osmerus mordax* (Mitchill, 1814)	A-F-P	rainbow smelt
Spirinchus starksi (Fisk, 1913)	P	night smelt
Spirinchus thaleichthys (Ayres, 1860)	F-P	longfin smelt
Thaleichthys pacificus (Richardson, 1836)	F-P	eulachon
	Salmonidae—trouts	
* *Coregonus artedi* Lesueur, 1818	F	cisco or lake herring
Coregonus autumnalis (Pallas, 1776)	F	Arctic cisco
Coregonus clupeaformis (Mitchill, 1818)	A-F	lake whitefish
Coregonus hoyi (Gill, 1872)	F	bloater
* *Coregonus huntsmani* Scott, 1987	A-F	Atlantic whitefish

SCIENTIFIC NAME	OCCURRENCE	COMMON NAME
* *Coregonus johannae* (Wagner, 1910)	F[X]	deepwater cisco
Coregonus kiyi (Koelz, 1921)	F	kiyi
Coregonus laurettae Bean, 1881	F	Bering cisco
Coregonus nasus (Pallas, 1776)	F	broad whitefish
+*Coregonus nigripinnis* (Gill, 1872)	F[X]	blackfin cisco
Coregonus pidschian (Gmelin, 1788)	F	humpback whitefish
Coregonus reighardi (Koelz, 1924)	F	shortnose cisco
Coregonus sardinella Valenciennes, 1848	F	least cisco
+*Coregonus zenithicus* (Jordan & Evermann, 1909)	F	shortjaw cisco
* *Oncorhynchus aguabonita* (Jordan, 1893)	F	golden trout
* *Oncorhynchus apache* (Miller, 1972)	F	Apache trout
* *Oncorhynchus clarki* (Richardson, 1836)	F-P	cutthroat trout
* *Oncorhynchus gilae* (Miller, 1950)	F	Gila trout
Oncorhynchus gorbuscha (Walbaum, 1792)	A-F-P	pink salmon
Oncorhynchus keta (Walbaum, 1792)	F-P	chum salmon
Oncorhynchus kisutch (Walbaum, 1792)	A-F-P	coho salmon
* *Oncorhynchus mykiss* (Walbaum, 1792)	A-F-P	rainbow trout[3]
Oncorhynchus nerka (Walbaum, 1792)	F-P	sockeye salmon[4]
Oncorhynchus tshawytscha (Walbaum, 1792)	F-P	chinook salmon
Prosopium abyssicola (Snyder, 1919)	F	Bear Lake whitefish
Prosopium coulteri (Eigenmann & Eigenmann, 1892)	F	pygmy whitefish
Prosopium cylindraceum (Pallas, 1784)	F	round whitefish
* *Prosopium gemmifer* (Snyder, 1919)	F	Bonneville cisco
Prosopium spilonotus (Snyder, 1919)	F	Bonneville whitefish
Prosopium williamsoni (Girard, 1856)	F	mountain whitefish
Salmo salar Linnaeus, 1758	A-F	Atlantic salmon[5]
Salmo trutta Linnaeus, 1758	A-F[I]	brown trout
Salvelinus alpinus (Linnaeus, 1758)	A-F-P	Arctic char[6]
Salvelinus confluentus (Suckley, 1858)	F-P	bull trout
Salvelinus fontinalis (Mitchill, 1814)	A-F	brook trout
Salvelinus malma (Walbaum, 1792)	F-P	Dolly Varden
Salvelinus namaycush (Walbaum, 1792)	F	lake trout
Stenodus leucichthys (Güldenstadt, 1772)	F	inconnu
Thymallus arcticus (Pallas, 1776)	F	Arctic grayling

*ORDER STOMIIFORMES

Gonostomatidae[7]—lightfishes

* *Pollichthys mauli* (Poll, 1953)	A	stareye lightfish

*Stomiidae—dragonfishes

Chauliodus macouni Bean, 1890	P	Pacific viperfish

[3] The term steelhead is applied to sea-run rainbow trout and some populations from large lakes.

[4] Lacustrine stocks of sockeye salmon are known as kokanee.

[5] Lake populations of Atlantic salmon are variously known as ouananiche, lake Atlantic salmon, landlocked salmon, and Sebago salmon.

[6] Sunapee trout, blueback trout, and Quebec red trout are regarded by some authors as species distinct from the Arctic char.

[7] The many species of lightfishes are mesopelagic, but occasional stragglers and early life history stages are found over the continental shelf.

SCIENTIFIC NAME	OCCURRENCE	COMMON NAME
* *Stomias boa* (Risso, 1810)	A	boa dragonfish
Tactostoma macropus Bolin, 1939	P	longfin dragonfish

*ORDER AULOPIFORMES

Aulopidae—aulopus

Aulopus nanae Mead, 1958	A	yellowfin aulopus

Chlorophthalmidae—greeneyes

Chlorophthalmus agassizi Bonaparte, 1840	A	shortnose greeneye
Parasudis truculenta (Goode & Bean, 1896)	A	longnose greeneye

Scopelarchidae—pearleyes

Benthalbella dentata (Chapman, 1939)	P	northern pearleye

Synodontidae—lizardfishes

Saurida brasiliensis Norman, 1935	A	largescale lizardfish
Saurida caribbaea Breder, 1927	A	smallscale lizardfish
Saurida normani Longley, 1935	A	shortjaw lizardfish
Synodus foetens (Linnaeus, 1766)	A	inshore lizardfish
Synodus intermedius (Agassiz, 1829)	A	sand diver
Synodus lucioceps (Ayres, 1855)	P	California lizardfish
Synodus poeyi Jordan, 1887	A	offshore lizardfish
Synodus synodus (Linnaeus, 1758)	A	red lizardfish
Trachinocephalus myops (Forster, 1801)	A	snakefish

Paralepidae—barracudinas

* *Notolepis rissoi* (Bonaparte, 1841)	A	white barracudina
* *Paralepis atlantica* Krøyer, 1891	A-P	duckbill barracudina

Anotopteridae—daggertooths

Anotopterus pharao Zugmayer, 1911	A-P	daggertooth

Alepisauridae—lancetfishes

Alepisaurus brevirostris Gibbs, 1960	A	shortnose lancetfish
Alepisaurus ferox Lowe, 1833	A-P	longnose lancetfish

ORDER MYCTOPHIFORMES

+Myctophidae—lanternfishes

* *Benthosema glaciale* (Reinhardt, 1837)	A	glacier lanternfish
Ceratoscopelus townsendi (Eigenmann & Eigenmann, 1889)	P	dogtooth lampfish
Diaphus theta Eigenmann & Eigenmann, 1890	P	California headlightfish
Diogenys laternatus (Garman, 1899)	P	Diogenes lanternfish
* *Lampadena speculigera* Goode & Bean, 1896	A	mirror lanternfish
* *Lampanyctus crocodilus* (Risso, 1810)	A	jewel lanternfish
Lampanyctus regalis (Gilbert, 1892)	P	pinpoint lampfish
* *Myctophum affine* (Lütken, 1892)	A	metallic lanternfish
* *Myctophum punctatum* Rafinesque, 1810	A	spotted lanternfish

SCIENTIFIC NAME	OCCURRENCE	COMMON NAME
Notoscopelus resplendens (Richardson, 1845)	P	patchwork lampfish
* *Protomyctophum crockeri* (Bolin, 1939)	P	California flashlightfish
Stenobrachius leucopsarus (Eigenmann & Eigenmann, 1890)	P	northern lampfish
Tarletonbeania crenularis (Jordan & Gilbert, 1880)	P	blue lanternfish
Triphoturus mexicanus (Gilbert, 1890)	P	Mexican lampfish

ORDER PERCOPSIFORMES

Percopsidae—trout-perches

Percopsis omiscomaycus (Walbaum, 1792)	F	trout-perch
Percopsis transmontana (Eigenmann & Eigenmann, 1892)	F	sand roller

Aphredoderidae—pirate perches

Aphredoderus sayanus (Gilliams, 1824)	F	pirate perch

Amblyopsidae—cavefishes

Amblyopsis rosae (Eigenmann, 1899)	F	Ozark cavefish
Amblyopsis spelaea DeKay, 1842	F	northern cavefish
Chologaster agassizi Putnam, 1872	F	spring cavefish
Chologaster cornuta Agassiz, 1853	F	swampfish
Speoplatyrhinus poulsoni Cooper & Kuehne, 1974	F	Alabama cavefish
Typhlichthys subterraneus Girard, 1859	F	southern cavefish

ORDER GADIFORMES

*Moridae—codlings

* *Antimora microlepis* Bean, 1890	P	Pacific flatnose
* *Physiculus fulvus* Bean, 1884	A	metallic codling
* *Physiculus rastrelliger* Gilbert, 1890	P	hundred-fathom codling

Bregmacerotidae—codlets

Bregmaceros atlanticus Goode & Bean, 1886	A	antenna codlet
* *Bregmaceros houdei* Saksena & Richards, 1986	A	stellate codlet

+Gadidae—cods

* *Arctogadus borisovi* Drjagin, 1932	A-P	toothed cod
* *Arctogadus glacialis* (Peters, 1874)	A-P	polar cod
Boreogadus saida (Lepechin, 1774)	A-P	Arctic cod
* *Brosme brosme* (Ascanius, 1772)	A	cusk
* *Ciliata septentrionalis* (Collett, 1875)	A	northern rockling
Eleginus gracilis (Tilesius, 1810)	P	saffron cod
Enchelyopus cimbrius (Linnaeus, 1766)	A	fourbeard rockling
Gadus macrocephalus Tilesius, 1810	P	Pacific cod
Gadus morhua Linnaeus, 1758	A	Atlantic cod
* *Gadus ogac* Richardson, 1836	A-P	Greenland cod
Lota lota (Linnaeus, 1758)	F	burbot
Melanogrammus aeglefinus (Linnaeus, 1758)	A	haddock
* *Merluccius albidus* (Mitchill, 1818)	A	offshore hake

SCIENTIFIC NAME	OCCURRENCE	COMMON NAME
Merluccius bilinearis (Mitchill, 1814)	A	silver hake
Merluccius productus (Ayres, 1855)	P	Pacific hake
Microgadus proximus (Girard, 1854)	P	Pacific tomcod
Microgadus tomcod (Walbaum, 1792)	A-F	Atlantic tomcod
* *Micromesistius poutassou* (Risso, 1826)	A	blue whiting
* *Molva molva* (Linnaeus, 1758)	A	European ling
Pollachius virens (Linnaeus, 1758)	A	pollock
Steindachneria argentea Goode & Bean, 1896	A	luminous hake
Theragra chalcogramma (Pallas, 1814)	P	walleye pollock
* *Urophycis chesteri* (Goode & Bean, 1878)	A	longfin hake
Urophycis chuss (Walbaum, 1792)	A	red hake
Urophycis cirrata (Goode & Bean, 1896)	A	gulf hake
Urophycis earlli (Bean, 1880)	A	Carolina hake
Urophycis floridana (Bean & Dresel, 1884)	A	southern hake
Urophycis regia (Walbaum, 1792)	A	spotted hake
Urophycis tenuis (Mitchill, 1814)	A	white hake
	Macrouridae—grenadiers	
* *Albatrossia pectoralis* (Gilbert, 1892)	P	giant grenadier
* *Caelorinchus caribbaeus* (Goode & Bean, 1885)	A	blackfin grenadier
* *Caelorinchus caelorhincus* (Risso, 1810)	A	saddled grenadier
* *Macrourus berglax* Lacepède, 1802	A	roughhead grenadier
Nezumia bairdi (Goode & Bean, 1877)	A	marlin-spike
Nezumia sclerorhynchus (Valenciennes, 1838)	A	bluntsnout grenadier
Nezumia stelgidolepis (Gilbert, 1890)	P	California grenadier
	+Ophidiidae—cusk-eels	
Brotula barbata (Schneider, 1801)	A	bearded brotula
Chilara taylori (Girard, 1858)	P	spotted cusk-eel
* *Lepophidium brevibarbe* (Cuvier, 1829)	A	blackedge cusk-eel
Lepophidium jeannae Fowler, 1941	A	mottled cusk-eel
* *Lepophidium profundorum* (Gill, 1863)	A	fawn cusk-eel
+ *Ophidion beani* Jordan & Gilbert, 1883	A	longnose cusk-eel
Ophidion grayi (Fowler, 1948)	A	blotched cusk-eel
Ophidion holbrooki (Putnam, 1874)	A	bank cusk-eel
Ophidion marginatum (DeKay, 1842)	A	striped cusk-eel
Ophidion scrippsae (Hubbs, 1916)	P	basketweave cusk-eel
Ophidion selenops Robins & Böhlke, 1959	A	mooneye cusk-eel
Ophidion welshi (Nichols & Breder, 1922)	A	crested cusk-eel
Otophidium dormitator Böhlke & Robins, 1959	A	sleeper cusk-eel
Otophidium omostigmum (Jordan & Gilbert, 1882)	A	polka-dot cusk-eel
Parophidion schmidti (Woods & Kanazawa, 1951)	A	dusky cusk-eel
* *Petrotyx sanguineus* (Meek & Hildebrand, 1928)	A	redfin brotula
	Carapidae—pearlfishes	
Carapus bermudensis (Jones, 1874)	A	pearlfish
* *Echiodon dawsoni* Williams & Shipp, 1982	A	chain pearlfish
	Bythitidae—viviparous brotulas	
Brosmophycis marginata (Ayres, 1854)	P	red brotula

SCIENTIFIC NAME	OCCURRENCE	COMMON NAME
Gunterichthys longipenis Dawson, 1966	A	gold brotula
Ogilbia cayorum Evermann & Kendall, 1897	A	key brotula
Oligopus claudei (Torre, 1930)	A	reef-cave brotula
Oligopus diagrammus (Heller & Snodgrass, 1903)	P	purple brotula
Stygnobrotula latebricola Böhlke, 1957	A	black brotula

ORDER BATRACHOIDIFORMES

Batrachoididae—toadfishes

SCIENTIFIC NAME	OCCURRENCE	COMMON NAME
Opsanus beta (Goode & Bean, 1879)	A	gulf toadfish
Opsanus pardus (Goode & Bean, 1879)	A	leopard toadfish
Opsanus tau (Linnaeus, 1766)	A	oyster toadfish
Porichthys myriaster Hubbs & Schultz, 1939	P	specklefin midshipman
Porichthys notatus Girard, 1854	P	plainfin midshipman
Porichthys plectrodon Jordan & Gilbert, 1882	A	Atlantic midshipman

ORDER LOPHIIFORMES

Lophiidae—goosefishes

SCIENTIFIC NAME	OCCURRENCE	COMMON NAME
* *Lophiodes caulinaris* (Garman, 1899)	P	spottedtail goosefish
Lophiodes reticulatus Caruso & Suttkus, 1979	A	reticulate goosefish
Lophius americanus Valenciennes, 1837	A	goosefish
Lophius gastrophysus Ribeiro, 1915	A	blackfin goosefish

Antennariidae—frogfishes

SCIENTIFIC NAME	OCCURRENCE	COMMON NAME
Antennarius avalonis Jordan & Starks, 1907	P	roughjaw frogfish
Antennarius multiocellatus (Valenciennes, 1837)	A	longlure frogfish
Antennarius ocellatus (Bloch & Schneider, 1801)	A	ocellated frogfish
Antennarius pauciradiatus Schultz, 1957	A	dwarf frogfish
Antennarius radiosus Garman, 1896	A	singlespot frogfish
* *Antennarius striatus* (Shaw & Nodder, 1794)	A	striated frogfish
Histrio histrio (Linnaeus, 1758)	A	sargassumfish

Chaunacidae—gapers

SCIENTIFIC NAME	OCCURRENCE	COMMON NAME
Chaunax stigmaeus Fowler, 1946	A	redeye gaper

Ogcocephalidae—batfishes

SCIENTIFIC NAME	OCCURRENCE	COMMON NAME
* *Dibranchus atlanticus* Peters, 1875	A	Atlantic batfish
Halieutichthys aculeatus (Mitchill, 1818)	A	pancake batfish
* *Ogcocephalus corniger* Bradbury, 1980	A	longnose batfish
* *Ogcocephalus declivirostris* Bradbury, 1980	A	slantbrow batfish
Ogcocephalus nasutus (Valenciennes, 1837)	A	shortnose batfish
* *Ogcocephalus pantostictus* Bradbury, 1980	A	spotted batfish
Ogcocephalus parvus Longley & Hildebrand, 1940	A	roughback batfish
+ *Ogcocephalus radiatus* (Mitchill, 1818)	A	polka-dot batfish
* *Ogcocephalus rostellum* Bradbury, 1980	A	palefin batfish
* *Zalieutes elater* (Jordan & Gilbert, 1882)	P	roundel batfish
Zalieutes mcgintyi (Fowler, 1952)	A	tricorn batfish

SCIENTIFIC NAME	OCCURRENCE	COMMON NAME
	Ceratiidae—seadevils	
* *Cryptopsaras couesi* Gill, 1883	A-P	triplewart seadevil
	Himantolophidae—footballfishes	
Himantolophus groenlandicus Reinhardt, 1837	A	Atlantic footballfish
	ORDER GOBIESOCIFORMES	
	Gobiesocidae—clingfishes	
Acyrtops beryllinus (Hildebrand & Ginsburg, 1927)	A	emerald clingfish
Gobiesox eugrammus Briggs, 1955	P	lined clingfish
Gobiesox maeandricus (Girard, 1858)	P	northern clingfish
Gobiesox papillifer Gilbert, 1890	P	bearded clingfish
Gobiesox punctulatus (Poey, 1875)	A	stippled clingfish
Gobiesox rhessodon Smith, 1881	P	California clingfish
Gobiesox strumosus Cope, 1870	A	skilletfish
* *Rimicola dimorpha* Briggs, 1955	P	southern clingfish
Rimicola eigenmanni (Gilbert, 1890)	P	slender clingfish
Rimicola muscarum (Meek & Pierson, 1895)	P	kelp clingfish
	ORDER ATHERINIFORMES (BELONIFORMES, CYPRINODONTIFORMES)	
	+Exocoetidae—flyingfishes	
Chriodorus atherinoides Goode & Bean, 1882	A	hardhead halfbeak
Cypselurus californicus (Cooper, 1863)	P	California flyingfish
Cypselurus comatus (Mitchill, 1815)	A	clearwing flyingfish
Cypselurus cyanopterus (Valenciennes, 1847)	A	margined flyingfish
Cypselurus exsiliens (Linnaeus, 1771)	A	bandwing flyingfish
Cypselurus furcatus (Mitchill, 1815)	A	spotfin flyingfish
Cypselurus hubbsi Parin, 1961	P	blotchwing flyingfish
Cypselurus melanurus (Valenciennes, 1847)	A	Atlantic flyingfish
Euleptorhamphus velox Poey, 1868	A	flying halfbeak
* *Euleptorhamphus viridis* (Van Hasselt, 1824)	P	ribbon halfbeak
Exocoetus obtusirostris Günther, 1866	A	oceanic two-wing flyingfish
Exocoetus volitans Linnaeus, 1758	A	tropical two-wing flyingfish
Fodiator acutus (Valenciennes, 1847)	A	sharpchin flyingfish
* *Hemiramphus balao* (Lesueur, 1821)	A	balao
Hemiramphus brasiliensis (Linnaeus, 1758)	A	ballyhoo
Hemiramphus saltator Gilbert & Starks, 1904	P	longfin halfbeak
Hirundichthys affinis (Günther, 1866)	A	fourwing flyingfish
Hirundichthys rondeleti (Valenciennes, 1847)	A-P	blackwing flyingfish
Hyporhamphus rosae (Jordan & Gilbert, 1880)	P	California halfbeak
* *Hyporhamphus unifasciatus* (Ranzani, 1842)	A-P	silverstripe halfbeak
Oxyporhamphus micropterus (Valenciennes, 1847)	A	smallwing flyingfish
Parexocoetus brachypterus (Richardson, 1846)	A	sailfin flyingfish
Prognichthys gibbifrons (Valenciennes, 1847)	A	bluntnose flyingfish
	Belonidae—needlefishes	
Ablennes hians (Valenciennes, 1846)	A	flat needlefish
Platybelone argalus (Lesueur, 1821)	A	keeltail needlefish

SCIENTIFIC NAME	OCCURRENCE	COMMON NAME
Strongylura exilis (Girard, 1854)	P	California needlefish
Strongylura marina (Walbaum,1792)	A-F	Atlantic needlefish
Strongylura notata (Poey, 1860)	A	redfin needlefish
Strongylura timucu (Walbaum, 1792)	A	timucu
Tylosurus acus (Lacepède, 1803)	A	agujon
Tylosurus crocodilus (Peron & Lesueur, 1821)	A	houndfish
	Scomberesocidae—sauries	
Cololabis saira (Brevoort, 1857)	P	Pacific saury
Scomberesox saurus (Walbaum, 1792)	A	Atlantic saury
	*Aplocheilidae—rivulins	
* *Rivulus harti* (Boulenger, 1890)	F[I]	giant rivulus
* *Rivulus marmoratus* Poey, 1880	A-F	mangrove rivulus
	+Cyprinodontidae—killifishes	
Adinia xenica (Jordan & Gilbert, 1882)	A	diamond killifish
+*Crenichthys baileyi* (Gilbert, 1893)	F	White River springfish
+*Crenichthys nevadae* Hubbs, 1932	F	Railroad Valley springfish
Cyprinodon bovinus Baird & Girard, 1853	F	Leon Springs pupfish
Cyprinodon diabolis Wales, 1930	F	Devils Hole pupfish
Cyprinodon elegans Baird & Girard, 1853	F	Comanche Springs pupfish
Cyprinodon eximius Girard, 1859	F	Conchos pupfish
Cyprinodon hubbsi Carr, 1936	F	Lake Eustis minnow
Cyprinodon macularius Baird & Girard, 1853	F	desert pupfish
Cyprinodon nevadensis Eigenmann & Eigenmann, 1889	F	Amargosa pupfish
Cyprinodon pecosensis Echelle & Echelle, 1978	F	Pecos pupfish
Cyprinodon radiosus Miller, 1948	F	Owens pupfish
Cyprinodon rubrofluviatilis Fowler, 1916	F	Red River pupfish
Cyprinodon salinus Miller, 1943	F	Salt Creek pupfish
Cyprinodon tularosa Miller & Echelle, 1975	F	White Sands pupfish
Cyprinodon variegatus Lacepède, 1803	A-F	sheepshead minnow
* *Empetrichthys latos* Miller, 1948	F	Pahrump poolfish
* *Empetrichthys merriami* Gilbert, 1893	F[X]	Ash Meadows poolfish
Floridichthys carpio (Günther, 1866)	A	goldspotted killifish
Fundulus albolineatus Gilbert, 1891	F[X]	whiteline topminnow
* *Fundulus bifax* Cashner & Rogers, 1988	F	stippled studfish
Fundulus catenatus (Storer, 1846)	F	northern studfish
Fundulus chrysotus (Günther, 1866)	F	golden topminnow
Fundulus cingulatus Valenciennes, 1846	F	banded topminnow
Fundulus confluentus Goode & Bean, 1879	A-F	marsh killifish
Fundulus diaphanus (Lesueur, 1817)	F	banded killifish
* *Fundulus dispar* (Agassiz, 1854)	F	starhead topminnow
* *Fundulus escambiae* (Bollman, 1897)	F	russetfin topminnow
* *Fundulus euryzonus* Suttkus & Cashner, 1981	F	broadstripe topminnow
Fundulus grandis Baird & Girard, 1853	A-F	gulf killifish
Fundulus heteroclitus (Linnaeus, 1766)	A-F	mummichog
Fundulus jenkinsi (Evermann, 1892)	A-F	saltmarsh topminnow
* *Fundulus julisia* Williams & Etnier, 1982	F	Barrens topminnow

SCIENTIFIC NAME	OCCURRENCE	COMMON NAME
Fundulus lineolatus (Agassiz, 1854)	F	lined topminnow
* *Fundulus luciae* (Baird, 1855)	A-F	spotfin killifish
+*Fundulus majalis* (Walbaum, 1792)	A	striped killifish
Fundulus notatus (Rafinesque, 1820)	F	blackstripe topminnow
* *Fundulus notti* (Agassiz, 1854)	F	bayou topminnow
Fundulus olivaceus (Storer, 1845)	F	blackspotted topminnow
Fundulus parvipinnis Girard, 1854	F-P	California killifish
Fundulus pulvereus (Evermann, 1892)	A-F	bayou killifish
Fundulus rathbuni Jordan & Meek, 1889	F	speckled killifish
Fundulus sciadicus Cope, 1865	F	plains topminnow
Fundulus seminolis Girard, 1859	F	Seminole killifish
+*Fundulus similis* (Baird & Girard, 1853)	A	longnose killifish
Fundulus stellifer (Jordan, 1877)	F	southern studfish
Fundulus waccamensis Hubbs & Raney, 1946	F	Waccamaw killifish
Fundulus zebrinus Jordan & Gilbert, 1883	F	plains killifish
Jordanella floridae Goode & Bean, 1879	F	flagfish
Leptolucania ommata (Jordan, 1884)	F	pygmy killifish
Lucania goodei Jordan, 1880	F	bluefin killifish
* *Lucania parva* (Baird & Girard, 1855)	A-F-P	rainwater killifish
	Poeciliidae—livebearers	
Belonesox belizanus Kner, 1860	A-F[I]	pike killifish
* *Gambusia affinis* (Baird & Girard, 1853)	A-F	western mosquitofish
* *Gambusia amistadensis* Peden, 1973	F[X]	Amistad gambusia
Gambusia gaigei Hubbs, 1929	F	Big Bend gambusia
Gambusia geiseri Hubbs & Hubbs, 1957	F	largespring gambusia
* *Gambusia georgei* Hubbs & Peden, 1969	F[X]	San Marcos gambusia
Gambusia heterochir Hubbs, 1957	F[X]	Clear Creek gambusia
* *Gambusia holbrooki* Girard, 1859	A-F	eastern mosquitofish
Gambusia nobilis (Baird & Girard, 1853)	F	Pecos gambusia
Gambusia rhizophorae Rivas, 1969	A-F	mangrove gambusia
Gambusia senilis Girard, 1859	F	blotched gambusia
Heterandria formosa Agassiz, 1855	F	least killifish
Poecilia formosa (Girard, 1859)	F	Amazon molly
Poecilia latipinna (Lesueur, 1821)	A-F	sailfin molly
Poecilia mexicana Steindachner, 1863	F[I]	shortfin molly
Poecilia reticulata Peters, 1859	F[I]	guppy
Poeciliopsis gracilis (Heckel, 1848)	F[I]	porthole livebearer
Poeciliopsis occidentalis (Baird & Girard, 1853)	F	Gila topminnow
Xiphophorus helleri Heckel, 1848	F[I]	green swordtail
Xiphophorus maculatus (Günther, 1866)	F[I]	southern platyfish
Xiphophorus variatus (Meek, 1904)	F[I]	variable platyfish
	Atherinidae—silversides	
Atherinomorus stipes (Müller & Troschel, 1847)	A	hardhead silverside
Atherinops affinis (Ayres, 1860)	P	topsmelt
Atherinopsis californiensis Girard, 1854	P	jacksmelt
Hypoatherina harringtonensis (Goode, 1877)	A	reef silverside
Labidesthes sicculus (Cope, 1865)	F	brook silverside
Leuresthes tenuis (Ayres, 1860)	P	California grunion

SCIENTIFIC NAME	OCCURRENCE	COMMON NAME
Membras martinica (Valenciennes, 1835)	A	rough silverside
Menidia beryllina (Cope, 1866)	A-F	inland silverside
* *Menidia clarkhubbsi* Echelle & Mosier, 1982	A	Texas silverside
Menidia conchorum Hildebrand & Ginsburg, 1927	A	key silverside
Menidia extensa Hubbs & Raney, 1946	F	Waccamaw silverside
Menidia menidia (Linnaeus, 1766)	A	Atlantic silverside
Menidia peninsulae (Goode & Bean, 1879)	A	tidewater silverside
ORDER LAMPRIFORMES		
Lampridae—opahs		
Lampris guttatus (Brünnich, 1788)	A-P	opah
Lophotidae—crestfishes		
Eumecichthys fiski (Günther, 1890)	A	unicornfish
* *Lophotus lacepede* Giorna, 1809	A-P	crestfish
Trachipteridae—ribbonfishes		
Desmodema lorum Rosenblatt & Butler, 1977	P	whiptail ribbonfish
Desmodema polystictum (Ogilby, 1897)	A	polka-dot ribbonfish
Trachipterus altivelis Kner, 1859	P	king-of-the-salmon
Trachipterus arcticus (Brünnich, 1788)	A	dealfish
Trachipterus fukuzakii Fitch, 1964	P	tapertail ribbonfish
Zu cristatus (Bonelli, 1820)	A-P	scalloped ribbonfish
Regalecidae—oarfishes		
Regalecus glesne (Ascanius, 1772)	A-P	oarfish
Stylephoridae—tube-eyes		
Stylephorus chordatus Shaw, 1791	A	tube-eye
ORDER BERYCIFORMES		
*Trachichthyidae—roughies		
* *Gephyroberyx darwini* (Johnson, 1866)	A	big roughy
*Berycidae—alfonsinos		
* *Beryx decadactylus* Cuvier, 1829	A	red bream
Holocentridae—squirrelfishes		
Corniger spinosus Agassiz, 1829	A	spinycheek soldierfish
* *Holocentrus adscensionis* (Osbeck, 1765)	A	squirrelfish
Holocentrus bullisi Woods, 1955	A	deepwater squirrelfish
Holocentrus coruscus (Poey, 1860)	A	reef squirrelfish
Holocentrus marianus (Cuvier, 1829)	A	longjaw squirrelfish
Holocentrus poco (Woods, 1965)	A	saddle squirrelfish
Holocentrus rufus (Walbaum, 1792)	A	longspine squirrelfish
Holocentrus vexillarius (Poey, 1860)	A	dusky squirrelfish
Myripristis jacobus Cuvier, 1829	A	blackbar soldierfish
Ostichthys trachypoma (Günther, 1859)	A	bigeye soldierfish
Plectrypops retrospinis (Guichenot, 1853)	A	cardinal soldierfish

SCIENTIFIC NAME	OCCURRENCE	COMMON NAME
	Polymixiidae—beardfishes	
Polymixia lowei Günther, 1859	A	beardfish
	ORDER ZEIFORMES	
	Zeidae—dories	
* *Cyttopsis rosea* (Goode & Bean, 1896)	A	red dory
Zenopsis conchifera (Lowe, 1852)	A	buckler dory
Zenopsis nebulosa (Temminck & Schlegel, 1845)	P	mirror dory
	Grammicolepidae—diamond dories	
* *Grammicolepis brachiusculus* Poey, 1873	A	thorny tinselfish
Xenolepidichthys dalgleishi Gilchrist, 1922	A	spotted tinselfish
	Caproidae—boarfishes	
Antigonia capros Lowe, 1843	A	deepbody boarfish
Antigonia combatia Berry & Rathjen, 1959	A	shortspine boarfish
	ORDER GASTEROSTEIFORMES	
	Gasterosteidae—sticklebacks	
Apeltes quadracus (Mitchill, 1815)	A-F	fourspine stickleback
Aulorhynchus flavidus Gill, 1861	P	tube-snout
Culaea inconstans (Kirtland, 1841)	F	brook stickleback
Gasterosteus aculeatus Linnaeus, 1758	A-F-P	threespine stickleback
Gasterosteus wheatlandi Putnam, 1867	A	blackspotted stickleback
Pungitius pungitius (Linnaeus, 1758)	A-F-P	ninespine stickleback
	Aulostomidae—trumpetfishes	
Aulostomus maculatus Valenciennes, 1845	A	trumpetfish
	Fistulariidae—cornetfishes	
Fistularia petimba Lacepède, 1803	A	red cornetfish
Fistularia tabacaria Linnaeus, 1758	A	bluespotted cornetfish
	Centriscidae—snipefishes	
Macroramphosus gracilis (Lowe, 1839)	A-P	slender snipefish
Macroramphosus scolopax (Linnaeus, 1758)	A	longspine snipefish
	Syngnathidae—pipefishes	
* *Acentronura dendritica* (Barbour, 1905)	A	pipehorse
* *Anarchopterus criniger* (Bean & Dresel, 1884)	A	fringed pipefish
* *Anarchopterus tectus* (Dawson, 1978)	A	insular pipefish
* *Bryx dunckeri* (Metzelaar, 1919)	A	pugnose pipefish
* *Cosmocampus albirostris* (Kaup, 1856)	A	whitenose pipefish
* *Cosmocampus arctus* (Jenkins & Evermann, 1889)	P	snubnose pipefish
Cosmocampus brachycephalus (Poey, 1868)	A	crested pipefish
* *Cosmocampus elucens* (Poey, 1868)	A	shortfin pipefish
* *Cosmocampus hildebrandi* (Herald, 1965)	A	dwarf pipefish

SCIENTIFIC NAME	OCCURRENCE	COMMON NAME
Cosmocampus profundus (Herald, 1965)	A	deepwater pipefish
Hippocampus erectus Perry, 1810	A	lined seahorse
Hippocampus ingens Girard, 1858	P	Pacific seahorse
Hippocampus reidi Ginsburg, 1933	A	longsnout seahorse
Hippocampus zosterae Jordan & Gilbert, 1882	A	dwarf seahorse
Micrognathus crinitus (Jenyns, 1842)	A	banded pipefish
+*Micrognathus ensenadae* (Silvester, 1916)	A	harlequin pipefish
* *Microphis brachyurus* (Bleeker, 1853)	A-F	opossum pipefish
Syngnathus affinis Günther, 1870	A	Texas pipefish
Syngnathus auliscus (Swain, 1882)	P	barred pipefish
Syngnathus californiensis Storer, 1845	P	kelp pipefish
Syngnathus euchrous Fritzche, 1980	P	chocolate pipefish
Syngnathus exilis (Osburn & Nichols, 1916)	P	barcheek pipefish
Syngnathus floridae (Jordan & Gilbert, 1882)	A	dusky pipefish
Syngnathus fuscus Storer, 1839	A	northern pipefish
Syngnathus leptorhynchus Girard, 1854	P	bay pipefish
Syngnathus louisianae Günther, 1870	A	chain pipefish
Syngnathus pelagicus Linnaeus, 1758	A	sargassum pipefish
Syngnathus scovelli (Evermann & Kendall, 1896)	A-F	gulf pipefish
Syngnathus springeri Herald, 1942	A	bull pipefish

*ORDER DACTYLOPTERIFORMES

Dactylopteridae—flying gurnards

SCIENTIFIC NAME	OCCURRENCE	COMMON NAME
Dactylopterus volitans (Linnaeus, 1758)	A	flying gurnard

*ORDER SCORPAENIFORMES

Scorpaenidae—scorpionfishes

SCIENTIFIC NAME	OCCURRENCE	COMMON NAME
Helicolenus dactylopterus (Delaroche, 1809)	A	blackbelly rosefish
Neomerinthe hemingwayi Fowler, 1935	A	spinycheek scorpionfish
Pontinus castor Poey, 1860	A	longsnout scorpionfish
Pontinus longispinis Goode & Bean, 1896	A	longspine scorpionfish
Pontinus nematophthalmus (Günther, 1860)	A	spinythroat scorpionfish
Pontinus rathbuni Goode & Bean, 1896	A	highfin scorpionfish
Scorpaena agassizi Goode & Bean, 1896	A	longfin scorpionfish
Scorpaena albifimbria Evermann & Marsh, 1900	A	coral scorpionfish
Scorpaena bergi Evermann & Marsh, 1900	A	goosehead scorpionfish
Scorpaena brachyptera Eschmeyer, 1965	A	shortfin scorpionfish
Scorpaena brasiliensis Cuvier, 1829	A	barbfish
Scorpaena calcarata Goode & Bean, 1882	A	smoothhead scorpionfish
Scorpaena dispar Longley & Hildebrand, 1940	A	hunchback scorpionfish
Scorpaena elachys Eschmeyer, 1965	A	dwarf scorpionfish
Scorpaena grandicornis Cuvier, 1829	A	plumed scorpionfish
Scorpaena guttata Girard, 1854	P	California scorpionfish
Scorpaena inermis Cuvier, 1829	A	mushroom scorpionfish
Scorpaena isthmensis Meek & Hildebrand, 1928	A	smoothcheek scorpionfish
* *Scorpaena mystes* Jordan & Starks, 1895	P	stone scorpionfish
Scorpaena plumieri Bloch, 1789	A	spotted scorpionfish
Scorpaenodes caribbaeus Meek & Hildebrand, 1928	A	reef scorpionfish

SCIENTIFIC NAME	OCCURRENCE	COMMON NAME
Scorpaenodes tredecimspinosus (Metzelaar, 1919)	A	deepreef scorpionfish
Scorpaenodes xyris (Jordan & Gilbert, 1882)	P	rainbow scorpionfish
Sebastes aleutianus (Jordan & Evermann, 1898)	P	rougheye rockfish
Sebastes alutus (Gilbert, 1890)	P	Pacific ocean perch
Sebastes atrovirens (Jordan & Gilbert, 1880)	P	kelp rockfish
Sebastes auriculatus Girard, 1854	P	brown rockfish
Sebastes aurora (Gilbert, 1890)	P	aurora rockfish
Sebastes babcocki (Thompson, 1915)	P	redbanded rockfish
Sebastes borealis Barsukov, 1970	P	shortraker rockfish
Sebastes brevispinis (Bean, 1884)	P	silvergray rockfish
Sebastes carnatus (Jordan & Gilbert, 1880)	P	gopher rockfish
Sebastes caurinus Richardson, 1845	P	copper rockfish
Sebastes chlorostictus (Jordan & Gilbert, 1880)	P	greenspotted rockfish
Sebastes chrysomelas (Jordan & Gilbert, 1881)	P	black-and-yellow rockfish
Sebastes ciliatus (Tilesius, 1810)	P	dusky rockfish
Sebastes constellatus (Jordan & Gilbert, 1880)	P	starry rockfish
Sebastes crameri (Jordan, 1897)	P	darkblotched rockfish
Sebastes dalli (Eigenmann & Beeson, 1894)	P	calico rockfish
Sebastes diploproa (Gilbert, 1890)	P	splitnose rockfish
Sebastes elongatus Ayres, 1859	P	greenstriped rockfish
Sebastes emphaeus (Starks, 1911)	P	Puget Sound rockfish
Sebastes ensifer Chen, 1971	P	swordspine rockfish
Sebastes entomelas (Jordan & Gilbert, 1880)	P	widow rockfish
Sebastes eos (Eigenmann & Eigenmann, 1890)	P	pink rockfish
* *Sebastes fasciatus* Storer, 1854	A	Acadian redfish
Sebastes flavidus (Ayres, 1863)	P	yellowtail rockfish
Sebastes gilli (Eigenmann, 1891)	P	bronzespotted rockfish
Sebastes goodei (Eigenmann & Eigenmann, 1890)	P	chilipepper
Sebastes helvomaculatus Ayres, 1859	P	rosethorn rockfish
Sebastes hopkinsi (Cramer, 1895)	P	squarespot rockfish
Sebastes jordani (Gilbert, 1896)	P	shortbelly rockfish
Sebastes lentiginosus Chen, 1971	P	freckled rockfish
* *Sebastes levis* (Eigenmann & Eigenmann, 1889)	P	cowcod
Sebastes macdonaldi (Eigenmann & Beeson, 1893)	P	Mexican rockfish
Sebastes maliger (Jordan & Gilbert, 1880)	P	quillback rockfish
Sebastes melanops Girard, 1856	P	black rockfish
Sebastes melanosema Lea & Fitch, 1979	P	semaphore rockfish
Sebastes melanostomus (Eigenmann & Eigenmann, 1890)	P	blackgill rockfish
+*Sebastes mentella* Travin, 1951	A	deepwater redfish
Sebastes miniatus (Jordan & Gilbert, 1880)	P	vermilion rockfish
Sebastes mystinus (Jordan & Gilbert, 1881)	P	blue rockfish
Sebastes nebulosus Ayres, 1854	P	China rockfish
Sebastes nigrocinctus Ayres, 1859	P	tiger rockfish
* *Sebastes norvegicus* (Ascanius, 1772)	A	golden redfish
Sebastes ovalis (Ayres, 1863)	P	speckled rockfish
Sebastes paucispinis Ayres, 1854	P	bocaccio
Sebastes phillipsi (Fitch, 1964)	P	chameleon rockfish
Sebastes pinniger (Gill, 1864)	P	canary rockfish
* *Sebastes polyspinis* (Taranetz & Moiseev, 1933)	P	northern rockfish

SCIENTIFIC NAME	OCCURRENCE	COMMON NAME
Sebastes proriger (Jordan & Gilbert, 1880)	P	redstripe rockfish
Sebastes rastrelliger (Jordan & Gilbert, 1880)	P	grass rockfish
Sebastes reedi (Westrheim & Tsuyuki, 1967)	P	yellowmouth rockfish
Sebastes rosaceus Girard, 1854	P	rosy rockfish
Sebastes rosenblatti Chen, 1971	P	greenblotched rockfish
Sebastes ruberrimus (Cramer, 1895)	P	yelloweye rockfish
Sebastes rubrivinctus (Jordan & Gilbert, 1880)	P	flag rockfish
Sebastes rufinanus Lea & Fitch, 1972	P	dwarf-red rockfish
Sebastes rufus (Eigenmann & Eigenmann, 1890)	P	bank rockfish
Sebastes saxicola (Gilbert, 1890)	P	stripetail rockfish
Sebastes semicinctus (Gilbert, 1897)	P	halfbanded rockfish
Sebastes serranoides (Eigenmann & Eigenmann, 1890)	P	olive rockfish
Sebastes serriceps (Jordan & Gilbert, 1880)	P	treefish
Sebastes simulator Chen, 1971	P	pinkrose rockfish
Sebastes umbrosus (Jordan & Gilbert, 1882)	P	honeycomb rockfish
Sebastes variegatus Quast, 1971	P	harlequin rockfish
Sebastes wilsoni (Gilbert, 1915)	P	pygmy rockfish
Sebastes zacentrus (Gilbert, 1890)	P	sharpchin rockfish
Sebastolobus alascanus Bean, 1890	P	shortspine thornyhead
Sebastolobus altivelis Gilbert, 1896	P	longspine thornyhead
* *Sebastolobus macrochir* (Günther, 1880)	P	broadbanded thornyhead
Trachyscorpia cristulata (Goode & Bean, 1896)	A	Atlantic thornyhead

Triglidae—searobins

SCIENTIFIC NAME	OCCURRENCE	COMMON NAME
Bellator brachychir (Regan, 1914)	A	shortfin searobin
Bellator egretta (Goode & Bean, 1896)	A	streamer searobin
Bellator militaris (Goode & Bean, 1896)	A	horned searobin
Bellator xenisma (Jordan & Bollman, 1890)	P	splitnose searobin
Peristedion brevirostre Günther, 1860	A	flathead searobin
Peristedion gracile Goode & Bean, 1896	A	slender searobin
Peristedion miniatum Goode, 1880	A	armored searobin
Peristedion thompsoni Fowler, 1952	A	rimspine searobin
Prionotus alatus Goode & Bean, 1883	A	spiny searobin
Prionotus carolinus (Linnaeus, 1771)	A	northern searobin
Prionotus evolans (Linnaeus, 1766)	A	striped searobin
* *Prionotus longispinosus* Teague, 1951	A	bigeye searobin
Prionotus martis Ginsburg, 1950	A	barred searobin
Prionotus ophryas Jordan & Swain, 1884	A	bandtail searobin
Prionotus paralatus Ginsburg, 1950	A	Mexican searobin
Prionotus roseus Jordan & Evermann, 1896	A	bluespotted searobin
* *Prionotus rubio* Jordan, 1886	A	blackwing searobin
Prionotus scitulus Jordan & Gilbert, 1882	A	leopard searobin
Prionotus stearnsi Jordan & Swain, 1884	A	shortwing searobin
Prionotus stephanophrys Lockington, 1881	P	lumptail searobin
Prionotus tribulus Cuvier, 1829	A	bighead searobin

Anoplopomatidae—sablefishes

SCIENTIFIC NAME	OCCURRENCE	COMMON NAME
Anoplopoma fimbria (Pallas, 1814)	P	sablefish
Erilepis zonifer (Lockington, 1880)	P	skilfish

SCIENTIFIC NAME	OCCURRENCE	COMMON NAME
Hexagrammidae—greenlings		
Hexagrammos decagrammus (Pallas, 1810)	P	kelp greenling
Hexagrammos lagocephalus (Pallas, 1810)	P	rock greenling
Hexagrammos octogrammus (Pallas, 1814)	P	masked greenling
Hexagrammos stelleri Tilesius, 1810	P	whitespotted greenling
Ophiodon elongatus Girard, 1854	P	lingcod
Oxylebius pictus Gill, 1862	P	painted greenling
Pleurogrammus monopterygius (Pallas, 1810)	P	Atka mackerel
Zaniolepis frenata Eigenmann & Eigenmann, 1889	P	shortspine combfish
Zaniolepis latipinnis Girard, 1857	P	longspine combfish
+Cottidae—sculpins		
Archaulus biseriatus Gilbert & Burke, 1912	P	scaled sculpin
Artediellus atlanticus Jordan & Evermann, 1898	A	Atlantic hookear sculpin
* *Artediellus pacificus* Gilbert, 1895	P	hookhorn sculpin
Artediellus scaber Knipowitsch, 1907	P	hamecon
Artediellus uncinatus (Reinhardt, 1835)	A	Arctic hookear sculpin
Artedius corallinus (Hubbs, 1926)	P	coralline sculpin
Artedius fenestralis Jordan & Gilbert, 1883	P	padded sculpin
Artedius harringtoni (Starks, 1896)	P	scalyhead sculpin
Artedius lateralis (Girard, 1854)	P	smoothhead sculpin
Artedius notospilotus Girard, 1856	P	bonehead sculpin
Ascelichthys rhodorus Jordan & Gilbert, 1880	P	rosylip sculpin
Asemichthys taylori Gilbert, 1912	P	spinynose sculpin
Blepsias bilobus Cuvier, 1829	P	crested sculpin
Blepsias cirrhosus (Pallas, 1814)	P	silverspotted sculpin
Chitonotus pugetensis (Steindachner, 1876)	P	roughback sculpin
Clinocottus acuticeps (Gilbert, 1896)	F-P	sharpnose sculpin
Clinocottus analis (Girard, 1857)	P	woolly sculpin
Clinocottus embryum (Jordan & Starks, 1895)	P	calico sculpin
Clinocottus globiceps (Girard, 1857)	P	mosshead sculpin
Clinocottus recalvus (Greeley, 1899)	P	bald sculpin
Cottus aleuticus Gilbert, 1896	F-P	coastrange sculpin
Cottus asper Richardson, 1836	F-P	prickly sculpin
Cottus asperrimus Rutter, 1908	F	rough sculpin
Cottus baileyi Robins, 1961	F	black sculpin
Cottus bairdi Girard, 1850	F	mottled sculpin
Cottus beldingi Eigenmann & Eigenmann, 1891	F	Paiute sculpin
Cottus carolinae (Gill, 1861)	F	banded sculpin
Cottus cognatus Richardson, 1836	F	slimy sculpin
Cottus confusus Bailey & Bond, 1963	F	shorthead sculpin
Cottus echinatus Bailey & Bond, 1963	F[X]	Utah Lake sculpin
Cottus extensus Bailey & Bond, 1963	F	Bear Lake sculpin
Cottus girardi Robins, 1961	F	Potomac sculpin
Cottus greenei (Gilbert & Culver, 1898)	F	Shoshone sculpin
Cottus gulosus (Girard, 1854)	F	riffle sculpin
* *Cottus hypselurus* Robins & Robison, 1985	F	Ozark sculpin
Cottus klamathensis Gilbert, 1898	F	marbled sculpin
Cottus leiopomus Gilbert & Evermann, 1894	F	Wood River sculpin

SCIENTIFIC NAME	OCCURRENCE	COMMON NAME
Cottus marginatus (Bean, 1881)	F	margined sculpin
Cottus perplexus Gilbert & Evermann, 1894	F	reticulate sculpin
Cottus pitensis Bailey & Bond, 1963	F	Pit sculpin
Cottus princeps Gilbert, 1898	F	Klamath Lake sculpin
Cottus pygmaeus Williams, 1968	F	pygmy sculpin
Cottus rhotheus (Smith, 1882)	F	torrent sculpin
Cottus ricei (Nelson, 1876)	F	spoonhead sculpin
Cottus tenuis (Evermann & Meek, 1898)	F	slender sculpin
+*Dasycottus setiger* Bean, 1890	P	spinyhead sculpin
Enophrys bison (Girard, 1854)	P	buffalo sculpin
Enophrys diceraus (Pallas, 1783)	P	antlered sculpin
Enophrys lucasi (Jordan & Gilbert, 1898)	P	leister sculpin
Enophrys taurina Gilbert, 1914	P	bull sculpin
* *Eurymen gyrinus* Gilbert & Burke, 1912	P	smoothcheek sculpin
* *Gymnocanthus galeatus* (Bean, 1881)	P	armorhead sculpin
* *Gymnocanthus pistilliger* (Pallas, 1814)	P	threaded sculpin
Gymnocanthus tricuspis (Reinhardt, 1832)	A-P	Arctic staghorn sculpin
Hemilepidotus hemilepidotus (Tilesius, 1811)	P	red Irish lord
Hemilepidotus jordani Bean, 1881	P	yellow Irish lord
* *Hemilepidotus papilio* (Bean, 1880)	P	butterfly sculpin
Hemilepidotus spinosus (Ayres, 1854)	P	brown Irish lord
Hemilepidotus zapus Gilbert & Burke, 1912	P	longfin Irish lord
Hemitripterus americanus (Gmelin, 1789)	A	sea raven
Hemitripterus bolini (Myers, 1934)	P	bigmouth sculpin
Icelinus borealis Gilbert, 1896	P	northern sculpin
Icelinus burchami Evermann & Goldsborough, 1907	P	dusky sculpin
Icelinus cavifrons Gilbert, 1890	P	pit-head sculpin
Icelinus filamentosus Gilbert, 1890	P	threadfin sculpin
Icelinus fimbriatus Gilbert, 1890	P	fringed sculpin
Icelinus oculatus Gilbert, 1890	P	frogmouth sculpin
Icelinus quadriseriatus (Lockington, 1880)	P	yellowchin sculpin
Icelinus tenuis Gilbert, 1890	P	spotfin sculpin
Icelus bicornis (Reinhardt, 1840)	A-P	twohorn sculpin
* *Icelus canaliculatus* Gilbert, 1896	P	blacknose sculpin
* *Icelus euryops* Bean, 1890	P	wide-eye sculpin
Icelus spatula Gilbert & Burke, 1912	A-P	spatulate sculpin
Icelus spiniger Gilbert, 1896	P	thorny sculpin
* *Icelus uncinalis* Gilbert & Burke, 1912	P	uncinate sculpin
Jordania zonope Starks, 1895	P	longfin sculpin
Leiocottus hirundo Girard, 1856	P	lavender sculpin
Leptocottus armatus Girard, 1854	F-P	Pacific staghorn sculpin
+*Malacocottus kincaidi* Gilbert & Thompson, 1905	P	blackfin sculpin
* *Malacocottus zonurus* Bean, 1890	P	darkfin sculpin
Megalocottus platycephalus (Pallas, 1814)	P	belligerent sculpin
Microcottus sellaris (Gilbert, 1893)	P	brightbelly sculpin
Myoxocephalus aenaeus (Mitchill, 1814)	A	grubby
Myoxocephalus jaok (Cuvier, 1829)	P	plain sculpin
Myoxocephalus niger (Bean, 1881)	P	warthead sculpin
Myoxocephalus octodecemspinosus (Mitchill, 1814)	A	longhorn sculpin

SCIENTIFIC NAME	OCCURRENCE	COMMON NAME
Myoxocephalus polyacanthocephalus (Pallas, 1814)	P	great sculpin
Myoxocephalus quadricornis (Linnaeus, 1758)	A-F-P	fourhorn sculpin
Myoxocephalus scorpioides (Fabricius, 1780)	A-P	Arctic sculpin
Myoxocephalus scorpius (Linnaeus, 1758)	A-P	shorthorn sculpin
Myoxocephalus thompsoni (Girard, 1851)	F	deepwater sculpin
* *Myoxocephalus verrucosus* (Bean, 1881)	P	warty sculpin
Nautichthys oculofasciatus (Girard, 1857)	P	sailfin sculpin
Nautichthys pribilovius (Jordan & Gilbert, 1898)	P	eyeshade sculpin
Nautichthys robustus Peden, 1970	P	shortmast sculpin
Oligocottus maculosus Girard, 1856	P	tidepool sculpin
Oligocottus rimensis (Greeley, 1899)	P	saddleback sculpin
Oligocottus rubellio (Greeley, 1899)	P	rosy sculpin
Oligocottus snyderi Greeley, 1898	P	fluffy sculpin
Orthonopias triacis Starks & Mann, 1911	P	snubnose sculpin
Paricelinus hopliticus Eigenmann & Eigenmann, 1889	P	thornback sculpin
Phallocottus obtusus Schultz, 1938	P	spineless sculpin
+*Psychrolutes paradoxus* Günther, 1861	P	tadpole sculpin
* *Psychrolutes sigalutes* (Jordan & Starks, 1895)	P	soft sculpin
Radulinus asprellus Gilbert, 1890	P	slim sculpin
Radulinus boleoides Gilbert, 1898	P	darter sculpin
Radulinus vinculus Bolin, 1950	P	smoothgum sculpin
* *Rastrinus scutiger* (Bean, 1891)	P	roughskin sculpin
Rhamphocottus richardsoni Günther, 1874	P	grunt sculpin
* *Ruscarius creaseri* (Hubbs, 1926)	P	roughcheek sculpin
* *Ruscarius meanyi* Jordan & Starks, 1895	P	Puget Sound sculpin
+*Scorpaenichthys marmoratus* (Ayres, 1854)	P	cabezon
Sigmistes caulias Rutter, 1898	P	kelp sculpin
Sigmistes smithi Schultz, 1938	P	arched sculpin
Synchirus gilli Bean, 1890	P	manacled sculpin
* *Thyriscus anoplus* Gilbert & Burke, 1912	P	sponge sculpin
* *Triglops forficatus* (Gilbert, 1896)	P	scissortail sculpin
Triglops macellus (Bean, 1883)	P	roughspine sculpin
Triglops murrayi Günther, 1888	A	moustache sculpin
* *Triglops nybelini* Jensen, 1944	A-P	bigeye sculpin
Triglops pingeli Reinhardt, 1838	A-P	ribbed sculpin
Triglops scepticus Gilbert, 1896	P	spectacled sculpin

Agonidae—poachers

SCIENTIFIC NAME	OCCURRENCE	COMMON NAME
Agonomalus mozinoi Wilimovsky & Wilson, 1979	P	kelp poacher
Agonopsis sterletus (Gilbert, 1898)	P	southern spearnose poacher
Agonopsis vulsa (Jordan & Gilbert, 1880)	P	northern spearnose poacher
Anoplagonus inermis (Günther, 1860)	P	smooth alligatorfish
Aspidophoroides bartoni Gilbert, 1896	P	Aleutian alligatorfish
Aspidophoroides monopterygius (Bloch, 1786)	A	alligatorfish
Aspidophoroides olriki Lütken, 1876	A-P	Arctic alligatorfish
Bathyagonus alascanus (Gilbert, 1896)	P	gray starsnout
Bathyagonus infraspinatus (Gilbert, 1904)	P	spinycheek starsnout
Bathyagonus nigripinnis Gilbert, 1890	P	blackfin poacher
Bathyagonus pentacanthus (Gilbert, 1890)	P	bigeye poacher

SCIENTIFIC NAME	OCCURRENCE	COMMON NAME
Bothragonus swani (Steindachner, 1876)	P	rockhead
Hypsagonus quadricornis (Cuvier, 1829)	P	fourhorn poacher
* *Leptagonus decagonus* (Bloch & Schneider, 1801)	A-P	Atlantic poacher
Occella dodecaedron (Tilesius, 1813)	P	Bering poacher
Occella impi Gruchy, 1970	P	pixie poacher
Occella verrucosa (Lockington, 1880)	P	warty poacher
Odontopyxis trispinosa Lockington, 1880	P	pygmy poacher
Pallasina barbata (Steindachner, 1876)	P	tubenose poacher
* *Percis japonica* (Pallas, 1772)	P	dragon poacher
* *Podothecus acipenserinus* (Tilesius, 1813)	P	sturgeon poacher
Sarritor frenatus (Gilbert, 1896)	P	sawback poacher
Sarritor leptorhynchus (Gilbert, 1896)	P	longnose poacher
Stellerina xyosterna (Jordan & Gilbert, 1880)	P	pricklebreast poacher
Xeneretmus latifrons (Gilbert, 1890)	P	blacktip poacher
Xeneretmus leiops Gilbert, 1915	P	smootheye poacher
Xeneretmus ritteri Gilbert, 1915	P	stripefin poacher
Xeneretmus triacanthus (Gilbert, 1890)	P	bluespotted poacher
	+Cyclopteridae—snailfishes	
Aptocyclus ventricosus (Pallas, 1770)	P	smooth lumpsucker
* *Careproctus candidus* Gilbert & Burke, 1912	P	bigeye snailfish
* *Careproctus furcellus* Gilbert & Burke, 1912	P	emarginate snailfish
* *Careproctus gilberti* Burke, 1912	P	smalldisk snailfish
Careproctus longipinnis Burke, 1912	A	longfin snailfish
Careproctus melanurus Gilbert, 1892	P	blacktail snailfish
* *Careproctus phasma* Gilbert, 1896	P	spectral snailfish
* *Careproctus rastrinus* Gilbert & Burke, 1912	P	salmon snailfish
* *Careproctus scottae* Chapman & DeLacy, 1939	P	peachskin snailfish
* *Careproctus spectrum* Bean, 1891	P	stippled snailfish
Crystallichthys cyclospilus Gilbert & Burke, 1912	P	blotched snailfish
Cyclopteropsis macalpini (Fowler, 1914)	A	Arctic lumpsucker
* *Cyclopteropsis phrynoides* (Gilbert & Burke, 1912)	P	toad lumpsucker
Cyclopterus lumpus Linnaeus, 1758	A	lumpfish
* *Eumicrotremus barbatus* (Lindberg & Legeza, 1955)	P	papillose lumpsucker
* *Eumicrotremus birulai* Popov, 1928	P	Siberian lumpsucker
Eumicrotremus derjugini Popov, 1926	A-P	leatherfin lumpsucker
* *Eumicrotremus gyrinops* (Garman, 1892)	P	Alaskan lumpsucker
Eumicrotremus orbis (Günther, 1861)	P	Pacific spiny lumpsucker
* *Eumicrotremus spinosus* (Müller, 1777)	A-P	Atlantic spiny lumpsucker
* *Lethotremus muticus* Gilbert, 1895	P	docked snailfish
* *Liparis atlanticus* (Jordan & Evermann, 1898)	A	Atlantic seasnail
* *Liparis beringianus* (Gilbert & Burke, 1912)	P	Bering snailfish
* *Liparis bristolensis* Burke, 1912	P	Bristol snailfish
Liparis callyodon (Pallas, 1814)	P	spotted snailfish
* *Liparis catharus* Vogt, 1973	P	purity snailfish
Liparis coheni Able, 1976	A	gulf snailfish
Liparis cyclopus Günther, 1861	A	ribbon snailfish
Liparis dennyi Jordan & Starks, 1895	P	marbled snailfish
Liparis fabricii Krøyer, 1847	A-P	gelatinous seasnail
Liparis florae (Jordan & Starks, 1895)	P	tidepool snailfish

SCIENTIFIC NAME	OCCURRENCE	COMMON NAME
Liparis fucensis Gilbert, 1895	P	slipskin snailfish
* *Liparis gibbus* Bean, 1881	A-P	variegated snailfish
* *Liparis greeni* (Jordan & Starks, 1895)	P	lobefin snailfish
+*Liparis inquilinus* Able, 1973	A	inquiline snailfish
* *Liparis megacephalus* (Burke, 1912)	P	bighead snailfish
* *Liparis micraspidophorus* (Burke, 1912)	P	thumbtack snailfish
Liparis mucosus Ayres, 1855	P	slimy snailfish
* *Liparis ochotensis* Schmidt, 1904	P	Okhotsk snailfish
Liparis pulchellus Ayres, 1855	P	showy snailfish
Liparis rutteri (Gilbert & Snyder, 1898)	P	ringtail snailfish
* *Liparis tunicatus* Reinhardt, 1837	A-P	kelp snailfish
* *Lipariscus nanus* Gilbert, 1915	P	pygmy snailfish
Nectoliparis pelagicus Gilbert & Burke 1912	P	tadpole snailfish
* *Paraliparis calidus* Cohen, 1968	A	lowfin snailfish
Paraliparis deani Burke, 1912	P	prickly snailfish

ORDER PERCIFORMES

Centropomidae—snooks

SCIENTIFIC NAME	OCCURRENCE	COMMON NAME
Centropomus ensiferus Poey, 1860	A-F	swordspine snook
Centropomus parallelus Poey, 1860	A-F	fat snook
Centropomus pectinatus Poey, 1860	A-F	tarpon snook
* *Centropomus undecimalis* (Bloch, 1792)	A-F	common snook

+Percichthyidae—temperate basses

SCIENTIFIC NAME	OCCURRENCE	COMMON NAME
Morone americana (Gmelin, 1789)	A-F	white perch
Morone chrysops (Rafinesque, 1820)	F	white bass
Morone mississippiensis Jordan & Eigenmann, 1887	F	yellow bass
Morone saxatilis (Walbaum, 1792)	A-F-P	striped bass
Polyprion americanus (Schneider, 1801)	A	wreckfish
Stereolepis gigas Ayres, 1859	P	giant sea bass
Synagrops bellus (Goode & Bean, 1896)	A	blackmouth bass
* *Synagrops spinosus* Schultz, 1940	A	keelcheek bass

+Serranidae—sea basses

SCIENTIFIC NAME	OCCURRENCE	COMMON NAME
Anthias nicholsi Firth, 1933	A	yellowfin bass
Anthias tenuis Nichols, 1920	A	threadnose bass
* *Bathyanthias mexicanus* (Schultz, 1958)	A	yellowtail bass
Centropristis fuscula (Poey, 1861)	A	twospot sea bass
Centropristis ocyurus (Jordan & Evermann, 1887)	A	bank sea bass
Centropristis philadelphica (Linnaeus, 1758)	A	rock sea bass
Centropristis striata (Linnaeus, 1758)	A	black sea bass
Diplectrum bivittatum (Valenciennes, 1828)	A	dwarf sand perch
Diplectrum formosum (Linnaeus, 1766)	A	sand perch
* *Epinephelus acanthistius* (Gilbert, 1892)	P	gulf coney
Epinephelus adscensionis (Osbeck, 1765)	A	rock hind
Epinephelus afer (Bloch, 1793)	A	mutton hamlet
Epinephelus analogus Gill, 1864	P	spotted cabrilla
Epinephelus cruentatus (Lacepède, 1802)	A	graysby
* *Epinephelus dermatolepis* Boulenger, 1895	P	leather bass

SCIENTIFIC NAME	OCCURRENCE	COMMON NAME
Epinephelus drummondhayi Goode & Bean, 1879	A	speckled hind
Epinephelus flavolimbatus Poey, 1865	A	yellowedge grouper
Epinephelus fulvus (Linnaeus, 1758)	A	coney
Epinephelus guttatus (Linnaeus, 1758)	A	red hind
Epinephelus inermis (Valenciennes, 1833)	A	marbled grouper
Epinephelus itajara (Lichtenstein, 1822)	A	jewfish
Epinephelus morio (Valenciennes, 1828)	A	red grouper
Epinephelus mystacinus (Poey, 1852)	A	misty grouper
Epinephelus nigritus (Holbrook, 1855)	A	warsaw grouper
Epinephelus niveatus (Valenciennes, 1828)	A-P	snowy grouper
Epinephelus striatus (Bloch, 1792)	A	Nassau grouper
Gonioplectrus hispanus (Cuvier, 1828)	A	Spanish flag
Hemanthias aureorubens (Longley, 1935)	A	streamer bass
Hemanthias leptus (Ginsburg, 1952)	A	longtail bass
* *Hemanthias signifer* (Garman, 1899)	P	splittail bass
Hemanthias vivanus (Jordan & Swain, 1884)	A	red barbier
Holanthias martinicensis (Guichenot, 1868)	A	roughtongue bass
Hypoplectrus unicolor (Walbaum, 1792)	A	butter hamlet
* *Liopropoma carmabi* (Randall, 1963)	A	candy basslet
Liopropoma eukrines (Starck & Courtenay, 1962)	A	wrasse bass
Liopropoma mowbrayi Woods & Kanazawa, 1951	A	cave bass
Liopropoma rubre Poey, 1861	A	peppermint bass
Mycteroperca bonaci (Poey, 1860)	A	black grouper
Mycteroperca interstitialis (Poey, 1860)	A	yellowmouth grouper
Mycteroperca jordani (Jenkins & Evermann, 1889)	P	gulf grouper
Mycteroperca microlepis (Goode & Bean, 1879)	A	gag
Mycteroperca phenax Jordan & Swain, 1884	A	scamp
Mycteroperca rubra (Bloch, 1793)	A	comb grouper
Mycteroperca tigris (Valenciennes, 1833)	A	tiger grouper
Mycteroperca venenosa (Linnaeus, 1758)	A	yellowfin grouper
Mycteroperca xenarcha Jordan, 1888	P	broomtail grouper
Paralabrax clathratus (Girard, 1854)	P	kelp bass
Paralabrax maculatofasciatus (Steindachner, 1868)	P	spotted sand bass
Paralabrax nebulifer (Girard, 1854)	P	barred sand bass
* *Paranthias furcifer* (Valenciennes, 1828)	A-P	creole-fish
Plectranthias garrupellus Robins & Starck, 1961	A	apricot bass
* *Pronotogrammus multifasciatus* Gill, 1863	P	threadfin bass
+*Pseudogramma gregoryi* (Breder, 1927)	A	reef bass
+*Rypticus bistrispinus* (Mitchill, 1818)	A	freckled soapfish
+*Rypticus maculatus* Holbrook, 1855	A	whitespotted soapfish
+*Rypticus saponaceus* (Schneider, 1801)	A	greater soapfish
+*Rypticus subbifrenatus* (Gill, 1861)	A	spotted soapfish
Schultzea beta (Hildebrand, 1940)	A	school bass
Serraniculus pumilio Ginsburg, 1952	A	pygmy sea bass
Serranus annularis (Günther, 1880)	A	orangeback bass
Serranus atrobranchus (Cuvier, 1829)	A	blackear bass
Serranus baldwini (Evermann & Marsh, 1900)	A	lantern bass
Serranus chionaraia Robins & Starck, 1961	A	snow bass
Serranus notospilus Longley, 1935	A	saddle bass
Serranus phoebe Poey, 1852	A	tattler

SCIENTIFIC NAME	OCCURRENCE	COMMON NAME
Serranus subligarius (Cope, 1870)	A	belted sandfish
Serranus tabacarius (Cuvier, 1829)	A	tobaccofish
Serranus tigrinus (Bloch, 1790)	A	harlequin bass
Serranus tortugarum Longley, 1935	A	chalk bass
	*Grammatidae—basslets	
* *Gramma loreto* Poey, 1868	A	royal gramma
* *Lipogramma anabantoides* Böhlke, 1960	A	dusky basslet
* *Lipogramma trilineatum* Randall, 1963	A	threeline basslet
	Centrarchidae—sunfishes	
Acantharchus pomotis (Baird, 1855)	F	mud sunfish
Ambloplites ariommus Viosca, 1936	F	shadow bass
Ambloplites cavifrons Cope, 1868	F	Roanoke bass
Ambloplites constellatus Cashner & Suttkus, 1977	F	Ozark bass
Ambloplites rupestris (Rafinesque, 1817)	F	rock bass
Archoplites interruptus (Girard, 1854)	F	Sacramento perch
Centrarchus macropterus (Lacepède, 1801)	F	flier
* *Elassoma boehlkei* Rohde & Arndt, 1987	F	Carolina pygmy sunfish
Elassoma evergladei Jordan, 1884	F	Everglades pygmy sunfish
* *Elassoma okatie* Rohde & Arndt, 1987	F	bluebarred pygmy sunfish
Elassoma okefenokee Böhlke, 1956	F	Okefenokee pygmy sunfish
Elassoma zonatum Jordan, 1877	F	banded pygmy sunfish
Enneacanthus chaetodon (Baird, 1855)	F	blackbanded sunfish
Enneacanthus gloriosus (Holbrook, 1855)	F	bluespotted sunfish
Enneacanthus obesus (Girard, 1854)	F	banded sunfish
+*Lepomis auritus* (Linnaeus, 1758)	F	redbreast sunfish
+*Lepomis cyanellus* Rafinesque, 1819	F	green sunfish
+*Lepomis gibbosus* (Linnaeus, 1758)	F	pumpkinseed
+*Lepomis gulosus* (Cuvier, 1829)	F	warmouth
Lepomis humilis (Girard, 1858)	F	orangespotted sunfish
+*Lepomis macrochirus* Rafinesque, 1819	F	bluegill
+*Lepomis marginatus* (Holbrook, 1855)	F	dollar sunfish
Lepomis megalotis (Rafinesque, 1820)	F	longear sunfish
Lepomis microlophus (Günther, 1859)	F	redear sunfish
+*Lepomis punctatus* (Valenciennes, 1831)	F	spotted sunfish
+*Lepomis symmetricus* Forbes, 1883	F	bantam sunfish
Micropterus coosae Hubbs & Bailey, 1940	F	redeye bass
* *Micropterus dolomieu* Lacepède, 1802	F	smallmouth bass
Micropterus notius Bailey & Hubbs, 1949	F	Suwannee bass
Micropterus punctulatus (Rafinesque, 1819)	F	spotted bass
Micropterus salmoides (Lacepède, 1802)	F	largemouth bass
Micropterus treculi (Vaillant & Bocourt, 1874)	F	Guadalupe bass
Pomoxis annularis Rafinesque, 1818	F	white crappie
Pomoxis nigromaculatus (Lesueur, 1829)	F	black crappie
	Percidae—perches	
Ammocrypta asprella (Jordan, 1878)	F	crystal darter
Ammocrypta beani Jordan, 1877	F	naked sand darter
Ammocrypta bifascia Williams, 1975	F	Florida sand darter

SCIENTIFIC NAME	OCCURRENCE	COMMON NAME
Ammocrypta clara Jordan & Meek, 1885	F	western sand darter
Ammocrypta meridiana Williams, 1975	F	southern sand darter
Ammocrypta pellucida (Putnam, 1863)	F	eastern sand darter
Ammocrypta vivax Hay, 1882	F	scaly sand darter
Etheostoma acuticeps Bailey, 1959	F	sharphead darter
Etheostoma aquali Williams & Etnier, 1978	F	coppercheek darter
Etheostoma asprigene (Forbes, 1878)	F	mud darter
* *Etheostoma baileyi* Page & Burr, 1982	F	emerald darter
Etheostoma barbouri Kuehne & Small, 1971	F	teardrop darter
* *Etheostoma barrenense* Burr & Page, 1982	F	splendid darter
Etheostoma bellum Zorach, 1968	F	orangefin darter
Etheostoma blennioides Rafinesque, 1819	F	greenside darter
Etheostoma blennius Gilbert & Swain, 1887	F	blenny darter
Etheostoma boschungi Wall & Williams, 1974	F	slackwater darter
Etheostoma caeruleum Storer, 1845	F	rainbow darter
Etheostoma camurum (Cope, 1870)	F	bluebreast darter
Etheostoma chlorobranchium Zorach, 1972	F	greenfin darter
Etheostoma chlorosomum (Hay, 1881)	F	bluntnose darter
Etheostoma cinereum Storer, 1845	F	ashy darter
Etheostoma collettei Birdsong & Knapp, 1969	F	creole darter
+*Etheostoma collis* (Hubbs & Cannon, 1935)	F	Carolina darter
Etheostoma coosae (Fowler, 1945)	F	Coosa darter
Etheostoma cragini Gilbert, 1885	F	Arkansas darter
* *Etheostoma crossopterum* Braasch & Mayden, 1985	F	fringed darter
Etheostoma davisoni Hay, 1885	F	Choctawhatchee darter
Etheostoma ditrema Ramsey & Suttkus, 1965	F	coldwater darter
* *Etheostoma duryi* Henshall, 1889	F	black darter
Etheostoma edwini (Hubbs & Cannon, 1935)	F	brown darter
Etheostoma etnieri Bouchard, 1977	F	cherry darter
Etheostoma euzonum (Hubbs & Black, 1940)	F	Arkansas saddled darter
Etheostoma exile (Girard, 1859)	F	Iowa darter
Etheostoma flabellare Rafinesque, 1819	F	fantail darter
* *Etheostoma flavum* Etnier & Bailey, 1989	F	saffron darter
Etheostoma fonticola (Jordan & Gilbert, 1886)	F	fountain darter
Etheostoma fricksium Hildebrand, 1923	F	Savannah darter
Etheostoma fusiforme (Girard, 1854)	F	swamp darter
Etheostoma gracile (Girard, 1859)	F	slough darter
Etheostoma grahami (Girard, 1859)	F	Rio Grande darter
Etheostoma histrio Jordan & Gilbert, 1887	F	harlequin darter
Etheostoma hopkinsi (Fowler, 1945)	F	Christmas darter
Etheostoma inscriptum (Jordan & Brayton, 1878)	F	turquoise darter
+*Etheostoma jessiae* (Jordan & Brayton, 1878)	F	blueside darter
* *Etheostoma jordani* Gilbert, 1891	F	greenbreast darter
Etheostoma juliae Meek, 1891	F	yoke darter
Etheostoma kanawhae (Raney, 1941)	F	Kanawha darter
Etheostoma kennicotti (Putnam, 1863)	F	stripetail darter
Etheostoma lepidum (Baird & Girard, 1853)	F	greenthroat darter
Etheostoma longimanum Jordan, 1888	F	longfin darter
Etheostoma luteovinctum Gilbert & Swain, 1887	F	redband darter
* *Etheostoma lynceum* Hay, 1885	F	brighteye darter

SCIENTIFIC NAME	OCCURRENCE	COMMON NAME
Etheostoma maculatum Kirtland, 1841	F	spotted darter
Etheostoma mariae (Fowler, 1947)	F	pinewoods darter
Etheostoma microlepidum Raney & Zorach, 1967	F	smallscale darter
Etheostoma microperca Jordan & Gilbert, 1888	F	least darter
Etheostoma moorei Raney & Suttkus, 1964	F	yellowcheek darter
Etheostoma neopterum Howell & Dingerkus, 1978	F	lollipop darter
Etheostoma nianguae Gilbert & Meek, 1887	F	Niangua darter
* *Etheostoma nigripinne* Braasch & Mayden, 1985	F	blackfin darter
Etheostoma nigrum Rafinesque, 1820	F	johnny darter
Etheostoma nuchale Howell & Caldwell, 1965	F	watercress darter
Etheostoma obeyense Kirsch, 1892	F	barcheek darter
Etheostoma okaloosae (Fowler, 1941)	F	Okaloosa darter
Etheostoma olivaceum Braasch & Page, 1979	F	sooty darter
Etheostoma olmstedi Storer, 1842	F	tessellated darter
* *Etheostoma osburni* (Hubbs & Trautman, 1932)	F	candy darter
Etheostoma pallididorsum Distler & Metcalf, 1962	F	paleback darter
Etheostoma parvipinne Gilbert & Swain, 1887	F	goldstripe darter
Etheostoma perlongum (Hubbs & Raney, 1946)	F	Waccamaw darter
Etheostoma podostemone Jordan & Jenkins, 1889	F	riverweed darter
Etheostoma proeliare (Hay, 1881)	F	cypress darter
Etheostoma punctulatum (Agassiz, 1854)	F	stippled darter
* *Etheostoma pyrrhogaster* Bailey & Etnier, 1988	F	firebelly darter
Etheostoma radiosum (Hubbs & Black, 1941)	F	orangebelly darter
* *Etheostoma rafinesquei* Burr & Page, 1982	F	Kentucky darter
Etheostoma rubrum Raney & Suttkus, 1966	F	bayou darter
Etheostoma rufilineatum (Cope, 1870)	F	redline darter
Etheostoma rupestre Gilbert & Swain, 1887	F	rock darter
Etheostoma sagitta (Jordan & Swain, 1883)	F	arrow darter
* *Etheostoma sanguifluum* (Cope, 1870)	F	bloodfin darter
Etheostoma sellare (Radcliffe & Welsh, 1913)	F	Maryland darter
* *Etheostoma serrifer* (Hubbs & Cannon, 1935)	F	sawcheek darter
* *Etheostoma simoterum* (Cope, 1868)	F	snubnose darter
Etheostoma smithi Page & Braasch, 1976	F	slabrock darter
Etheostoma spectabile (Agassiz, 1854)	F	orangethroat darter
Etheostoma squamiceps Jordan, 1877	F	spottail darter
Etheostoma stigmaeum (Jordan, 1877)	F	speckled darter
Etheostoma striatulum Page & Braasch, 1977	F	striated darter
Etheostoma swaini (Jordan, 1884)	F	gulf darter
Etheostoma swannanoa Jordan & Evermann, 1889	F	Swannanoa darter
Etheostoma tetrazonum (Hubbs & Black, 1940)	F	Missouri saddled darter
Etheostoma thalassinum (Jordan & Brayton, 1878)	F	seagreen darter
Etheostoma tippecanoe Jordan & Evermann, 1890	F	Tippecanoe darter
Etheostoma trisella Bailey & Richards, 1963	F	trispot darter
Etheostoma tuscumbia Gilbert & Swain, 1887	F	Tuscumbia darter
Etheostoma variatum Kirtland, 1838	F	variegate darter
Etheostoma virgatum (Jordan, 1880)	F	striped darter
Etheostoma vitreum (Cope, 1870)	F	glassy darter
* *Etheostoma vulneratum* (Cope, 1870)	F	wounded darter
* *Etheostoma wapiti* Etnier & Williams, 1989	F	boulder darter
Etheostoma whipplei (Girard, 1859)	F	redfin darter

SCIENTIFIC NAME	OCCURRENCE	COMMON NAME
Etheostoma zonale (Cope, 1868)	F	banded darter
* *Etheostoma zonifer* (Hubbs & Cannon, 1935)	F	backwater darter
* *Etheostoma zonistium* Bailey & Etnier, 1988	F	bandfin darter
* *Gymnocephalus cernuus* (Linnaeus, 1758)	F[I]	ruffe
Perca flavescens (Mitchill, 1814)	F	yellow perch
Percina antesella Williams & Etnier, 1977	F	amber darter
Percina aurantiaca (Cope, 1868)	F	tangerine darter
Percina aurolineata Suttkus & Ramsey, 1967	F	goldline darter
Percina burtoni Fowler, 1945	F	blotchside darter
Percina caprodes (Rafinesque, 1818)	F	logperch
* *Percina carbonaria* (Baird & Girard, 1853)	F	Texas logperch
Percina copelandi (Jordan, 1877)	F	channel darter
Percina crassa Jordan & Brayton, 1878	F	Piedmont darter
Percina cymatotaenia (Gilbert & Meek, 1887)	F	bluestripe darter
Percina evides (Jordan & Copeland, 1877)	F	gilt darter
Percina gymnocephala Beckham, 1980	F	Appalachia darter
* *Percina jenkinsi* Thompson, 1985	F	Conasauga logperch
Percina lenticula Richards & Knapp, 1964	F	freckled darter
Percina macrocephala (Cope, 1869)	F	longhead darter
Percina macrolepida Stevenson, 1971	F	bigscale logperch
Percina maculata (Girard, 1859)	F	blackside darter
Percina nasuta (Bailey, 1941)	F	longnose darter
Percina nigrofasciata (Agassiz, 1854)	F	blackbanded darter
Percina notogramma (Raney & Hubbs, 1948)	F	stripeback darter
* *Percina oxyrhynchus* (Hubbs & Raney, 1939)	F	sharpnose darter
Percina palmaris (Bailey, 1940)	F	bronze darter
Percina pantherina (Moore & Reeves, 1955)	F	leopard darter
Percina peltata (Stauffer, 1864)	F	shield darter
Percina phoxocephala (Nelson, 1876)	F	slenderhead darter
Percina rex (Jordan & Evermann, 1889)	F	Roanoke logperch
Percina roanoka (Jordan & Jenkins, 1889)	F	Roanoke darter
Percina sciera (Swain, 1883)	F	dusky darter
Percina shumardi (Girard, 1859)	F	river darter
Percina squamata (Gilbert & Swain, 1887)	F	olive darter
Percina tanasi Etnier, 1976	F	snail darter
Percina uranidea (Jordan & Gilbert, 1887)	F	stargazing darter
* *Percina vigil* (Hay, 1882)	F	saddleback darter
Stizostedion canadense (Smith, 1834)	F	sauger
* *Stizostedion vitreum* (Mitchill, 1818)	F	walleye

Priacanthidae—bigeyes

SCIENTIFIC NAME	OCCURRENCE	COMMON NAME
* *Cookeolus japonicus* (Cuvier, 1829)	A	bulleye
Priacanthus arenatus Cuvier, 1829	A	bigeye
+*Priacanthus cruentatus* (Lacepède, 1801)	A	glasseye snapper
Pristigenys alta (Gill, 1862)	A	short bigeye
Pristigenys serrula (Gilbert, 1891)	P	popeye catalufa

Apogonidae—cardinalfishes

SCIENTIFIC NAME	OCCURRENCE	COMMON NAME
Apogon affinis (Poey, 1875)	A	bigtooth cardinalfish
Apogon aurolineatus (Mowbray, 1927)	A	bridle cardinalfish

SCIENTIFIC NAME	OCCURRENCE	COMMON NAME
Apogon binotatus (Poey, 1867)	A	barred cardinalfish
Apogon guadalupensis (Osburn & Nichols, 1916)	P	Guadalupe cardinalfish
Apogon lachneri Böhlke, 1959	A	whitestar cardinalfish
Apogon leptocaulus Gilbert, 1972	A	slendertail cardinalfish
Apogon maculatus (Poey, 1860)	A	flamefish
Apogon phenax Böhlke & Randall, 1968	A	mimic cardinalfish
Apogon pillionatus Böhlke & Randall, 1968	A	broadsaddle cardinalfish
Apogon planifrons Longley & Hildebrand, 1940	A	pale cardinalfish
Apogon pseudomaculatus Longley, 1932	A	twospot cardinalfish
Apogon quadrisquamatus Longley, 1934	A	sawcheek cardinalfish
Apogon townsendi (Breder, 1927)	A	belted cardinalfish
Astrapogon alutus (Jordan & Gilbert, 1882)	A	bronze cardinalfish
Astrapogon puncticulatus (Poey, 1887)	A	blackfin cardinalfish
Astrapogon stellatus (Cope, 1869)	A	conchfish
Phaeoptyx conklini (Silvester, 1916)	A	freckled cardinalfish
Phaeoptyx pigmentaria (Poey, 1860)	A	dusky cardinalfish
Phaeoptyx xenus (Böhlke & Randall, 1968)	A	sponge cardinalfish
	Malacanthidae—tilefishes	
Caulolatilus chrysops (Valenciennes, 1833)	A	goldface tilefish
Caulolatilus cyanops Poey, 1866	A	blackline tilefish
Caulolatilus intermedius Howell Rivero, 1936	A	anchor tilefish
Caulolatilus microps Goode & Bean, 1878	A	blueline tilefish
Caulolatilus princeps (Jenyns, 1842)	P	ocean whitefish
Lopholatilus chamaeleonticeps Goode & Bean, 1879	A	tilefish
Malacanthus plumieri (Bloch, 1787)	A	sand tilefish
	Pomatomidae—bluefishes	
+*Pomatomus saltatrix* (Linnaeus, 1766)	A	bluefish
	Rachycentridae—cobias	
Rachycentron canadum (Linnaeus, 1766)	A	cobia
	Echeneidae—remoras	
* *Echeneis naucrates* Linnaeus, 1758	A-P	sharksucker
Echeneis neucratoides Zuieuw, 1789	A	whitefin sharksucker
* *Phtheirichthys lineatus* (Menzies, 1791)	A-P	slender suckerfish
Remora australis (Bennett, 1840)	A-P	whalesucker
Remora brachyptera (Lowe, 1839)	A-P	spearfish remora
Remora osteochir (Cuvier, 1829)	A-P	marlinsucker
Remora remora (Linnaeus, 1758)	A-P	remora
Remorina albescens (Temminck & Schlegel, 1845)	A-P	white suckerfish
	Carangidae—jacks	
Alectis ciliaris (Bloch, 1787)	A	African pompano
+*Caranx bartholomaei* Cuvier, 1833	A	yellow jack
Caranx caballus Günther, 1868	P	green jack
Caranx caninus Günther, 1868	P	Pacific crevalle jack
Caranx crysos (Mitchill, 1815)	A	blue runner
* *Caranx dentex* (Bloch & Schneider, 1801)	A	white trevally

SCIENTIFIC NAME	OCCURRENCE	COMMON NAME
Caranx hippos (Linnaeus, 1766)	A	crevalle jack
Caranx latus Agassiz, 1831	A	horse-eye jack
Caranx lugubris Poey, 1860	A	black jack
+*Caranx ruber* (Bloch, 1793)	A	bar jack
Chloroscombrus chrysurus (Linnaeus, 1766)	A	Atlantic bumper
Chloroscombrus orqueta Jordan & Gilbert, 1883	P	Pacific bumper
Decapterus macarellus (Cuvier, 1833)	A	mackerel scad
* *Decapterus punctatus* (Cuvier, 1829)	A	round scad
Decapterus scombrinus (Valenciennes, 1846)	P	Mexican scad
Decapterus tabl Berry, 1968	A	redtail scad
Elagatis bipinnulata (Quoy & Gaimard, 1824)	A	rainbow runner
Hemicaranx amblyrhynchus (Cuvier, 1833)	A	bluntnose jack
Naucrates ductor (Linnaeus, 1758)	A-P	pilotfish
* *Oligoplites saurus* (Schneider, 1801)	A	leatherjack
Selar crumenophthalmus (Bloch, 1793)	A	bigeye scad
Selene peruviana (Guichenot, 1865)	P	Pacific moonfish
Selene setapinnis (Mitchill, 1815)	A	Atlantic moonfish
Selene vomer (Linnaeus, 1758)	A	lookdown
Seriola dumerili (Risso, 1810)	A	greater amberjack
Seriola fasciata (Bloch, 1797)	A	lesser amberjack
* *Seriola lalandi* Valenciennes, 1833	P	yellowtail
* *Seriola rivoliana* Valenciennes, 1833	A-P	almaco jack
Seriola zonata (Mitchill, 1815)	A	banded rudderfish
Trachinotus carolinus (Linnaeus, 1766)	A	Florida pompano
Trachinotus falcatus (Linnaeus, 1758)	A	permit
Trachinotus goodei Jordan & Evermann, 1896	A	palometa
Trachinotus paitensis Cuvier, 1832	P	paloma pompano
Trachinotus rhodopus (Gill, 1863)	P	gafftopsail pompano
Trachurus lathami Nichols, 1920	A	rough scad
Trachurus symmetricus (Ayres, 1855)	P	jack mackerel
Uraspis secunda (Poey, 1860)	A-P	cottonmouth jack
	*Nematistiidae—roosterfishes	
Nematistius pectoralis Gill, 1862	P	roosterfish
	Coryphaenidae—dolphins	
Coryphaena equisetis Linnaeus, 1758	A	pompano dolphin
Coryphaena hippurus Linnaeus, 1758	A-P	dolphin
	Bramidae—pomfrets	
Brama brama (Bonnaterre, 1758)	A	Atlantic pomfret
Brama caribbea Mead, 1972	A	Caribbean pomfret
Brama dussumieri Cuvier, 1831	A	lowfin pomfret
Brama japonica Hilgendorf, 1878	P	Pacific pomfret
Brama orcini Cuvier, 1831	P	bigtooth pomfret
Pteraclis aesticola (Jordan & Snyder, 1901)	P	Pacific fanfish
Pterycombus brama Fries, 1837	A	Atlantic fanfish
Taractes asper Lowe, 1843	P	rough pomfret
Taratichthys longipinnis (Lowe, 1843)	A	bigscale pomfret
Taratichthys steindachneri (Döderlein, 1883)	P	sickle pomfret

SCIENTIFIC NAME	OCCURRENCE	COMMON NAME
	Emmelichthyidae—rovers	
Erythrocles monodi Poll & Cadenat, 1954	A	crimson rover
	Lutjanidae—snappers	
Apsilus dentatus Guichenot, 1853	A	black snapper
Etelis oculatus (Valenciennes, 1828)	A	queen snapper
Lutjanus analis (Cuvier, 1828)	A	mutton snapper
Lutjanus apodus (Walbaum, 1892)	A	schoolmaster
Lutjanus argentiventris (Peters, 1869)	P	amarillo snapper
Lutjanus buccanella (Cuvier, 1828)	A	blackfin snapper
Lutjanus campechanus (Poey, 1860)	A	red snapper
Lutjanus colorado Jordan & Gilbert, 1882	P	colorado snapper
Lutjanus cyanopterus (Cuvier, 1828)	A	cubera snapper
Lutjanus griseus (Linnaeus, 1758)	A-F	gray snapper
Lutjanus jocu (Schneider, 1801)	A	dog snapper
Lutjanus mahogoni (Cuvier, 1828)	A	mahogany snapper
* *Lutjanus peru* (Nichols & Murphy, 1922)	P	Pacific red snapper
* *Lutjanus purpureus* Poey, 1867	A	Caribbean red snapper
Lutjanus synagris (Linnaeus, 1758)	A	lane snapper
Lutjanus vivanus (Cuvier, 1828)	A	silk snapper
Ocyurus chrysurus (Bloch, 1791)	A	yellowtail snapper
Pristipomoides aquilonaris (Goode & Bean, 1896)	A	wenchman
* *Pristipomoides freemani* Anderson, 1966	A	yelloweye wenchman
Rhomboplites aurorubens (Cuvier, 1829)	A	vermilion snapper
* *Symphysanodon berryi* Anderson, 1970	A	slope bass
	Lobotidae—tripletails	
Lobotes surinamensis (Bloch, 1790)	A	tripletail
	Gerreidae—mojarras	
Diapterus auratus Ranzani, 1840	A	Irish pompano
Diapterus plumieri (Cuvier, 1830)	A-F	striped mojarra
* *Eucinostomus argenteus* Baird & Girard, 1855	A-F-P	spotfin mojarra
Eucinostomus gracilis (Gill, 1862)	P	Pacific flagfin mojarra
Eucinostomus gula (Quoy & Gaimard, 1824)	A	silver jenny
* *Eucinostomus harengulus* Goode & Bean, 1879	A	tidewater mojarra
Eucinostomus havana (Nichols, 1912)	A	bigeye mojarra
Eucinostomus jonesi (Günther, 1879)	A	slender mojarra
Eucinostomus lefroyi (Goode, 1874)	A	mottled mojarra
Eucinostomus melanopterus (Bleeker, 1863)	A	flagfin mojarra
Gerres cinereus (Walbaum, 1792)	A	yellowfin mojarra
	+Haemulidae—grunts	
Anisotremus davidsoni (Steindachner, 1875)	P	sargo
Anisotremus surinamensis (Bloch, 1790)	A	black margate
Anisotremus virginicus (Linnaeus, 1758)	A	porkfish
Conodon nobilis (Linnaeus, 1758)	A	barred grunt
Haemulon album Cuvier, 1830	A	margate
Haemulon aurolineatum Cuvier, 1830	A	tomtate
Haemulon carbonarium Poey, 1860	A	caesar grunt

SCIENTIFIC NAME	OCCURRENCE	COMMON NAME
Haemulon chrysargyreum Günther, 1859	A	smallmouth grunt
Haemulon flavolineatum (Desmarest, 1823)	A	French grunt
Haemulon macrostomum Günther, 1859	A	Spanish grunt
Haemulon melanurum (Linnaeus, 1758)	A	cottonwick
* *Haemulon parra* (Desmarest, 1823)	A	sailors choice
Haemulon plumieri (Lacepède, 1801)	A	white grunt
Haemulon sciurus (Shaw, 1803)	A	bluestriped grunt
Haemulon striatum (Linnaeus, 1758)	A	striped grunt
Microlepidotus inornatus Gill, 1862	P	wavyline grunt
Orthopristis chrysoptera (Linnaeus, 1766)	A-F	pigfish
Pomadasys crocro (Cuvier, 1830)	A	burro grunt
Xenistius californiensis (Steindachner, 1875)	P	salema
	Inermiidae—bonnetmouths	
Emmelichthyops atlanticus Schultz, 1945	A	bonnetmouth
Inermia vittata Poey, 1861	A	boga
	Sparidae—porgies	
Archosargus probatocephalus (Walbaum, 1792)	A-F	sheepshead
Archosargus rhomboidalis (Linnaeus, 1758)	A	sea bream
Calamus arctifrons Goode & Bean, 1882	A	grass porgy
Calamus bajonado (Schneider, 1801)	A	jolthead porgy
Calamus brachysomus (Lockington, 1880)	P	Pacific porgy
Calamus calamus (Valenciennes, 1830)	A	saucereye porgy
Calamus leucosteus Jordan & Gilbert, 1885	A	whitebone porgy
Calamus nodosus Randall & Caldwell, 1966	A	knobbed porgy
Calamus penna (Valenciennes, 1830)	A	sheepshead porgy
Calamus proridens Jordan & Gilbert, 1884	A	littlehead porgy
Diplodus argenteus (Valenciennes, 1830)	A	silver porgy
Diplodus holbrooki (Bean, 1878)	A	spottail pinfish
Lagodon rhomboides (Linnaeus, 1766)	A-F	pinfish
* *Pagrus pagrus* (Linnaeus, 1758)	A	red porgy
Stenotomus caprinus Bean, 1882	A	longspine porgy
Stenotomus chrysops (Linnaeus, 1766)	A	scup
	Sciaenidae—drums	
Aplodinotus grunniens Rafinesque, 1819	F	freshwater drum
Atractoscion nobilis (Ayres, 1860)	P	white seabass
Bairdiella batabana (Poey, 1860)	A	blue croaker
Bairdiella chrysoura (Lacepède, 1802)	A-F	silver perch
Bairdiella icistia (Jordan & Gilbert, 1882)	[I][8]	bairdiella
Bairdiella sanctaeluciae (Jordan, 1890)	A	striped croaker
Cheilotrema saturnum (Girard, 1858)	P	black croaker
Cynoscion arenarius Ginsburg, 1929	A	sand seatrout
Cynoscion nebulosus (Cuvier, 1830)	A-F	spotted seatrout
Cynoscion nothus (Holbrook, 1855)	A	silver seatrout
Cynoscion parvipinnis Ayres, 1862	P	shortfin corvina
Cynoscion regalis (Bloch & Schneider, 1801)	A	weakfish

[8] In our area confined to Salton Sea, California, where it was introduced.

SCIENTIFIC NAME	OCCURRENCE	COMMON NAME
Cynoscion xanthulus Jordan & Gilbert, 1882	[I][8]	orangemouth corvina
Equetus acuminatus (Schneider, 1801)	A	high-hat
* *Equetus iwamotoi* (Miller & Woods, 1988)	A	blackbar drum
Equetus lanceolatus (Linnaeus, 1758)	A	jackknife-fish
Equetus punctatus (Schneider, 1801)	A	spotted drum
Equetus umbrosus Jordan & Eigenmann, 1889	A	cubbyu
Genyonemus lineatus (Ayres, 1855)	P	white croaker
Larimus fasciatus Holbrook, 1855	A	banded drum
Leiostomus xanthurus Lacepède, 1802	A-F	spot
Menticirrhus americanus (Linnaeus, 1758)	A	southern kingfish
Menticirrhus littoralis (Holbrook, 1855)	A	gulf kingfish
Menticirrhus saxatilis (Bloch & Schneider, 1801)	A	northern kingfish
Menticirrhus undulatus (Girard, 1854)	P	California corbina
Micropogonias undulatus (Linnaeus, 1766)	A-F	Atlantic croaker
Odontoscion dentex (Cuvier, 1830)	A	reef croaker
Pogonias cromis (Linnaeus, 1766)	A	black drum
Roncador stearnsi (Steindachner, 1875)	P	spotfin croaker
Sciaenops ocellatus (Linnaeus, 1766)	A-F	red drum
Seriphus politus Ayres, 1860	P	queenfish
Stellifer lanceolatus (Holbrook, 1855)	A	star drum
Umbrina coroides Cuvier, 1830	A	sand drum
Umbrina roncador Jordan & Gilbert, 1882	P	yellowfin croaker
	Mullidae—goatfishes	
+*Mulloidichthys dentatus* (Gill, 1862)	P	Mexican goatfish
+*Mulloidichthys martinicus* (Cuvier, 1829)	A	yellow goatfish
Mullus auratus Jordan & Gilbert, 1882	A	red goatfish
Pseudupeneus grandisquamis (Gill, 1863)	P	bigscale goatfish
Pseudupeneus maculatus (Bloch, 1793)	A	spotted goatfish
Upeneus parvus Poey, 1853	A	dwarf goatfish
	Pempheridae—sweepers	
Pempheris schomburgki Müller & Troschel, 1848	A	glassy sweeper
	Kyphosidae—sea chubs	
Girella nigricans (Ayres, 1860)	P	opaleye
Hermosilla azurea Jenkins & Evermann, 1889	P	zebra perch
Kyphosus analogus (Gill, 1862)	P	blue-bronze chub
Kyphosus incisor (Cuvier, 1831)	A	yellow chub
Kyphosus sectatrix (Linnaeus, 1758)	A	Bermuda chub
Medialuna californiensis (Steindachner, 1875)	P	halfmoon
Sectator ocyurus (Jordan & Gilbert, 1882)	P	bluestriped chub
	Ephippidae—spadefishes	
Chaetodipterus faber (Broussonet, 1782)	A	Atlantic spadefish
Chaetodipterus zonatus (Girard, 1858)	P	Pacific spadefish
	Chaetodontidae—butterflyfishes	
Chaetodon aculeatus (Poey, 1860)	A	longsnout butterflyfish
Chaetodon aya Jordan, 1886	A	bank butterflyfish

SCIENTIFIC NAME	OCCURRENCE	COMMON NAME
Chaetodon capistratus Linnaeus, 1758	A	foureye butterflyfish
Chaetodon falcifer Hubbs & Rechnitzer, 1958	P	scythe butterflyfish
* *Chaetodon humeralis* Günther, 1860	P	threeband butterflyfish
Chaetodon ocellatus Bloch, 1787	A	spotfin butterflyfish
Chaetodon sedentarius Poey, 1860	A	reef butterflyfish
Chaetodon striatus Linnaeus, 1758	A	banded butterflyfish
Pomacanthidae—angelfishes		
Centropyge argi Woods & Kanazawa, 1951	A	cherubfish
Holacanthus bermudensis Goode, 1876	A	blue angelfish
Holacanthus ciliaris (Linnaeus, 1758)	A	queen angelfish
Holacanthus tricolor (Bloch, 1795)	A	rock beauty
Pomacanthus arcuatus (Linnaeus, 1758)	A	gray angelfish
Pomacanthus paru (Bloch, 1787)	A	French angelfish
* *Pomacanthus zonipectus* (Gill, 1862)	P	Cortez angelfish
Pentacerotidae—armorheads		
* *Pentaceros pectoralis* (Hardy, 1983)	P	longfin armorhead
+Cichlidae—cichlids		
Astronotus ocellatus (Agassiz, 1831)	F[I]	oscar
* *Cichla ocellaris* Bloch & Schneider, 1801	F[I]	peacock cichlid
Cichlasoma bimaculatum (Linnaeus, 1758)	F[I]	black acara
* *Cichlasoma citrinellum* (Günther, 1864)	F[I]	midas cichlid
Cichlasoma cyanoguttatum (Baird & Girard, 1854)	F	Rio Grande cichlid
* *Cichlasoma managuense* (Günther, 1867)	F[I]	jaguar guapote
* *Cichlasoma meeki* (Brind, 1918)	F[I]	firemouth cichlid
Cichlasoma nigrofasciatum (Günther, 1867)	F[I]	convict cichlid
Cichlasoma octofasciatum (Regan, 1903)	F[I]	Jack Dempsey
* *Cichlasoma urophthalmus* (Günther, 1862)	A-F[I]	Mayan cichlid
* *Geophagus surinamensis* (Bloch, 1791)	F[I]	redstriped eartheater
* *Hemichromis bimaculatus* Gill, 1862	F[I]	African jewelfish
Tilapia aurea (Steindachner, 1864)	F[I]	blue tilapia
Tilapia mariae (Boulenger, 1899)	F[I]	spotted tilapia
Tilapia melanotheron (Rüppell, 1852)	F[I]	blackchin tilapia
Tilapia mossambica (Peters, 1852)	F-P[I]	Mozambique tilapia
* *Tilapia urolepis* Norman, 1923	F[I]	Wami tilapia
Tilapia zilli (Gervais, 1848)	F[I]	redbelly tilapia
Embiotocidae—surfperches		
Amphistichus argenteus Agassiz, 1854	P	barred surfperch
Amphistichus koelzi (Hubbs, 1933)	P	calico surfperch
Amphistichus rhodoterus (Agassiz, 1854)	P	redtail surfperch
Brachyistius frenatus Gill, 1862	P	kelp perch
+ *Cymatogaster aggregata* Gibbons, 1854	F-P	shiner perch
Embiotoca jacksoni Agassiz, 1853	P	black perch
Embiotoca lateralis Agassiz, 1854	P	striped seaperch
Hyperprosopon anale Agassiz, 1861	P	spotfin surfperch
Hyperprosopon argenteum Gibbons, 1854	P	walleye surfperch
Hyperprosopon ellipticum (Gibbons, 1854)	P	silver surfperch

SCIENTIFIC NAME	OCCURRENCE	COMMON NAME
Hypsurus caryi (Agassiz, 1853)	P	rainbow seaperch
Hysterocarpus traski Gibbons, 1854	F	tule perch
Micrometrus aurora (Jordan & Gilbert, 1880)	P	reef perch
Micrometrus minimus (Gibbons, 1854)	P	dwarf perch
Phanerodon atripes (Jordan & Gilbert, 1880)	P	sharpnose seaperch
Phanerodon furcatus Girard, 1854	P	white seaperch
Rhacochilus toxotes Agassiz, 1854	P	rubberlip seaperch
Rhacochilus vacca (Girard, 1855)	P	pile perch
Zalembius rosaceus (Jordan & Gilbert, 1880)	P	pink seaperch
	Pomacentridae—damselfishes	
Abudefduf saxatilis (Linnaeus, 1758)	A	sergeant major
Abudefduf taurus (Müller & Troschel, 1848)	A	night sergeant
* *Chromis cyanea* (Poey, 1860)	A	blue chromis
Chromis enchrysurus Jordan & Gilbert, 1882	A	yellowtail reeffish
* *Chromis insolata* (Cuvier, 1830)	A	sunshinefish
* *Chromis multilineata* (Guichenot, 1853)	A	brown chromis
Chromis punctipinnis (Cooper, 1863)	P	blacksmith
Chromis scotti Emery, 1968	A	purple reeffish
Hypsypops rubicundus (Girard, 1854)	P	garibaldi
Microspathodon chrysurus (Cuvier, 1830)	A	yellowtail damselfish
Pomacentrus diencaeus (Jordan & Rutter, 1897)	A	longfin damselfish
Pomacentrus fuscus Cuvier, 1830	A	dusky damselfish
Pomacentrus leucostictus Müller & Troschel, 1848	A	beaugregory
Pomacentrus partitus Poey, 1868	A	bicolor damselfish
Pomacentrus planifrons Cuvier, 1830	A	threespot damselfish
* *Pomacentrus variabilis* Castelnau, 1855	A	cocoa damselfish
	Cirrhitidae—hawkfishes	
Amblycirrhitus pinos (Mowbray, 1927)	A	redspotted hawkfish
	Mugilidae—mullets	
Agonostomus monticola (Bancroft, 1836)	A-F	mountain mullet
Mugil cephalus Linnaeus, 1758	A-F-P	striped mullet
* *Mugil curema* Valenciennes, 1836	A-F-P	white mullet
Mugil gaimardianus Desmarest, 1831	A	redeye mullet
* *Mugil gyrans* (Jordan & Gilbert, 1884)	A	fantail mullet
Mugil liza Valenciennes, 1836	A	liza
	Sphyraenidae—barracudas	
Sphyraena argentea Girard, 1854	P	Pacific barracuda
Sphyraena barracuda (Walbaum, 1792)	A	great barracuda
Sphyraena borealis DeKay, 1842	A	northern sennet
Sphyraena guachancho Cuvier, 1829	A	guaguanche
Sphyraena picudilla Poey, 1860	A	southern sennet
	Polynemidae—threadfins	
Polydactylus approximans (Lay & Bennett, 1839)	P	blue bobo
Polydactylus octonemus (Girard, 1858)	A	Atlantic threadfin
Polydactylus oligodon (Günther, 1860)	A	littlescale threadfin

SCIENTIFIC NAME	OCCURRENCE	COMMON NAME
Polydactylus opercularis (Gill, 1863)	P	yellow bobo
Polydactylus virginicus (Linnaeus, 1758)	A	barbu
	Labridae—wrasses	
Bodianus pulchellus (Poey, 1860)	A	spotfin hogfish
Bodianus rufus (Linnaeus, 1758)	A	Spanish hogfish
* *Clepticus parrae* (Bloch & Schneider, 1801)	A	creole wrasse
Decodon puellaris (Poey, 1860)	A	red hogfish
Doratonotus megalepis Günther, 1862	A	dwarf wrasse
Halichoeres bathyphilus (Beebe & Tee-Van, 1932)	A	greenband wrasse
Halichoeres bivittatus (Bloch, 1791)	A	slippery dick
Halichoeres caudalis (Poey, 1860)	A	painted wrasse
Halichoeres cyanocephalus (Bloch, 1791)	A	yellowcheek wrasse
Halichoeres garnoti (Valenciennes, 1839)	A	yellowhead wrasse
Halichoeres maculipinna (Müller & Troschel, 1848)	A	clown wrasse
Halichoeres pictus (Poey, 1860)	A	rainbow wrasse
Halichoeres poeyi (Steindachner, 1867)	A	blackear wrasse
Halichoeres radiatus (Linnaeus, 1758)	A	puddingwife
Halichoeres semicinctus (Ayres, 1859)	P	rock wrasse
Hemipteronotus martinicensis (Valenciennes, 1839)	A	rosy razorfish
Hemipteronotus novacula (Linnaeus, 1758)	A	pearly razorfish
Hemipteronotus splendens (Castelnau, 1855)	A	green razorfish
Lachnolaimus maximus (Walbaum, 1792)	A	hogfish
Oxyjulis californica (Günther, 1861)	P	senorita
Semicossyphus pulcher (Ayres, 1854)	P	California sheephead
Tautoga onitis (Linnaeus, 1758)	A	tautog
Tautogolabrus adspersus (Walbaum, 1792)	A	cunner
Thalassoma bifasciatum (Bloch, 1791)	A	bluehead
	Scaridae—parrotfishes	
Cryptotomus roseus Cope, 1871	A	bluelip parrotfish
Nicholsina usta (Valenciennes, 1839)	A	emerald parrotfish
Scarus coelestinus Valenciennes, 1839	A	midnight parrotfish
Scarus coeruleus (Bloch, 1786)	A	blue parrotfish
Scarus croicensis Bloch, 1790	A	striped parrotfish
Scarus guacamaia Cuvier, 1829	A	rainbow parrotfish
Scarus taeniopterus Desmarest, 1831	A	princess parrotfish
Scarus vetula Schneider, 1801	A	queen parrotfish
Sparisoma atomarium (Poey, 1861)	A	greenblotch parrotfish
Sparisoma aurofrenatum (Valenciennes, 1839)	A	redband parrotfish
Sparisoma chrysopterum (Bloch & Schneider, 1801)	A	redtail parrotfish
Sparisoma radians (Valenciennes, 1839)	A	bucktooth parrotfish
Sparisoma rubripinne (Valenciennes, 1839)	A	redfin parrotfish
Sparisoma viride (Bonnaterre, 1788)	A	stoplight parrotfish
	Bathymasteridae—ronquils	
Bathymaster caeruleofasciatus Gilbert & Burke, 1912	P	Alaskan ronquil
Bathymaster leurolepis McPhail, 1965	P	smallmouth ronquil
Bathymaster signatus Cope, 1873	P	searcher

SCIENTIFIC NAME	OCCURRENCE	COMMON NAME
* *Rathbunella hypoplecta* (Gilbert, 1890)	P	stripedfin ronquil
Ronquilus jordani (Gilbert, 1889)	P	northern ronquil
	Zoarcidae—eelpouts	
* *Bothrocara brunneum* (Bean, 1890)	P	twoline eelpout
Bothrocara pusillum (Bean, 1890)	P	Alaska eelpout
* *Eucryphycus californicus* (Starks & Mann, 1911)	P	persimmon eelpout
* *Gymnelus hemifasciatus* Andriashev, 1937	P	halfbarred pout
* *Gymnelus popovi* (Taranets & Andriashev, 1935)	P	Aleutian pout
* *Gymnelus retrodorsalis* Le Danois, 1913	A-P	aurora pout
* *Gymnelus viridis* (Fabricius, 1780)	A-P	fish doctor
* *Lycenchelys paxillus* (Goode & Bean, 1879)	A	common wolf eel
Lycenchelys verrilli (Goode & Bean, 1877)	A	wolf eelpout
Lycodapus fierasfer Gilbert, 1890	P	blackmouth eelpout
Lycodapus mandibularis Gilbert, 1915	P	pallid eelpout
Lycodapus parviceps Gilbert, 1896	P	smallhead eelpout
* *Lycodapus psarostomatus* Peden & Anderson, 1981	P	specklemouth eelpout
Lycodes brevipes Bean, 1890	P	shortfin eelpout
* *Lycodes concolor* Gill & Townsend, 1897	P	ebony eelpout
* *Lycodes cortezianus* (Gilbert, 1890)	P	bigfin eelpout
Lycodes diapterus Gilbert, 1892	P	black eelpout
* *Lycodes esmarki* Collett, 1875	A	greater eelpout
Lycodes jugoricus Knipowitsch, 1906	P	shulupaoluk
Lycodes lavalaei Vladykov & Tremblay, 1936	A	Newfoundland eelpout
* *Lycodes mucosus* Richardson, 1855	A-P	saddled eelpout
Lycodes palearis Gilbert, 1896	P	wattled eelpout
Lycodes pallidus Collett, 1878	A-P	pale eelpout
* *Lycodes polaris* (Sabine, 1824)	A-P	Canadian eelpout
* *Lycodes raridens* Taranets & Andriashev, 1937	P	marbled eelpout
* *Lycodes reticulatus* Reinhardt, 1835	A-P	Arctic eelpout
Lycodes rossi Malmgren, 1864	P	threespot eelpout
Lycodes sagittarius McAllister, 1976	P	archer eelpout
Lycodes turneri Bean, 1879	A-P	polar eelpout
* *Lycodes vahli* Reinhardt, 1831	A	checker eelpout
Lycodopsis pacifica (Collett, 1879)	P	blackbelly eelpout
Lyconema barbatum Gilbert, 1896	P	bearded eelpout
Macrozoarces americanus (Schneider, 1801)	A	ocean pout
Melanostigma atlanticum Koefoed, 1952	A	Atlantic soft pout
	Stichaeidae—pricklebacks	
Acantholumpenus mackayi (Gilbert, 1896)	P	pighead prickleback
Alectrias alectrolophus (Pallas, 1814)	P	stone cockscomb
Alectridium aurantiacum Gilbert & Burke, 1912	P	lesser prickleback
Allolumpenus hypochromus Hubbs & Schultz, 1932	P	Y-prickleback
Anoplarchus insignis Gilbert & Burke, 1912	P	slender cockscomb
Anoplarchus purpurescens Gill, 1861	P	high cockscomb
Bryozoichthys lysimus (Jordan & Snyder, 1902)	P	nutcracker prickleback
Bryozoichthys marjorius McPhail, 1970	P	pearly prickleback
Cebidichthys violaceus (Girard, 1854)	P	monkeyface prickleback
Chirolophis ascanii (Walbaum, 1792)	A	Atlantic warbonnet

SCIENTIFIC NAME	OCCURRENCE	COMMON NAME
Chirolophis decoratus (Jordan & Snyder, 1902)	P	decorated warbonnet
Chirolophis nugator (Jordan & Williams,1895)	P	mosshead warbonnet
Chirolophis tarsodes (Jordan & Snyder, 1902)	P	matcheek warbonnet
* *Ernogrammus walkeri* Follett & Powell, 1988	P	masked prickleback
* *Esselenia carli* Follett & Anderson, 1990	P	threeline prickleback
* *Esselenia laurae* Follett & Anderson, 1990	P	twoline prickleback
Eumesogrammus praecisus (Krøyer, 1837)	A-P	fourline snakeblenny
Gymnoclinus cristulatus Gilbert & Burke, 1912	P	trident prickleback
Lumpenella longirostris (Evermann & Goldsborough, 1907)	P	longsnout prickleback
Lumpenus fabricii (Valenciennes, 1836)	A-P	slender eelblenny
Lumpenus lumpretaeformis (Walbaum, 1792)	A	snakeblenny
Lumpenus maculatus (Fries, 1837)	A-P	daubed shanny
* *Lumpenus medius* (Reinhardt, 1837)	A-P	stout eelblenny
Lumpenus sagitta Wilimovsky, 1956	P	snake prickleback
Phytichthys chirus (Jordan & Gilbert, 1880)	P	ribbon prickleback
Plagiogrammus hopkinsi Bean, 1894	P	crisscross prickleback
Plectobranchus evides Gilbert, 1890	P	bluebarred prickleback
Poroclinus rothrocki Bean, 1890	P	whitebarred prickleback
Stichaeus punctatus (Fabricius, 1780)	A-P	Arctic shanny
Ulvaria subbifurcata (Storer, 1839)	A	radiated shanny
Xiphister atropurpureus (Kittlitz, 1858)	P	black prickleback
Xiphister mucosus (Girard, 1858)	P	rock prickleback

Cryptacanthodidae—wrymouths

SCIENTIFIC NAME	OCCURRENCE	COMMON NAME
* *Cryptacanthodes aleutensis* (Gilbert, 1896)	P	dwarf wrymouth
* *Cryptacanthodes giganteus* (Kittlitz, 1858)	P	giant wrymouth
Cryptacanthodes maculatus Storer, 1839	A	wrymouth

+Pholidae—gunnels

SCIENTIFIC NAME	OCCURRENCE	COMMON NAME
Apodichthys flavidus Girard, 1854	P	penpoint gunnel
* *Apodichthys fucorum* Jordan & Gilbert, 1880	P	rockweed gunnel
Pholis clemensi Rosenblatt, 1964	P	longfin gunnel
* *Pholis fasciata* (Bloch & Schneider, 1801)	A-P	banded gunnel
Pholis gilli Evermann & Goldsborough, 1907	P	Bering gunnel
Pholis gunnellus (Linnaeus, 1758)	A	rock gunnel
Pholis laeta (Cope, 1873)	P	crescent gunnel
Pholis ornata (Girard, 1854)	P	saddleback gunnel
Pholis schultzi Schultz, 1931	P	red gunnel
* *Rhodymenichthys dolichogaster* (Pallas, 1814)	P	stippled gunnel
Ulvicola sanctaerosae Gilbert & Starks, 1897	P	kelp gunnel

Anarhichadidae—wolffishes

SCIENTIFIC NAME	OCCURRENCE	COMMON NAME
* *Anarhichas denticulatus* Krøyer, 1845	A-P	northern wolffish
Anarhichas lupus Linnaeus, 1758	A	Atlantic wolffish
Anarhichas minor Olafsen, 1772	A	spotted wolffish
Anarhichas orientalis Pallas, 1814	P	Bering wolffish
Anarrhichthys ocellatus Ayres, 1855	P	wolf-eel

SCIENTIFIC NAME	OCCURRENCE	COMMON NAME
Ptilichthyidae—quillfishes		
Ptilichthys goodei Bean, 1881	P	quillfish
Zaproridae—prowfishes		
Zaprora silenus Jordan, 1896	P	prowfish
Scytalinidae—graveldivers		
Scytalina cerdale Jordan & Gilbert, 1880	P	graveldiver
Opistognathidae—jawfishes		
Lonchopisthus micrognathus (Poey, 1860)	A	swordtail jawfish
Opistognathus aurifrons (Jordan & Thompson, 1905)	A	yellowhead jawfish
Opistognathus lonchurus (Jordan & Gilbert, 1882)	A	moustache jawfish
* *Opistognathus macrognathus* (Poey, 1860)	A	banded jawfish
* *Opistognathus maxillosus* (Poey, 1860)	A	mottled jawfish
Opistognathus melachasme Smith-Vaniz, 1972	A	yellowmouth jawfish
+ *Opistognathus* sp.	A	spotfin jawfish
Opistognathus whitehursti (Longley, 1931)	A	dusky jawfish
Trichodontidae—sandfishes		
Arctoscopus japonicus (Steindachner, 1881)	P	sailfin sandfish
Trichodon trichodon (Tilesius, 1813)	P	Pacific sandfish
Uranoscopidae—stargazers		
Astroscopus guttatus Abbott, 1861	A	northern stargazer
Astroscopus y-graecum (Cuvier, 1829)	A	southern stargazer
Gnathagnus egregius (Jordan & Thompson, 1905)	A	freckled stargazer
Kathetostoma albigutta (Bean, 1892)	A	lancer stargazer
Kathetostoma averruncus Jordan & Bollman, 1890	P	smooth stargazer
Percophidae—flatheads		
Bembrops anatirostris Ginsburg, 1955	A	duckbill flathead
Bembrops gobioides (Goode, 1880)	A	goby flathead
***Tripterygiidae—triplefins**		
Enneanectes altivelis Rosenblatt, 1960	A	lofty triplefin
Enneanectes boehlkei Rosenblatt, 1960	A	roughhead triplefin
Enneanectes pectoralis (Fowler, 1941)	A	redeye triplefin
Dactyloscopidae—sand stargazers		
Dactyloscopus crossotus Starks, 1913	A	bigeye stargazer
* *Dactyloscopus moorei* (Fowler, 1906)	A	speckled stargazer
Dactyloscopus tridigitatus Gill, 1859	A	sand stargazer
Gillellus greyae Kanazawa, 1952	A	arrow stargazer
* *Gillellus healae* Dawson, 1982	A	masked stargazer
Gillellus uranidea Böhlke, 1968	A	warteye stargazer
* *Platygillellus rubrocinctus* (Longley, 1934)	A	saddle stargazer

SCIENTIFIC NAME	OCCURRENCE	COMMON NAME
	Clinidae—clinids	
Acanthemblemaria aspera (Longley, 1927)	A	roughhead blenny
Acanthemblemaria chaplini Böhlke, 1957	A	papillose blenny
Alloclinus holderi (Lauderbach, 1907)	P	island kelpfish
Chaenopsis alepidota (Gilbert, 1890)	P	orangethroat pikeblenny
Chaenopsis limbaughi Robins & Randall, 1965	A	yellowface pikeblenny
Chaenopsis ocellata Poey, 1865	A	bluethroat pikeblenny
* *Coralliozetus bahamensis* (Stephens, 1961)	A	blackhead blenny
* *Coralliozetus diaphanus* (Longley, 1927)	A	glass blenny
Cryptotrema corallinum Gilbert, 1890	P	deepwater blenny
Emblemaria atlantica Jordan & Evermann, 1898	A	banner blenny
Emblemaria pandionis Evermann & Marsh, 1899	A	sailfin blenny
Emblemaria piratula Ginsburg & Reid, 1942	A	pirate blenny
Gibbonsia elegans (Cooper, 1864)	P	spotted kelpfish
Gibbonsia metzi Hubbs, 1927	P	striped kelpfish
+*Gibbonsia montereyensis* Hubbs, 1927	P	crevice kelpfish
Hemiemblemaria simulus Longley & Hildebrand, 1940	A	wrasse blenny
Heterostichus rostratus Girard, 1854	P	giant kelpfish
Labrisomus bucciferus (Poey, 1868)	A	puffcheek blenny
Labrisomus gobio (Valenciennes, 1836)	A	palehead blenny
Labrisomus guppyi (Norman, 1922)	A	mimic blenny
Labrisomus haitiensis Beebe & Tee-Van, 1928	A	longfin blenny
Labrisomus kalisherae (Jordan, 1904)	A	downy blenny
Labrisomus nigricinctus Howell Rivero, 1936	A	spotcheek blenny
Labrisomus nuchipinnis (Quoy & Gaimard, 1824)	A	hairy blenny
Malacoctenus aurolineatus Smith, 1957	A	goldline blenny
Malacoctenus macropus (Poey, 1868)	A	rosy blenny
Malacoctenus triangulatus Springer, 1959	A	saddled blenny
Nemaclinus atelestos Böhlke & Springer, 1975	A	threadfin blenny
Neoclinus blanchardi Girard, 1858	P	sarcastic fringehead
Neoclinus stephensae Hubbs, 1953	P	yellowfin fringehead
Neoclinus uninotatus Hubbs, 1953	P	onespot fringehead
Paraclinus cingulatus (Evermann & Marsh, 1899)	A	coral blenny
Paraclinus fasciatus (Steindachner, 1876)	A	banded blenny
Paraclinus grandicomis (Rosén, 1911)	A	horned blenny
Paraclinus infrons Böhlke, 1960	A	bald blenny
Paraclinus integripinnis (Smith, 1880)	P	reef finspot
Paraclinus marmoratus (Steindachner, 1876)	A	marbled blenny
Paraclinus nigripinnis (Steindachner, 1867)	A	blackfin blenny
Starksia ocellata (Steindachner, 1876)	A	checkered blenny
Starksia starcki Gilbert, 1971	A	key blenny
Stathmonotus hemphilli Bean, 1885	A	blackbelly blenny
Stathmonotus stahli (Evermann & Marsh, 1899)	A	eelgrass blenny
	Blenniidae—combtooth blennies	
Chasmodes bosquianus (Lacepède, 1800)	A	striped blenny
Chasmodes saburrae Jordan & Gilbert, 1882	A	Florida blenny
Entomacrodus nigricans Gill, 1859	A	pearl blenny
Hypleurochilus aequipinnis (Günther, 1861)	A	oyster blenny

SCIENTIFIC NAME	OCCURRENCE	COMMON NAME
Hypleurochilus bermudensis Beebe & Tee-Van, 1933	A	barred blenny
Hypleurochilus geminatus (Wood, 1825)	A	crested blenny
Hypleurochilus springeri Randall, 1966	A	orangespotted blenny
Hypsoblennius gentilis (Girard, 1854)	P	bay blenny
Hypsoblennius gilberti (Jordan, 1882)	P	rockpool blenny
* *Hypsoblennius hentz* (Lesueur, 1825)	A	feather blenny
* *Hypsoblennius invemar* Smith-Vaniz & Acero, 1980	A	tessellated blenny
Hypsoblennius ionthas (Jordan & Gilbert, 1882)	A	freckled blenny
* *Hypsoblennius jenkinsi* (Jordan & Evermann, 1896)	P	mussel blenny
Lupinoblennius dispar Herre, 1942	A	mangrove blenny
Lupinoblennius nicholsi (Tavolga, 1954)	A	highfin blenny
Ophioblennius atlanticus (Valenciennes, 1836)	A	redlip blenny
Parablennius marmoreus (Poey, 1876)	A	seaweed blenny
Scartella cristata (Linnaeus, 1758)	A	molly miller
	Icosteidae—ragfishes	
Icosteus aenigmaticus Lockington, 1880	P	ragfish
	Ammodytidae—sand lances	
+*Ammodytes americanus* DeKay, 1842	A	American sand lance
Ammodytes dubius Reinhardt, 1837	A	northern sand lance
* *Ammodytes hexapterus* Pallas, 1814	P	Pacific sand lance
	Callionymidae—dragonets	
* *Diplogrammus pauciradiatus* (Gill, 1865)	A	spotted dragonet
* *Foetorepus agassizi* (Goode & Bean, 1888)	A	spotfin dragonet
* *Paradiplogrammus bairdi* (Jordan, 1887)	A	lancer dragonet
	Eleotridae—sleepers	
Dormitator latifrons (Richardson, 1844)	P	Pacific fat sleeper
Dormitator maculatus (Bloch, 1785)	A-F	fat sleeper
Eleotris picta Kner & Steindachner, 1863	F	spotted sleeper
Eleotris pisonis (Gmelin, 1788)	A-F	spinycheek sleeper
Erotelis smaragdus (Valenciennes, 1837)	A	emerald sleeper
Gobiomorus dormitor Lacepède, 1800	A-F	bigmouth sleeper
	Gobiidae—gobies	
Acanthogobius flavimanus (Temminck & Schlegel, 1845)	F-P[I]	yellowfin goby
Awaous tajasica (Lichtenstein, 1822)	A-F	river goby
Barbulifer ceuthoecus (Jordan & Gilbert, 1884)	A	bearded goby
Bathygobius curacao (Metzelaar, 1919)	A	notchtongue goby
Bathygobius mystacium Ginsburg, 1947	A	island frillfin
Bathygobius soporator (Valenciennes, 1837)	A	frillfin goby
Bollmannia boqueronensis Evermann & Marsh, 1899	A	white-eye goby
Bollmannia communis Ginsburg, 1942	A	ragged goby
* *Bollmannia eigenmanni* (Garman, 1896)	A	shelf goby
Clevelandia ios (Jordan & Gilbert, 1882)	F-P	arrow goby

SCIENTIFIC NAME	OCCURRENCE	COMMON NAME
Coryphopterus alloides Böhlke & Robins, 1960	A	barfin goby
Coryphopterus dicrus Böhlke & Robins, 1960	A	colon goby
Coryphopterus eidolon Böhlke & Robins, 1960	A	pallid goby
Coryphopterus glaucofraenum Gill, 1863	A	bridled goby
Coryphopterus hyalinus Böhlke & Robins, 1962	A	glass goby
Coryphopterus lipernes Böhlke & Robins, 1962	A	peppermint goby
Coryphopterus nicholsi (Bean, 1882)	P	blackeye goby
Coryphopterus personatus (Jordan & Thompson, 1904)	A	masked goby
Coryphopterus punctipectophorus Springer, 1960	A	spotted goby
Coryphopterus thrix Böhlke & Robins, 1960	A	bartail goby
* *Coryphopterus tortugae* (Jordan, 1904)	A	sand goby
Eucyclogobius newberryi (Girard, 1856)	F-P	tidewater goby
Evermannichthys spongicola (Radcliffe, 1917)	A	sponge goby
Evorthodus lyricus (Girard, 1858)	A	lyre goby
Gillichthys mirabilis Cooper, 1864	F-P	longjaw mudsucker
Gnatholepis thompsoni Jordan, 1902	A	goldspot goby
Gobioides broussoneti Lacepède, 1800	A-F	violet goby
Gobionellus atripinnis Gilbert & Randall, 1979	A	blackfin goby
Gobionellus boleosoma (Jordan & Gilbert, 1882)	A-F	darter goby
+ *Gobionellus oceanicus* (Pallas, 1770)	A	highfin goby
* *Gobionellus pseudofasciatus* Gilbert & Randall, 1979	A-F	slashcheek goby
Gobionellus saepepallens Gilbert & Randall, 1968	A	dash goby
* *Gobionellus sagittula* (Günther, 1861)	P	longtail goby
Gobionellus shufeldti (Jordan & Eigenmann, 1886)	A-F	freshwater goby
Gobionellus smaragdus (Valenciennes, 1837)	A	emerald goby
Gobionellus stigmalophius Mead & Böhlke, 1958	A	spotfin goby
Gobionellus stigmaticus (Poey, 1860)	A	marked goby
Gobionellus stigmaturus (Goode & Bean, 1882)	A	spottail goby
* *Gobiosoma bosc* (Lacepède, 1800)	A-F	naked goby
Gobiosoma ginsburgi Hildebrand & Schroeder, 1928	A	seaboard goby
Gobiosoma grosvenori (Robins, 1964)	A	rockcut goby
Gobiosoma horsti Metzelaar, 1922	A	yellowline goby
Gobiosoma longipala Ginsburg, 1933	A	twoscale goby
Gobiosoma macrodon Beebe & Tee-Van, 1928	A	tiger goby
Gobiosoma oceanops (Jordan, 1904)	A	neon goby
Gobiosoma robustum Ginsburg, 1933	A-F	code goby
Gobiosoma xanthiprora Böhlke & Robins, 1968	A	yellowprow goby
Gobulus myersi Ginsburg, 1939	A	paleback goby
Ilypnus gilberti (Eigenmann & Eigenmann, 1889)	P	cheekspot goby
Ioglossus calliurus Bean, 1882	A	blue goby
* *Ioglossus helenae* Randall, 1968	A	hovering goby
Lepidogobius lepidus (Girard, 1858)	P	bay goby
Lethops connectens Hubbs, 1926	P	halfblind goby
Lophogobius cyprinoides (Pallas, 1770)	A	crested goby
Lythrypnus dalli (Gilbert, 1890)	P	bluebanded goby
* *Lythrypnus elasson* Böhlke & Robins, 1960	A	dwarf goby
Lythrypnus nesiotes Böhlke & Robins, 1960	A	island goby
Lythrypnus phorellus Böhlke & Robins, 1960	A	convict goby

SCIENTIFIC NAME	OCCURRENCE	COMMON NAME
Lythrypnus spilus Böhlke & Robins, 1960	A	bluegold goby
Lythrypnus zebra (Gilbert, 1890)	P	zebra goby
Microgobius carri Fowler, 1945	A	Seminole goby
Microgobius gulosus (Girard, 1858)	A-F	clown goby
Microgobius microlepis Longley & Hildebrand, 1940	A	banner goby
Microgobius thalassinus (Jordan & Gilbert, 1883)	A	green goby
Nes longus (Nichols, 1914)	A	orangespotted goby
Palatogobius paradoxus Gilbert, 1971	A	mauve goby
* *Priolepis hipoliti* (Metzelaar, 1922)	A	rusty goby
Quietula y-cauda (Jenkins & Evermann, 1889)	P	shadow goby
Risor ruber (Rosén, 1911)	A	tusked goby
Tridentiger trigonocephalus (Gill, 1859)	P[I]	chameleon goby
Typhlogobius californiensis Steindachner, 1879	P	blind goby
Varicus marilynae Gilmore, 1979	A	orangebelly goby
Microdesmidae—wormfishes		
Cerdale floridana Longley, 1934	A	pugjaw wormfish
Microdesmus lanceolatus Dawson, 1962	A	lancetail wormfish
Microdesmus longipinnis (Weymouth, 1910)	A	pink wormfish
Acanthuridae—surgeonfishes		
Acanthurus bahianus Castelnau, 1855	A	ocean surgeon
Acanthurus chirurgus (Bloch, 1787)	A	doctorfish
Acanthurus coeruleus Schneider, 1801	A	blue tang
Acanthurus randalli Briggs & Caldwell, 1957	A	gulf surgeonfish
Luvaridae—louvars		
Luvarus imperialis Rafinesque, 1810	A-P	louvar
***Trichiuridae—snake mackerels**		
Assurger anzac (Alexander, 1917)	P	razorback scabbardfish
* *Benthodesmus elongatus* (Clarke, 1879)	A-P	frostfish
Epinnula orientalis Gilchrist & von Bonde, 1924	A	sackfish
Gempylus serpens Cuvier, 1829	A-P	snake mackerel
Lepidocybium flavobrunneum (Smith, 1843)	A-P	escolar
* *Lepidopus fitchi* Rosenblatt & Wilson, 1987	P	Pacific scabbardfish
Nealotus tripes Johnson, 1865	A	black snake mackerel
* *Nesiarchus nasutus* Johnson, 1862	A	black gemfish
Ruvettus pretiosus Cocco, 1829	A-P	oilfish
Trichiurus lepturus Linnaeus, 1758	A	Atlantic cutlassfish
Trichiurus nitens Garman, 1899	P	Pacific cutlassfish
+Scombridae—mackerels		
* *Acanthocybium solandri* (Cuvier, 1832)	A	wahoo
Allothunnus fallai Serventy, 1948	P	slender tuna
+*Auxis rochei* (Risso, 1810)	A-P	bullet mackerel
+*Auxis thazard* (Lacepède, 1800)	A-P	frigate mackerel
Euthynnus affinis (Cantor, 1849)	P	kawakawa
Euthynnus alletteratus (Rafinesque, 1810)	A	little tunny
Euthynnus lineatus Kishinouye, 1920	P	black skipjack

SCIENTIFIC NAME	OCCURRENCE	COMMON NAME
* *Katsuwonus pelamis* (Linnaeus, 1758)	A-P	skipjack tuna
Sarda chiliensis (Cuvier, 1832)	P	Pacific bonito
Sarda sarda (Bloch, 1793)	A	Atlantic bonito
Scomber japonicus Houttuyn, 1782	A-P	chub mackerel
Scomber scombrus Linnaeus, 1758	A	Atlantic mackerel
Scomberomorus cavalla (Cuvier, 1829)	A	king mackerel
Scomberomorus concolor (Lockington, 1879)	P	gulf sierra
Scomberomorus maculatus (Mitchill, 1815)	A	Spanish mackerel
Scomberomorus regalis (Bloch, 1793)	A	cero
Scomberomorus sierra Jordan & Starks, 1895	P	Pacific sierra
Thunnus alalunga (Bonnaterre, 1788)	A-P	albacore
Thunnus albacares (Bonnaterre, 1788)	A-P	yellowfin tuna
Thunnus atlanticus (Lesson, 1830)	A	blackfin tuna
Thunnus obesus (Lowe, 1839)	A-P	bigeye tuna
Thunnus thynnus (Linnaeus, 1758)	A-P	bluefin tuna
	Xiphiidae—swordfishes	
Xiphias gladius Linnaeus, 1758	A-P	swordfish
	Istiophoridae—billfishes	
Istiophorus platypterus (Shaw & Nodder, 1792)	A-P	sailfish
Makaira indica (Cuvier, 1832)	P	black marlin
Makaira nigricans Lacepède, 1802	A-P	blue marlin
Tetrapturus albidus Poey, 1860	A	white marlin
Tetrapturus angustirostris Tanaka, 1915	P	shortbill spearfish
Tetrapturus audax (Philippi, 1887)	P	striped marlin
Tetrapturus pfluegeri Robins & de Sylva, 1963	A	longbill spearfish
	Stromateidae—butterfishes	
Ariomma bondi Fowler, 1930	A	silver-rag
Ariomma melanum (Ginsburg, 1954)	A	brown driftfish
Ariomma regulus (Poey, 1868)	A	spotted driftfish
Centrolophus medusophagus (Cocco, 1839)	A	brown ruff
Centrolophus niger (Gmelin, 1788)	A	black ruff
Cubiceps paradoxus Butler, 1979	P	longfin cigarfish
* *Cubiceps pauciradiatus* Günther, 1872	A	bigeye cigarfish
Hyperoglyphe bythites (Ginsburg, 1954)	A	black driftfish
Hyperoglyphe perciformis (Mitchill, 1818)	A	barrelfish
Icichthys lockingtoni Jordan & Gilbert, 1880	P	medusafish
Nomeus gronovii (Gmelin, 1788)	A	man-of-war fish
Peprilus alepidotus (Linnaeus, 1766)	A	harvestfish
Peprilus burti Fowler, 1944	A	gulf butterfish
Peprilus simillimus (Ayres, 1860)	P	Pacific pompano
Peprilus triacanthus (Peck, 1804)	A	butterfish
Psenes cyanophrys Valenciennes, 1833	A	freckled driftfish
* *Psenes maculatus* Lütken, 1880	A	silver driftfish
Psenes pellucidus Lütken, 1880	A-P	bluefin driftfish
Tetragonurus atlanticus Lowe, 1839	A	bigeye squaretail
Tetragonurus cuvieri Risso, 1810	P	smalleye squaretail

SCIENTIFIC NAME	OCCURRENCE	COMMON NAME
	Anabantidae—gouramies	
* *Trichopsis vittata* (Cuvier, 1831)	F[I]	croaking gourami
	ORDER PLEURONECTIFORMES	
	+Bothidae—lefteye flounders	
Ancylopsetta dilecta (Goode & Bean, 1883)	A	three-eye flounder
Ancylopsetta quadrocellata Gill, 1884	A	ocellated flounder
Bothus lunatus (Linnaeus, 1758)	A	peacock flounder
Bothus ocellatus (Agassiz, 1831)	A	eyed flounder
Bothus robinsi Topp & Hoff, 1972	A	twospot flounder
Chascanopsetta lugubris Alcock, 1894	A	pelican flounder
Citharichthys arctifrons Goode, 1880	A	Gulf Stream flounder
Citharichthys arenaceus Evermann & Marsh, 1900	A	sand whiff
Citharichthys cornutus (Günther, 1880)	A	horned whiff
* *Citharichthys fragilis* Gilbert, 1890	P	gulf sanddab
Citharichthys gymnorhinus Gutherz & Blackman, 1970	A	anglefin whiff
Citharichthys macrops Dresel, 1885	A	spotted whiff
Citharichthys sordidus (Girard, 1854)	P	Pacific sanddab
Citharichthys spilopterus Günther, 1862	A-F	bay whiff
Citharichthys stigmaeus Jordan & Gilbert, 1882	P	speckled sanddab
Citharichthys xanthostigma Gilbert, 1890	P	longfin sanddab
Cyclopsetta chittendeni Bean, 1895	A	Mexican flounder
Cyclopsetta fimbriata (Goode & Bean, 1885)	A	spotfin flounder
Engyophrys senta Ginsburg, 1933	A	spiny flounder
Etropus crossotus Jordan & Gilbert, 1882	A	fringed flounder
* *Etropus cyclosquamus* Leslie & Stewart, 1986	A	shelf flounder
Etropus microstomus (Gill, 1864)	A	smallmouth flounder
Etropus rimosus Goode & Bean, 1885	A	gray flounder
Gastropsetta frontalis Bean, 1895	A	shrimp flounder
Hippoglossina stomata Eigenmann & Eigenmann, 1890	P	bigmouth sole
Monolene antillarum Norman, 1933	A	slim flounder
Monolene sessilicauda Goode, 1880	A	deepwater flounder
Paralichthys albigutta Jordan & Gilbert, 1882	A	gulf flounder
Paralichthys californicus (Ayres, 1859)	P	California halibut
Paralichthys dentatus (Linnaeus, 1766)	A	summer flounder
Paralichthys lethostigma Jordan & Gilbert, 1884	A-F	southern flounder
Paralichthys oblongus (Mitchill, 1815)	A	fourspot flounder
Paralichthys squamilentus Jordan & Gilbert, 1882	A	broad flounder
Scophthalmus aquosus (Mitchill, 1815)	A	windowpane
Syacium gunteri Ginsburg, 1933	A	shoal flounder
Syacium micrurum Ranzani, 1840	A	channel flounder
Syacium papillosum (Linnaeus, 1758)	A	dusky flounder
Trichopsetta ventralis (Goode & Bean, 1885)	A	sash flounder
Xystreurys liolepis Jordan & Gilbert, 1880	P	fantail sole
	Pleuronectidae—righteye flounders	
Atheresthes evermanni Jordan & Starks, 1904	P	Kamchatka flounder

SCIENTIFIC NAME	OCCURRENCE	COMMON NAME
Atheresthes stomias (Jordan & Gilbert, 1880)	P	arrowtooth flounder
Embassichthys bathybius (Gilbert, 1890)	P	deepsea sole
* *Eopsetta exilis* (Jordan & Gilbert, 1880)	P	slender sole
Eopsetta jordani (Lockington, 1879)	P	petrale sole
* *Errex zachirus* (Lockington, 1879)	P	rex sole
Glyptocephalus cynoglossus (Linnaeus, 1758)	A	witch flounder
Hippoglossoides elassodon Jordan & Gilbert, 1880	P	flathead sole
Hippoglossoides platessoides (Fabricius, 1780)	A	American plaice
Hippoglossoides robustus Gill & Townsend, 1897	P	Bering flounder
Hippoglossus hippoglossus (Linnaeus, 1758)	A	Atlantic halibut
Hippoglossus stenolepis Schmidt, 1904	P	Pacific halibut
Hypsopsetta guttulata (Girard, 1856)	P	diamond turbot
Microstomus pacificus (Lockington, 1879)	P	Dover sole
Platichthys stellatus (Pallas, 1787)	F-P	starry flounder
* *Pleuronectes americanus* Walbaum, 1792	A	winter flounder
* *Pleuronectes asper* Pallas, 1814	P	yellowfin sole
* *Pleuronectes bilineatus* (Ayres, 1855)	P	rock sole
* *Pleuronectes ferrugineus* (Storer, 1839)	A	yellowtail flounder
* *Pleuronectes glacialis* Pallas, 1776	P	Arctic flounder
* *Pleuronectes isolepis* (Lockington, 1880)	P	butter sole
* *Pleuronectes proboscideus* (Gilbert, 1896)	P	longhead dab
* *Pleuronectes putnami* (Gill, 1864)	A	smooth flounder
Pleuronectes quadrituberculatus Pallas, 1814	P	Alaska plaice
* *Pleuronectes vetulus* (Girard, 1854)	P	English sole
Pleuronichthys coenosus Girard, 1854	P	C-O sole
Pleuronichthys decurrens Jordan & Gilbert, 1881	P	curlfin sole
Pleuronichthys ritteri Starks & Morris, 1907	P	spotted turbot
Pleuronichthys verticalis Jordan & Gilbert, 1880	P	hornyhead turbot
Psettichthys melanostictus Girard, 1854	P	sand sole
Reinhardtius hippoglossoides (Walbaum, 1792)	A-P	Greenland halibut[9]

+Soleidae—soles

SCIENTIFIC NAME	OCCURRENCE	COMMON NAME
Achirus lineatus (Linnaeus, 1758)	A	lined sole
* *Gymnachirus melas* (Nichols, 1916)	A	naked sole
* *Gymnachirus texae* (Gunter, 1936)	A	fringed sole
Symphurus arawak Robins & Randall, 1965	A	Caribbean tonguefish
Symphurus atricauda (Jordan & Gilbert, 1880)	P	California tonguefish
Symphurus civitatus Ginsburg, 1951	A	offshore tonguefish
Symphurus diomedianus (Goode & Bean, 1886)	A	spottedfin tonguefish
Symphurus minor Ginsburg, 1951	A	largescale tonguefish
Symphurus nebulosus (Goode & Bean, 1883)	A	freckled tonguefish
Symphurus parvus Ginsburg, 1951	A	pygmy tonguefish
Symphurus pelicanus Ginsburg, 1951	A	longtail tonguefish
Symphurus piger (Goode & Bean, 1888)	A	deepwater tonguefish
Symphurus plagiusa (Linnaeus, 1766)	A	blackcheek tonguefish
Symphurus pusillus (Goode & Bean, 1885)	A	northern tonguefish

[9] For a discussion of the reasons for retention of this name see the Annual Report of the Committee on Names of Fishes, 1969, Trans. Am. Fish. Soc. 98(1):179. The current "official" market name both in the United States and Canada is Greenland turbot.

SCIENTIFIC NAME	OCCURRENCE	COMMON NAME
Symphurus urospilus (Ginsburg, 1951)	A	spottail tonguefish
Trinectes inscriptus (Gosse, 1851)	A	scrawled sole
Trinectes maculatus (Bloch & Schneider, 1801)	A-F	hogchoker

ORDER TETRAODONTIFORMES

Triacanthodidae—spikefishes

SCIENTIFIC NAME	OCCURRENCE	COMMON NAME
Hollardia meadi Tyler, 1966	A	spotted spikefish
Parahollardia lineata (Longley, 1935)	A	jambeau

Balistidae—leatherjackets

SCIENTIFIC NAME	OCCURRENCE	COMMON NAME
Aluterus heudeloti Hollard, 1855	A	dotterel filefish
Aluterus monoceros (Linnaeus, 1758)	A	unicorn filefish
Aluterus schoepfi (Walbaum, 1792)	A	orange filefish
Aluterus scriptus (Osbeck, 1765)	A	scrawled filefish
Balistes capriscus Gmelin, 1789	A	gray triggerfish
Balistes polylepis Steindachner, 1876	P	finescale triggerfish
Balistes vetula Linnaeus, 1758	A	queen triggerfish
Cantherhines macrocerus (Hollard, 1854)	A	whitespotted filefish
Cantherhines pullus (Ranzani, 1842)	A	orangespotted filefish
* *Canthidermis maculata* (Bloch, 1786)	A	rough triggerfish
Canthidermis sufflamen (Mitchill, 1815)	A	ocean triggerfish
Melichthys niger (Bloch, 1786)	A-P	black durgon
Monacanthus ciliatus (Mitchill, 1818)	A	fringed filefish
Monacanthus hispidus (Linnaeus, 1766)	A	planehead filefish
Monacanthus setifer Bennett, 1830	A	pygmy filefish
Monacanthus tuckeri Bean, 1906	A	slender filefish
Xanthichthys mento (Jordan & Gilbert, 1882)	P	redtail triggerfish
Xanthichthys ringens (Linnaeus, 1758)	A	sargassum triggerfish

Ostraciidae—boxfishes

SCIENTIFIC NAME	OCCURRENCE	COMMON NAME
Lactophrys bicaudalis (Linnaeus, 1758)	A	spotted trunkfish
Lactophrys polygonia (Poey, 1876)	A	honeycomb cowfish
Lactophrys quadricornis (Linnaeus, 1758)	A	scrawled cowfish
Lactophrys trigonus (Linnaeus, 1758)	A	trunkfish
Lactophrys triqueter (Linnaeus, 1758)	A	smooth trunkfish
Ostracion diaphanum Bloch & Schneider, 1801	P	spiny boxfish

+Tetraodontidae—puffers

SCIENTIFIC NAME	OCCURRENCE	COMMON NAME
Canthigaster rostrata (Bloch, 1782)	A	sharpnose puffer
Chilomycterus affinis Günther, 1870	P	Pacific burrfish
Chilomycterus antennatus (Cuvier, 1818)	A	bridled burrfish
Chilomycterus antillarum Jordan & Rutter, 1897	A	web burrfish
Chilomycterus atinga (Linnaeus, 1758)	A	spotted burrfish
Chilomycterus schoepfi (Walbaum, 1792)	A	striped burrfish
Diodon holocanthus Linnaeus, 1758	A-P	balloonfish
Diodon hystrix Linnaeus, 1758	A-P	porcupinefish
Lagocephalus laevigatus (Linnaeus, 1766)	A	smooth puffer
Lagocephalus lagocephalus (Linnaeus, 1758)	A-P	oceanic puffer
Sphoeroides annulatus (Jenyns, 1842)	P	bullseye puffer

SCIENTIFIC NAME	OCCURRENCE	COMMON NAME
Sphoeroides dorsalis Longley, 1934	A	marbled puffer
Sphoeroides lobatus (Steindachner, 1870)	P	longnose puffer
Sphoeroides maculatus (Bloch & Schneider, 1801)	A	northern puffer
Sphoeroides nephelus (Goode & Bean, 1882)	A	southern puffer
Sphoeroides pachygaster (Müller & Troschel, 1848)	A	blunthead puffer
Sphoeroides parvus Shipp & Yerger, 1969	A	least puffer
Sphoeroides spengleri (Bloch, 1782)	A	bandtail puffer
Sphoeroides testudineus (Linnaeus, 1758)	A	checkered puffer
Molidae—molas		
Mola lanceolata (Lienard, 1840)	A	sharptail mola
Mola mola (Linnaeus, 1758)	A-P	ocean sunfish
Ranzania laevis (Pennant, 1776)	A-P	slender mola

PART II

Appendix 1
Changes from 1980 List and Comments

The comments and explanatory notes below are keyed to the appropriate scientific name as indicated by an asterisk (*) or plus sign (+) in the main list, Part I. Entries are in the same order as in the list and are grouped, for convenience, by page. Information provided in the Appendix in the Third Edition, 1970, Am. Fish. Soc. Spec. Publ. 6:65–87, and in Appendix 1 in the Fourth Edition, 1980, Am. Fish. Soc. Spec. Publ. 12:68–92, is not repeated here. Abbreviations of journal names are those used in "Serial Sources for the Biosis Data Base."

Page 11

Petromyzontiformes, Petromyzontidae. Opinion 1171 of the International Commission on Zoological Nomenclature, 1981, Bull. Zool. Nomencl. 38(2):98, ruled that the stem of the generic name *Petromyzon* is Petromyzont-. These spellings, consistently used by the Committee, are correct.

Lampetra macrostoma. R. J. Beamish, 1982, Can. J. Fish. Aquat. Sci. 39:736, described this parasitic lamprey (subgenus *Entosphenus*) from two lakes, Cowichan and Mesachie, on Vancouver Island, British Columbia.

Lampetra richardsoni. C. E. Bond and T. T. Kan, 1985, Proceedings, Second International Conference on Indo-Pacific Fishes, Ichthyological Society of Japan, Tokyo, p. 919, suggested that *L. pacifica* Vladykov, 1973, Pacific brook lamprey, cannot be distinguished from *L. richardsoni*. This committee has reviewed the data and agree that *pacifica* is a junior synonym of *richardsoni*.

Lampetra similis. V. D. Vladykov and E. Kott, 1979, Can. J. Zool. 57:809, described this new species from the Klamath River system of Oregon and California. Although regarded by some authors as a subspecies of *L. tridentata*, it is here accorded species status on the advice of C. E. Bond.

Page 12

Notorynchus cepedianus. Merger of the several nominal species of *Notorynchus* into one calls for replacement of *N. maculatus* by *N. cepedianus*, L. J. V. Compagno, 1984, Sharks of the World, part 1, Hexanchiformes to Lamniformes, FAO Fish. Synop. 125 (vol. 4, part 1):22, and others.

Lamniformes. We follow the common practice (e.g., J. S. Nelson, 1984, Fishes of the World, 2nd edition, Wiley & Sons, pp. 50, 56) of dividing those sharks assigned to the Squaliformes in the 1980 edition of this list into two orders. The Lamniformes have an anal fin; the Squaliformes lack an anal fin.

Rhincodontidae. Opinion 1278 of the International Commission on Zoological Nomenclature, 1984, Bull. Zool. Nomencl. 41(4):215, conserved the names *Rhincodon* and Rhincodontidae. These spellings, therefore, are unchanged from the previous list. This small family is divided by many ichthyologists into two to seven families. As noted by G. Dingerkus, 1985, Am. Soc. Ichthyol. Herpetol., Annual Meeting Abstracts, p. 56, *Rhincodon* and *Ginglymostoma* belong together. We prefer to interpret the family to include all of the Orectolobidae of authors, and we use the name carpet sharks.

Rhincodon typus. See Rhincodontidae.

Odontaspis noronhai. S. Branstetter and J. D. McEachran, 1986, Northeast Gulf Sci. 8(2):153, recorded this species in the upper 100 m of water, about 110 km east of Port Isabel, Texas.

Cetorhinidae. We follow J. G. Maisey, 1985, Copeia (1):228, in recognizing this family to include *Cetorhinus* and the newly described *Megachasma*.

Megachasma pelagios. The megamouth shark was reported from California by R. J. Lavenberg and J. A. Seigel, 1985, Terra 23(4):29. This new genus and species was assigned by its describers, L. R. Taylor, L. J. V. Compagno, and P. L. Struhsaker, 1983, Proc. Calif. Acad. Sci. 43:87, to a monotypic family, Megachasmidae. J. G. Maisey, 1985, Copeia (1):228, grouped it with *Cetorhinus maximus* in the family Cetorhinidae, a placement here adopted.

Page 13

Carcharhinus longimanus. This shark was called *C. maou* (Lesson, 1830) by J. E. Randall, 1980, U.S. Natl. Mar. Fish. Serv. Fish. Bull. 78:206. However, the junior synonym *Squalus longimanus* Poey, 1861, is on the official list of species names in zoology under Opinion 723 of the International Commission on Zoological Nomenclature.

Galeocerdo cuvier. R. M. Bailey and C. R. Robins, 1988, Bull. Zool. Nomencl. 45(2):98, noted that patronymic names proposed in apposition with the generic name are approved by the 1985 Code (Article 31a) and that, therefore, the "*i*," previously added to such names is to be dropped. We therefore adopt the original spelling.

Galeorhinus zyopterus. L. J. V. Compagno, 1984, FAO Fish. Synop. 125 (vol. 4, part 2):386, synonymized the soupfin shark, *G. zyopterus*, with the tope, *G. galeus* (Linnaeus, 1758), but did not provide data to support this synonymy. Because both taxa are important commercially and recreationally, we regard this change as premature. If this change proves to be correct, we would urge adoption of the name tope for the combined entity.

Squaliformes. See Lamniformes (p. 12).

Squalus asper. F. C. Rohde informs us (pers. comm.) that this shark, which is relatively common in deeper waters from North Carolina to the Florida Keys, has been captured in waters as shallow as 200 m off North Carolina.

Page 14

Squatina dumeril. See *Galeocerdo cuvier* (p. 13).

Pristis pristis. G. Dingerkus, 1983, Am. Soc. Ichthyol. Herpetol., Program and Abstracts, p. 25, concluded that *P. perotteti* is a junior synonym of *P. pristis*, an action followed by us and many others.

Bathyraja aleutica. R. Ishiyama and C. L. Hubbs, 1968, Copeia (2):407, recognized *Bathyraja* as a separate genus. Five species, *aleutica*, *interrupta*, *parmifera*, *rosispinis*, and *trachura* previously placed in *Raja* on our list, belong in this genus.

Bathyraja hubbsi. This new skate from the North Pacific and Bering Sea (depth, 190–590 m) was described by H. Ishihara and R. Ishiyama, 1985, Jpn. J. Ichthyol. 32(2):148.

Bathyraja interrupta. See *B. aleutica*.

Bathyraja parmifera. See *B. aleutica*.

Bathyraja rosispinis. See *B. aleutica*.

Bathyraja trachura. See *B. aleutica*.

Raja erinacea. This species, *R. rhina*, and *R. stellulata* were originally described in *Raia*; therefore, the authorities for these names are placed in parentheses.

Raja rhina. See *R. erinacea*.

Raja stellulata. See *R. erinacea*.

Dasyatis say. See *Galeocerdo cuvier* (p. 13).

Page 15

Urolophidae. The round stingrays are more closely allied to the Potamotrygonidae than to the Dasyatidae. We follow J. D. McEachran (and most recent authorities), 1983, Chondrichthyes, *in* Synopsis and Classification of Living Organisms, McGraw Hill, p. 840, in recognizing this family.

Manta birostris. We follow C. L. Hubbs, W. I. Follett, and L. J. Dempster, 1979, Occas. Pap. Calif. Acad. Sci. 133:5, and others in placing *M. hamiltoni* (Newman) in the synonymy of *M. birostris*, and Atlantic is dropped from the common name.

Mobula thurstoni. G. Notobartolo-di-Sciara, 1987, Zool. J. Linn. Soc. 91:1, placed *lucasana* in the synonymy of *thurstoni*.

Lepisosteiformes. We follow J. S. Nelson, 1984, Fishes of the World, 2nd ed., Wiley & Sons, p. 83, in using this ordinal name instead of Semionotiformes for the gars and their allies.

Page 16

Albuliformes. C. R. Robins, 1989, Memoir, Sears Found. Mar. Res. no. 1, part 9:19, recognized this order and combined the Notacanthiformes with it.

Chlopsidae. D. G. Smith, 1989, Memoir, Sears Found. Mar. Res. no. 1, part 9:72, noted that Chlopsidae had priority over Xenocongridae.

Anarchias similis. D. G. Smith, 1989, Memoir, Sears Found. Mar. Res. no. 1, part 9:118, placed *A. yoshiae* in the synonymy of *A. similis*.

Gymnothorax conspersus. E. B. Böhlke, J. E. McCosker, and J. E. Böhlke, 1989, Memoir,

Sears Found. Mar. Res. no. 1, part 9:161, recorded this moray from coastal waters of North Carolina.

Gymnothorax kolpos. J. E. Böhlke and E. B. Böhlke, 1980, Proc. Acad. Nat. Sci. Phila. 132:223, described this species from coastal waters of the northern Gulf of Mexico and Florida.

Gymnothorax madeirensis. E. B. Böhlke, J. E. McCosker, and J. E. Böhlke, 1989, Memoir, Sears Found. Mar. Res. no. 1, part 9:154, recorded this moray from North Carolina.

Gymnothorax miliaris. E. B. Böhlke, J. E. McCosker, and J. E. Böhlke, 1989, Memoir, Sears Found. Mar. Res. no. 1, part 9:155, transferred this species to *Gymnothorax* from *Muraena*.

Page 17

Gymnothorax polygonius. E. B. Böhlke, J. E. McCosker, and J. E. Böhlke, 1989, Memoir, Sears Found. Mar. Res. no. 1, part 9:184, recorded this species in waters shallower than 100 m off North Carolina.

Gymnothorax saxicola. We follow E. B. Böhlke, J. E. McCosker, and J. E. Böhlke, 1989, Memoir, Sears Found. Mar. Res. no. 1, part 9:167, in adopting the name honeycomb moray for this species and restricting the name ocellated moray to the extralimital *G. ocellatus*.

Muraena robusta. E. B. Böhlke and S. W. Ross, 1981, Northeast Gulf Sci. 4(2):123, recorded this species from North Carolina and Florida.

Uropterygius macularius. E. B. Böhlke, J. E. McCosker, and J. E. Böhlke, 1989, Memoir, Sears Found. Mar. Res. no. 1, part 9:126, showed that this is the earliest name for the species previously known as *U. diopus*.

Synaphobranchus kaupi. C. H. Robins and C. R. Robins, 1989, Memoir, Sears Found. Mar. Res. no. 1, part 9:223, recorded this species from depths as shallow as 131 m off Nova Scotia.

Aplatophis chauliodus. J. E. McCosker, E. B. Böhlke, and J. E. Böhlke, 1989, Memoir, Sears Found. Mar. Res. no. 1, part 9:356, recorded this species from shelf waters of the northwestern Gulf of Mexico.

Callechelys guiniensis. J. E. McCosker, E. B. Böhlke, and J. E. Böhlke, 1989, Memoir, Sears Found. Mar. Res. no. 1, part 9:308, synonymized *C. perryae* with *C. guiniensis*.

Echiophis punctifer. J. E. McCosker, E. B. Böhlke, and J. E. Böhlke, 1989, Memoir, Sears Found. Mar. Res. no. 1, part 9:362, synonymized *E. mordax*, snapper eel, with *E. punctifer*, stippled spoon-nose eel, both of which were on our previous list. We select snapper eel for the combined species.

Ethadophis akkistikos. J. E. McCosker and J. E. Böhlke, 1984, Proc. Acad. Nat. Sci. Phila. 136:41, described this new species whose range includes shallow waters of the northern Gulf of Mexico.

Gordiichthys ergodes. J. E. McCosker, E. B. Böhlke, and J. E. Böhlke, 1989, Memoir, Sears Found. Mar. Res. no. 1, part 9:344, described this new species from waters shallower than 200 m from the northeastern Gulf of Mexico.

Gordiichthys leibyi. J. E. McCosker and J. E. Böhlke, 1984, Proc. Acad. Nat. Sci. Phila. 136:36, described this new species from the Gulf Coast of Florida.

Lethogaleos andersoni. J. E. McCosker and J. E. Böhlke, 1982, Proc. Acad. Nat. Sci. Phila. 134:114, described this new species from South Carolina in waters less than 200 m deep.

Myrichthys breviceps. J. E. McCosker, E. B. Böhlke, and J. E. Böhlke, 1989, Memoir, Sears Found. Mar. Res., no. 1, part 9:374, synonymized *M. acuminatus* with *M. breviceps*.

Myrichthys ocellatus. J. E. McCosker, E. B. Böhlke, and J. E. Böhlke, 1989, Memoir, Sears Found. Mar. Res., no. 1, part 9:377, noted that this name, previously associated with a species of *Ophichthus*, is a senior synonym of *M. oculatus*.

Ophichthus hyposagmatus. J. E. McCosker and E. B. Böhlke, 1984, Proc. Acad. Nat. Sci. Phila. 136:24, described this new species from the Gulf Coast of Florida.

Ophichthus omorgmus. J. E. McCosker and E. B. Böhlke, 1984, Proc. Acad. Nat. Sci. Phila. 136:26, described this new species from northwestern Florida in waters less than 200 m deep.

Ophichthus puncticeps. J. E. McCosker, E. B. Böhlke, and J. E. Böhlke, 1989, Memoir, Sears Found. Mar. Res., no. 1, part 9:402, noted that the name *ocellatus* did not apply to this genus and that the first available name for this species was *puncticeps*.

Ophichthus rex. J. E. Böhlke and J. H. Caruso, 1980, Proc. Acad. Nat. Sci. Phila. 132:239, described this new species from off the Louisiana coast.

Pseudomyrophis fugesae. J. E. McCosker, E. B. Böhlke, and J. E. Böhlke, 1989, Memoir, Sears Found. Mar. Res., no. 1, part 9:292, described this new species from southeastern Florida and Brazil.

Page 18

Saurenchelys cognita. D. G. Smith, 1989, Memoir, Sears Found. Mar. Res., no. 1, part 9:591, included records from shelf waters of the southeastern United States in the distribution of this new species.

Heteroconger halis. D. G. Smith, 1989. Memoir, Sears Found. Mar. Res., no. 1, part 9:484, synonymized *Nystactichthys* with *Heteroconger*. The term "garden eel" is applied broadly to all eels of the subfamily Heterocongrinae. We therefore add the modifier "brown" to the common name of this species.

Heteroconger luteolus. D. G. Smith, 1989, Memoir, Sears Found. Mar. Res., no. 1, part 9:488, described this new species from the Gulf Coast of Florida in 30–40 m depth.

Xenomystax congroides. D. G. Smith and R. H. Kanazawa, in D. G. Smith, 1989, Memoir, Sears Found. Mar. Res., no. 1, part 9:561, described this species, which occurs in our area in the Gulf of Mexico including depths shallower that 200 m.

Clupea harengus. W. S. Grant, 1986, Copeia (3):714, recognized *C. harengus* and *C. pallasi* as distinct species based on a study of their biochemical genetics, an action followed here.

Clupea pallasi. See *C. harengus*.

Page 19

Opisthonema libertate. C. L. Hubbs, W. I. Follett, and L. J. Dempster, 1979, Occas. Pap. Calif. Acad. Sci. 133:6, included this species in their list of California fishes without explanation. We are assured by R. N. Lea (pers. comm.) that this species does occur in California waters, and it is added to our list.

Engraulidae. The New Jersey anchovy, *Anchoa duodecim* (Cope), is dropped from the list because it is based on a specimen of an extralimital species, *Thryssina encrasicholoides*, with erroneous locality data, G. J. Nelson, 1983, Copeia (1):50.

Order Gonorynchiformes. This order is added because of the discovery of *Chanos chanos* within our boundaries (see below).

Chanidae. See Gonorynchiformes.

Chanos chanos. J. M. Duffy and H. J. Bernard, 1985, Calif. Fish Game 71:122–125, noted that this tropical species occasionally strays into southern Californian waters.

Cyprinidae. Recent and continuing systematic study of the American cyprinids has indicated the necessity for substantial change from the classification of earlier editions of this list. Although not all investigators are in agreement, the corrections here recommended are consensus choices of committee members based on published work or conclusions from advanced research. They are not necessarily definitive; further changes may be anticipated as study of new suites of characters is extended. We prefer to be conservative and suggest changes only where the data are compelling. Many but not all changes here adopted have been proposed by R. L. Mayden (1989, Univ. Kans. Mus. Nat. Hist. Misc. Publ. 80) or M. M. Coburn and T. M. Cavender (in press, *in* R. L. Mayden, ed., Systematics, Historical Ecology, and North American Fishes, Stanford Univ. Press, various publications, and pers. comm.), to whom we are grateful for their instructive insights.

Campostoma pauciradii. This stoneroller was described as a new species from parts of Alabama and Georgia by B. M. Burr and R. C. Cashner, 1983, Copeia (1):101.

Cyprinella analostana. *Cyprinella* Girard, 1856, previously treated as a subgenus of *Notropis*, was ranked as a genus by R. L. Mayden, 1989, Univ. Kans. Mus. Nat. Hist. Misc. Publ. 80:45. Twenty-one species in our area are therefore transferred from *Notropis* to *Cyprinella*. In as much as *Notropis* has been ruled to be masculine (see Opinion 1230 of the International Commission on Zoological Nomenclature, 1982, Bull. Zool. Nomencl. 39(4):241) and *Cyprinella* is feminine, adjectival endings are emended accordingly.

Cyprinella caerulea. See *C. analostana*.

Cyprinella callisema. See *C. analostana*.

Cyprinella callistia. See *C. analostana*.

Cyprinella callitaenia. See *C. analostana*.

Cyprinella camura. See *C. analostana*.

Cyprinella chloristia. See *C. analostana*.

Cyprinella formosa. See *C. analostana*.

Page 20

Cyprinella galactura. See *C. analostana*.

Cyprinella gibbsi. See *C. analostana*.

Cyprinella labrosa. In addition to the 21 species transferred from *Notropis* to *Cyprinella* (see *C. analostana*), three barbeled minnows formerly assigned to *Hybopsis* (*labrosa*, *monacha*, and *zanema*) are now referred to *Cyprinella* on the advice of T. M. Cavender, M. M. Coburn, and R. E. Jenkins (pers. comm.).

Cyprinella leedsi. See *C. analostana*.

Cyprinella lepida. The plateau shiner has been included in and excluded from different editions of this list. It has been studied recently by W. J. Mathews, 1987, Copeia (3):616, and R. L. Mayden, 1989, Univ. Kans. Mus. Nat. Hist. Misc. Publ. 80:45, who regarded it as a valid endemic species from the Edwards Plateau, Texas.

Cyprinella lutrensis. See *C. analostana*.

Cyprinella monacha. See *C. labrosa* and *Erimystax cahni*.

Cyprinella nivea. See *C. analostana*.

Cyprinella proserpina. See *C. analostana*.

Cyprinella pyrrhomelas. See *C. analostana*.

Cyprinella spiloptera. See *C. analostana*.

Cyprinella trichroistia. See *C. analostana*.

Cyprinella venusta. See *C. analostana*.

Cyprinella whipplei. See *C. analostana*.

Cyprinella xaenura. See *C. analostana*.

Cyprinella zanema. See *C. labrosa*.

Erimystax cahni. Four species of chubs of the genus *Hybopsis* (subgenus *Erimystax*) on the 1980 list (*cahni*, *dissimilis*, *insignis*, and *x-punctata*) are now placed in the genus *Erimystax* (gender masculine) on the basis of genealogical analysis by M. M. Coburn and T. M. Cavender, in press, *in* R. L. Mayden, ed., Systematics, Historical Ecology, and North American Fishes, Stanford Univ. Press. R. L. Mayden, 1989, Univ. Kans. Mus. Nat. Hist. Misc. Publ. 80:11, also placed these species in *Erimystax* along with *monacha*, which species we refer to *Cyprinella* (see above).

Erimystax dissimilis. See *E. cahni*.

Erimystax harryi. The Ozarkian subspecies of *E. dissimilis* is raised to specific status on the advice of D. A. Etnier who cites the findings of a dissertation study of the group by J. L. Harris, Univ. Tenn. Specimens from west of the Mississippi River differ from eastern material as noted by C. L. Hubbs and W. R. Crowe, 1956, Occas. Pap. Mus. Zool. Univ. Mich. 578:1, in higher vertebral count and in the much longer gut.

Erimystax insignis. See *E. cahni*.

Erimystax x-punctatus. See *E. cahni*.

Gila intermedia. This form, regarded by some authors and in the 1980 edition of this list (p. 73) as a subspecies of *G. robusta*, is given specific status in agreement with the views of W. L. Minckley (1973, Fishes of Arizona, Arizona Game and Fish Dept., p. 104) and J. N. Rinne (1976, Wasmann J. Biol. 34(1):85).

Hesperoleucas symmetricus. This species was placed in the genus *Lavinia* by J. C. Avise, J. J. Smith, and F. J. Ayala (1975, Evolution 29:411) because of the genetic similarity of the two. D. G. Buth (1984, *in* B. J. Turner, ed., Evolutionary Genetics of Fishes, Plenum, p. 583) argued plausibly that as sister taxa the two-species lineage (*H. symmetricus* and *L. exilicauda*) would retain more information if treated as a single genus. Pending elucidation of the problem, we retain the genera as separate.

Hybognathus amarus. This form, earlier regarded by some as a subspecies of *H. nuchalis*, was raised to species rank by C. P. Hlohowskyj, M. M. Coburn, and T. M. Cavender, 1989, Copeia (1):172.

Page 21

Hypophthalmichthys molitrix. The silver carp has been taken at so many localities in the central United States (e.g., see H. W. Robison and T. M. Buchanan, 1984, Fishes of Arkansas, Univ. Arkansas Press, p. 190) that its establishment seems assured. See Appendix 2 (p. 97 and Table 2).

Hypophthalmichthys nobilis. W. L. Pflieger, 1989, Am. Fish. Soc., Introduced Fish Section Newsletter 9(4):9, documented that the bighead carp was reproducing in natural waters of Missouri.

Lavinia exilicauda. See *Hesperoleucas symmetricus*.

Luxilus albeolus. Customarily treated as a subgenus of *Notropis*, *Luxilus*, with nine included species, was raised to generic status by R. L. Mayden, 1989, Univ. Kans. Mus. Nat. Hist. Misc. Publ. 80:38, an action supported by M. M. Coburn and T. M. Cavender (in press, *in* R. L. Mayden, ed., Systematics, Historical Ecology, and North American Fishes, Stanford Univ. Press) in their phyletic studies of the American Cyprinidae, and here adopted.

Luxilus cardinalis. This new species from the Arkansas and Red river drainages of Arkansas, Kansas, Missouri, and Oklahoma was described by R. L. Mayden, 1988, Copeia (1):156. See *L. albeolus*.

Luxilus cerasinus. See *L. albeolus*.

Luxilus chrysocephalus. See *L. albeolus*.

Luxilus coccogenis. See *L. albeolus*.

Luxilus cornutus. See *L. albeolus*.
Luxilus pilsbryi. See *L. albeolus*.
Luxilus zonatus. See *L. albeolus*.
Luxilus zonistius. See *L. albeolus*.
Lythrurus ardens. Formerly classified as a subgenus of *Notropis*, *Lythrurus*, with eight species, was raised to generic rank by R. L. Mayden, 1989, Univ. Kans. Mus. Nat. Hist. Misc. Publ. 80:34, a judgment corroborated by M. M. Coburn and T. M. Cavender (in press, *in* R. L. Mayden, ed., Systematics, Historical Ecology, and North American Fishes, Stanford Univ. Press) in their phyletic studies of the Cyprinidae and here adopted.
Lythrurus atrapiculus. See *L. ardens*.
Lythrurus bellus. See *L. ardens*.
Lythrurus fumeus. See *L. ardens*.
Lythrurus lirus. See *L. ardens*.
Lythrurus roseipinnis. See *L. ardens*.
Lythrurus snelsoni. This new species was described from upland streams of the Little River system in Arkansas and Oklahoma, by H. W. Robison, 1985, Copeia (1):126, as the Ouachita Mountain shiner. See *L. ardens*.
Lythrurus umbratilis. See *L. ardens*.
Macrhybopsis aestivalis. In a rearrangement of the species of the obviously polyphyletic "genus" *Hybopsis* (of the 1980 list), M. M. Coburn and T. M. Cavender (in press, *in* R. L. Mayden, ed., Systematics, Historical Ecology, and North American Fishes, Stanford Univ. Press) resurrect the genus *Macrhybopsis* for four species of barbeled minnows (*aestivalis*, *gelida*, *meeki*, and *storeriana*) of the Mississippi River and adjacent drainages. Among them, *aestivalis* and *gelida* are viewed as particularly close relatives. R. L. Mayden, 1989, Univ. Kans. Nat. Hist. Misc. Publ. 80:10, also placed three of these four species in *Macrhybopsis*, but assigned *aestivalis* to the monotypic genus *Extrarius*. We follow the Coburn and Cavender classification.
Macrhybopsis gelida. See *M. aestivalis*.
Macrhybopsis meeki. See *M. aestivalis*.
Macrhybopsis storeriana. See *M. aestivalis*.
Margariscus margarita. The relationships of the pearl dace are uncertain, but they are more likely with *Couesius*, *Phoxinus*, or perhaps *Hemitremia* than with *Semotilus*. Until the phylogeny is clarified, we follow M. M. Coburn and T. M. Cavender (in press, *in* R. L. Mayden, ed., Systematics, Historical Ecology, and North American Fishes, Stanford Univ. Press) in resurrecting *Margariscus* for this species.
Notropis amblops. In the compound "genus" *Hybopsis* of the 1980 edition of this list (p. 22) are four nominal species (*amblops*, *hypsinotus*, *lineapunctata*, and "*rubrifrons*"), which, together with *Hybopsis winchelli* (formerly treated as a subspecies of *amblops*) and *Notropis amnis*, were regarded by G. H. Clemmer (unpublished thesis) as an intimately interrelated group. These six forms were also accepted as a monophyletic group by R. L. Mayden (1989, Univ. Kans. Nat. Hist. Misc. Publ. 80: 12), and they are classified by M. M. Coburn and T. M. Cavender (in press, *in* R. L. Mayden, ed., Systematics, Historical Ecology, and North American Fishes, Stanford Univ. Press) as a subgenus of *Notropis*, an action we follow. Since *Notropis* (*Hybopsis*) *amblops*, as *Hybopsis gracilis* Agassiz, 1854, is the type species of *Hybopsis*, this move restricts the name to these six species as a subgenus (i.e., a "genus" *Hybopsis* is no longer recognized).
Notropis ammophilus. This new species from Alabama, Mississippi, and Tennessee was described by R. D. Suttkus and H. T. Boschung, 1990, Tulane Stud. Zool. Bot. 27(2):49.

Page 22

Notropis amnis. See *N. amblops*.
Notropis buccatus. Formerly placed in the monotypic genus *Ericymba*, this species is closely related to several species of *Notropis* (R. L. Mayden, 1989, Univ. Kans. Nat. Hist. Misc. Publ. 80:12), and we follow M. M. Coburn and T. M. Cavender (in press, *in* R. L. Mayden, ed., Systematics, Historical Ecology, and North American Fishes, Stanford Univ. Press) in the merger of these genera.
Notropis cahabae. This new species, related to *N. volucellus* and restricted to the Cahaba River, Alabama, was described by R. L. Mayden and B. R. Kuhajda, 1989, Bull. Alabama Mus. Nat. Hist. 9:1.
Notropis hypsinotus. See *N. amblops*.
Notropis lineapunctatus. See *N. amblops*. The ending is emended to agree with the arbitrarily ruled masculine gender of *Notropis*.
Notropis melanostomus. This diminutive new species was described from western Florida by S. A. Bortone, 1989, Copeia (3):737.
Notropis orca. The phantom shiner from the Rio Grande of New Mexico, Texas, and Mexico has been resurrected from the synonymy of *Notropis simus* by B. Chernoff, R. R. Miller, and C.

R. Gilbert, 1982, Occas. Pap. Mus. Zool. Univ. Mich. 698:15. The species is believed to be extinct, not having been collected since 1975 (R. R. Miller, J. D. Williams, and J. E. Williams, 1989, Fisheries (Bethesda) 14(6):26).

Page 23

Notropis rubescens R. M. Bailey, new name. This name replaces *Nocomis rubrifrons* D. S. Jordan, 1877 (Ann. Lyc. Nat. Hist. N.Y. 11(1876): 330), from Ocmulgee River, Flat Rock, Georgia. Most recent authors, and the 1980 edition of this list (p. 22), termed it rosyface chub, *Hybopsis rubrifrons* (Jordan). However, the name is preoccupied in *Notropis* by *Alburnus rubifrons* E. D. Cope, 1865 (Proc. Acad. Nat. Sci. Phila. 17:85), from the Kiskiminitas River, Pennsylvania, a synonym of *Alburnus rubellus* Agassiz, 1850 (=*Notropis rubellus*). *Notropis rubescens* is a Latin present participle of rubescere, to grow red. See *N. amblops*.

Notropis rupestris. This new species was described by Page, *in* L. M. Page and E. C. Beckham, 1987, Copeia (3):659, from the Middle Cumberland River, Tennessee.

Notropis stramineus. R. L. Mayden and C. R. Gilbert, 1989, Copeia (4):1084, showed that this name is a junior synonym of *Cyprinella ludibunda* Girard, 1856 (=*Notropis ludibundus*). However, this name has been unused since its proposal. A petition has been submitted to the International Commission on Zoological Nomenclature to conserve the familiar name *stramineus*. Until a decision is rendered, existing usage is retained under Article 80 of the Code.

Notropis topeka. R. L. Mayden and C. R. Gilbert, 1989, Copeia (4):1086, showed that this is a junior synonym of *Moniana tristis* Girard, 1856, a name unused since its proposal. A proposal has been submitted to the International Commission on Zoological Nomenclature to conserve the name *topeka*, which has been used exclusively for the species for more than a century. Until a decision is rendered, existing usage is retained under Article 80 of the Code.

Notropis wickliffi. This species was long regarded as a subspecies of *N. volucellus*. Several ichthyologists, including T. M. Cavender, D. A. Etnier, and C. R. Gilbert, have expressed confidence that these taxa are full species that are sometimes sympatric. We accept their judgment, which agrees with that of the original describer (M. B. Trautman, 1981, The Fishes of Ohio, rev. ed., Ohio State Univ. Press, p. 372).

Notropis winchelli. See *N. amblops*. The clear chub was not included in the 1980 edition because it was commonly regarded as a subspecies of *Hybopsis amblops*. N. H. Douglas, 1974, Freshwater Fishes of Louisiana, Baton Rouge, p. 106, adopted the unpublished findings of G. H. Clemmer that *amblops* and *winchelli* are specifically separable. In the partition of *Hybopsis*, both nominal taxa are assigned to subgenus *Hybopsis* of *Notropis*.

Opsopoeodus emiliae. The pugnose minnow, traditionally placed in the monotypic genus *Opsopoeodus*, has in recent years usually been regarded as a subgenus of *Notropis* (C. R. Gilbert and R. M. Bailey, 1972, Occas. Pap. Mus. Zool. Univ. Mich. 664). Recent discoveries in breeding behavior (L. M. Page and C. E. Johnston, 1990, Copia (4):1176) and osteology (M. M. Coburn and T. M. Cavender, in press, *in* R. L. Mayden, ed., Systematics, Historical Ecology, and North American Fishes, Stanford Univ. Press) point to a sister-group relationship with *Pimephales* (or with *Pimephales* and *Codoma*). These investigators recommend that *Opsopoeodus* again be recognized as a genus.

Oregonichthys crameri. In the reordering of *Hybopsis*, it is recommended by M. M. Coburn and T. M. Cavender (in press, *in* R. L. Mayden, ed., Systematics, Historical Ecology, and North American Fishes, Stanford Univ. Press,) that *crameri* again be placed in the monotypic genus *Oregonichthys*.

Phoxinus tennesseensis. This new species was described from the upper Tennessee River system of Tennessee and Virginia by W. C. Starnes and R. E. Jenkins, 1988, Proc. Biol. Soc. Wash. 101:518.

Platygobio gracilis. The flathead chub is returned to the monotypic genus *Platygobio* by R. L. Mayden (1989, Univ. Kans. Nat. Hist. Misc. Publ. 80:10) and by M. M. Coburn and T. M. Cavender (in press, *in* R. L. Mayden, ed., Systematics, Historical Ecology, and North American Fishes, Stanford Univ. Press,) although these authors disagree on its phyletic position. See also *Notropis amblops* (p. 21).

Pogonichthys ciscoides. The original publication for this species is dated 1973, but the California Academy of Sciences copy has the notation that the correct distribution date was 28 March 1974.

Page 24

Rhinichthys cobitis. Assigned to the genus *Tiaroga* since its original proposal, the loach minnow is now placed in *Rhinichthys* on the basis of study by M. M. Coburn and T. M. Cavender (in press, *in* R. L. Mayden, ed., Systematics, Historical Ecology, and North American Fishes, Stanford Univ. Press) and D. A. Woodman (1989, Am. Soc. Ichthyol. Herpetol., Annual Meeting Abstracts, p. 163).

Rhinichthys deaconi. A dace population from Las Vegas, Nevada, now believed to be extinct, was named by R. R. Miller, 1984, Occas. Pap. Mus. Zool. Univ. Mich. 707:1, as a species distinct from the widespread *R. osculus*.

Rhinichthys osculus. A. E. Peden and G. W. Hughes, 1988, Can. J. Zool. 66:1846, noted that *R. osculus* and *R. umatilla* (Gilbert & Evermann, 1894) are sympatric in certain parts of the Columbia River system in Canada and, therefore, they elevated *umatilla*, usually regarded as a subspecies of *osculus*, to a full species. *Rhinichthys osculus* is notoriously variable, local populations are difficult to evaluate, and the type locality of *umatilla* (Umatilla, Oregon) is much farther south in the Columbia system than the Canadian localities. Until this problem can be studied on a larger geographic scale, we continue to withhold species recognition of *umatilla*.

Semotilus thoreauianus. The Dixie chub, formerly regarded as a subspecies of *S. atromaculatus*, has been raised to full species status by C. E. Johnston and J. S. Ramsey, 1990, Copeia (1):119.

Cobitidae. Opinion 1500 of the International Commission on Zoological Nomenclature, 1988, Bull. Zool. Nomencl. 45(2):178, conserved this spelling of the family group name.

Catostomidae. Gerald R. Smith is investigating the phylogeny of the suckers. His findings and recommendations for systematic change (in press) were not available in time for evaluation for this list. They include a proposed merger of *Lagochila* in *Moxostoma*, and the elevation of *Thoburnia* and *Scartomyzon* from subgeneric rank in *Moxostoma* to full genera.

The webug sucker, *Catostomus fecundus* Cope & Yarrow, 1875, from Utah Lake, Utah, was included on previous editions of this list. The holotype has been identified as a hybrid between *Catostomus ardens* and *Chasmistes liorus*, the only two catostomid species in the lake. Under Article 23h of the International Code of Zoological Nomenclature, such names must not be used as valid for either parental species, and the entry is therefore dropped from the list.

Page 25

Chasmistes muriei. R. R. Miller and G. R. Smith, 1981, Occas. Pap. Mus. Zool. Univ. Mich. 696:17, described this new species from the Snake River below Jackson Lake dam in Wyoming. It was presumed to be extinct at the time of its description.

Deltistes luxatus. This species was placed in *Catostomus* in the 1980 list, and is now referred to the monotypic genus *Deltistes* on the recommendation of G. R. Smith and C. E. Bond (pers. comm.).

Moxostoma austrinum. This sucker from western Mexico was reported from Alamito Creek in the Big Bend region of the Rio Grande, Texas, by R. E. Jenkins, *in* D. G. Lee et al., 1980, Atlas of North American Freshwater Fishes, N.C. State Mus. Nat. Hist., p. 413.

Moxostoma pappillosum. The common name is changed to V-lip redhorse on the advice of R. E. Jenkins (pers. comm.) because "suckermouth" typifies all species of this family.

Characiformes. We follow J. S. Nelson, 1984, Fishes of the World, 2nd ed., Wiley & Sons, p. 130, and most other recent workers, in recognizing a separate order for the characins.

Page 26

Ameiurus brunneus. R. M. Bailey and C. R. Robins, 1988, Bull. Zool. Nomencl. 45:100, noted that, under the provisions of the 1985 Code of Zoological Nomenclature, names proposed for divisions of genera are valid. Thus, *Ameiurus*, held to be invalid under previous codes, is valid and available. J. G. Lundberg (1989, Am. Soc. Ichthyol. Herpetol., Annual Meeting Abstracts, p. 113) separated *Ameiurus* from *Ictalurus*, an action followed here.

Ameiurus catus. See *A. brunneus*. The relationships of *catus*, almost always associated with *Ictalurus* even by those who recognized two genera, are with *Ameiurus* (J. G. Lundberg and others, pers. comm.).

Ameiurus melas. See *A. brunneus*.

Ameiurus natalis. See *A. brunneus*.

Ameiurus nebulosus. See *A. brunneus*.

Ameiurus platycephalus. See *A. brunneus*.
Ameiurus serracanthus. See *A. brunneus*.

Page 27

Loricariidae. The common name suckermouth catfishes is adopted.

Pterygoplichthys multiradiatus. This South American species has been introduced and established in Florida. See Appendix 2, Table 1.

Esox lucius. This species is known simply as "pike" in English-speaking Europe. However, pike is used in other families of fishes and northern pike is widely used in North America, even in dictionaries; therefore, we have retained this common name.

Leuroglossus schmidti. M. J. Allen and G. B. Smith, 1988, NOAA Tech. Rep. NMFS 66:19, recorded this species from as shallow as 150 m along the Aleutian Islands and in the Bering Sea.

Leuroglossus stilbius. A. E. Peden, 1981, Can. J. Zool. 59(12):2396 placed *Bathylagus stilbius* in *Leuroglossus*.

Osmerus mordax. J. Lanteigne and D. E. McAllister, 1983, Syllogeus 45:1, recognized a lacustrine morph of the rainbow smelt from southern Quebec, New Brunswick, and Maine as a separate species, the pygmy smelt, *O. spectrum* Cope, 1870. We do not believe that this sibling form merits inclusion as a separate species.

Coregonus artedi. See *Galeocerdo cuvier* (p. 13).

Coregonus huntsmani. W. B. Scott, 1987, Can. J. Zool. 65:1856, proposed this replacement name for *C. canadensis* Scott, 1967, which was preoccupied and therefore not included in our 1980 list (see Am. Fish. Soc. Spec. Publ. 12:72). The species occurs in Nova Scotia.

Page 28

Coregonus johannae. The deepwater cisco, a member of the *zenithicus* group, is now listed as extinct on the recommendation of T. N. Todd (pers. comm.). See Am. Fish. Soc. Spec. Publ. 12:99.

Coregonus nigripinnis. The blackfin cisco is retained on this list provisionally, although there is considerable doubt as to whether it was a valid taxon. Lake Superior stocks (called subspecies *cyanopterus* by W. Koelz) were identified as *zenithicus* by T. N. Todd and G. R. Smith, 1980, Can. J. Fish. Aquat. Sci. 37:2228. Lake Ontario type material (nominal subspecies *prognathus*) restudied by T. N. Todd, 1981, Copeia (2):489, was a mixture of species, with the holotype considered a nomen dubium (probably *C. artedi* or *C. hoyi*, pers. comm., 1990). Collections from Lake Nipigon (subspecies *regalis*) and inland lakes in Canada were probably *C. artedi* (R. M. Clarke, 1973, Doctoral disser., Univ. Winnipeg; W. B. Scott and E. J. Crossman, 1973, Fish. Res. Board Can. Bull. 184: 257). Recent workers agree that the stocks from Lakes Michigan (the type locality of *nigripinnis*) and Huron are extinct (Am. Fish. Soc. Spec. Publ. 12:99–100). These fish were probably large dark-finned adults of *C. artedi* living in deep water.

Coregonus zenithicus. The status of *Coregonus alpenae* was discussed in the 1980 edition of this list (p. 99). Since then, we know of no new records of its occurrence. T. N. Todd, G. R. Smith, and L. E. Cable, 1981, Can. J. Fish. Aquat. Sci. 38:59–67, presented evidence that *C. alpenae*, longjaw cisco, is a specific synonym of *C. zenithicus*, so it is deleted from the list.

Oncorhynchus aguabonita. G. R. Smith and R. F. Stearley, 1989, Fisheries (Bethesda) 14(1):4, showed that the relationships of the trouts of the cutthroat and rainbow series lie with *Oncorhynchus* rather than with *Salmo*. The Committee earlier noted its endorsement of this change, 1989, Fisheries (Bethesda) 14(1):5.

Oncorhynchus apache. See *O. aguabonita*.

Oncorhynchus clarki. See *O. aguabonita*.

Oncorhynchus gilae. See *O. aguabonita*.

Oncorhynchus mykiss. See *O. aguabonita*. This species, previously known as *gairdneri* in North America, occurs also in Kamchatka, where it was first described as *mykiss*. This matter is discussed in detail by G. R. Smith and R. F. Stearley, 1989, Fisheries (Bethesda) 14(1):5.

Prosopium gemmifer. The spelling of the species name is returned to the original (*Leucichthys gemmifer*) to conform with the direction of Article 31b (i) of the International Code of Zoological Nomenclature, 1985.

Stomiiformes. We follow J. S. Nelson, 1984, Fishes of the World, 2nd ed., Wiley & Sons, p. 172, in adopting this ordinal name, also used in many other recent publications.

Pollichthys mauli. W. B. Scott and M. G. Scott, 1988, Can. Bull. Fish. Aquat. Sci. 219:167, recorded this species in waters less than 200 m deep over the Scotian Shelf, Canada.

Stomiidae. This family as here used includes the Astronesthidae, Chauliodontidae (viperfishes), Idiacanthidae, Malacosteidae, Melanostomiidae (scaleless dragonfishes), and Stomiidae, following W. L. Fink, 1985, Misc. Publ. Mus. Zool. Univ. Mich. 171:1–127.

Page 29

Stomias boa. W. B. Scott and M. G. Scott, 1988, Can. Bull. Fish. Aquat. Sci. 219:184, recorded this species in waters 137 m deep off southeastern Canada.

Aulopiformes. This order is separated from the Myctophiformes by many ichthyologists (e.g., J. S. Nelson, 1984, Fishes of the World, 2nd ed., Wiley & Sons, p. 185), an action adopted here.

Notolepis rissoi. W. B. Scott and M. G. Scott, 1988, Can. Bull. Fish. Aquat. Sci. 219:194, recorded this species in waters as shallow as 64 m on the Scotian Shelf, Canada.

Paralepis atlantica. W. B. Scott and M. G. Scott, 1988, Can. Bull. Fish. Aquat. Sci. 219:196, recorded this species from the Atlantic coast of Canada at depths less than 200 m; an "A" is therefore added to the occurrence column.

Myctophidae. Many additional species of this family enter waters shallower than 200 m along our coastal shelf.

Benthosema glaciale. W. B. Scott and M. G. Scott, 1988, Can. Bull. Fish. Aquat. Sci. 219: 206, recorded this species from surface waters at the edge of the shelf in eastern Canada.

Lampadena speculigera. W. B. Scott and M. G. Scott, 1988, Can. Bull. Fish. Aquat. Sci. 219: 220, recorded this species from along the edge of the Scotian Shelf, Canada, in about 200 m.

Lampanyctus crocodilus. W. B. Scott and M. G. Scott, 1988, Can. Bull. Fish. Aquat. Sci. 219: 221, reported on records of this species from as shallow as 46 m in Ungava Bay, Canada, as well as from other locations along eastern Canada.

Myctophum affine. W. B. Scott and M. G. Scott, 1988, Can. Bull. Fish. Aquat. Sci. 219:226, noted that this species occurs in less than 200 m along the edge of the Scotian Shelf, Canada.

Myctophum punctatum. W. B. Scott and M. G. Scott, 1988, Can. Bull. Fish. Aquat. Sci. 219: 227, noted many records of this species from the Atlantic region of southeastern Canada.

Page 30

Protomyctophum crockeri. California is added to the common name because flashlightfish is also applied to various species of the Anomalopidae, a family now rather commonly exhibited in larger aquariums.

Moridae. This family is added because of the discovery of the following three species in our region inside the 200 m isobath.

Antimora microlepis. M. J. Allen and G. B. Smith, 1988, NOAA Tech. Rep. NMFS 66:33, recorded this species from numerous localities in the Bering Sea and along the Aleutian Islands. One capture site was in 175 m.

Physiculus fulvus. C. D. Paulin, 1989, N. Z. J. Zool. 16(1):110, included several records from our Atlantic and Gulf coasts in waters as shallow as 140 m.

Physiculus rastrelliger. W. N. Eschmeyer, E. S. Herald, and H. Hamman, 1983, A Field Guide to Pacific Coast Fishes, Houghton Mifflin, p. 100, recorded this species from depths of 128–518 m along the Pacific Coast of California.

Bregmaceros houdei. V. P. Saksena and W. J. Richards, 1986, Bull. Mar. Sci. 38(2):285, described this new species which occurs in our region in the eastern Gulf of Mexico, including waters less than 200 m deep.

Gadidae. There is considerable disagreement as to the systematic limits of the family Gadidae, see D. M. Cohen, ed., 1989, Papers on the Systematics of Gadiform Fishes, Contrib. Sci. Nat. Hist. Mus. Los Angeles Co. 32. We follow tradition until such time as these problems are resolved.

Arctogadus borisovi. J. G. Hunter, S. T. Leach, D. E. McAllister, and M. B. Steigerwald, 1984, Syllogeus 52, recorded the following nine species, previously known from the Atlantic Arctic (and hence designated with an "A" on previous lists), from west of the Boothia Peninsula (95°W longitude) in the Pacific Arctic. The species (and page reference) are: *Arctogadus borisovi* (p. 19), *A. glacialis* (p. 19), *Gadus ogac* (p. 20), *Triglops nybelini* (p. 29), *Leptagonus decagonus* (p. 30), *Eumicrotremus spinosus* (p. 31), *Lycodes reticulatus* (p. 23), *Pholis fasciata* (p. 26), and *Anarhichas denticulatus* (p. 24). A "P" is therefore added to the occurrence column for each of these species.

Arctogadus glacialis. See *A. borisovi*.

Brosme brosme. This name was incorrectly attributed to Müller in previous editions.

Ciliata septentrionalis. This species has been recorded from Greenland by many authors (e.g., A. N. Svetovidov, 1948, Fauna SSSR, Ryby 9(4):91), a fact overlooked in previous editions of this list.

Gadus ogac. See *Arctogadus borisovi*, above.

Merluccius albidus. W. B. Scott and M. G. Scott, 1988, Can. Bull. Fish. Aquat. Sci. 219:277, recorded this species from Canadian waters in less than 200 m. It occurs commonly along the Atlantic and Gulf coasts of the United States but usually in deeper water.

Page 31

Micromesistius poutassou. This species has been recorded from Canadian waters as shallow as 189 m by W. B. Scott and M. G. Scott, 1988, Can. Bull. Fish. Aquat. Sci. 219:283, and in 200 m by D. Miller, 1966, Copeia (2):301.

Molva molva. W. B. Scott and M. G. Scott, 1988, Can. Bull. Fish. Aquat. Sci. 219:285, noted that a large specimen of this species was captured on the Grand Bank in 88–100 m depth.

Urophycis chesteri. We follow W. B. Scott and M. G. Scott, 1988, Can. Bull. Fish. Aquat. Sci. 219:288, and others, who placed *Phycis chesteri* in *Urophycis*.

Albatrossia pectoralis. M. J. Allen and G. B. Smith, 1988, NOAA Tech. Rep. NMFS 66:25, recorded this species from numerous localities in the Aleutian Islands and Bering Sea. Although generally a species of waters deeper than 300 m, it has been recorded in 200 m and perhaps shallower.

Caelorinchus caribbaeus. See *C. caelorhincus*, below.

Caelorinchus caelorhincus. Considerable confusion exists concerning the spelling of both the generic and specific name of this grenadier. Giorna spelled his genus as given here but with the ligatured "æ," which is difficult to distinguish from an "œ." He says that his name means beak (snout) notched. Risso in describing his species also uses the ligatured "æ," but unequivocally spells the French vernacular Caelorinque without ligatured letters in text and places the vernacular (with ligature) in the index in an alphabetical sequence indicating "æ." The word is apparently derived from the Latin "caelum," which is an old engraving tool or chisel resembling the snout of this fish. Unfortunately the last half of the generic and specific names are spelled differently.

Macrourus berglax. W. B. Scott and M. G. Scott 1988, Can. Bull. Fish. Aquat. Sci. 219:300, reported capture of this species from depths as shallow as 183 m in the eastern Grand Bank area of southeastern Canada.

Ophidiidae. We continue to accept provisionally the family definition proposed by D. M. Cohen and J. G. Nielsen, 1978, NOAA Tech. Rep. NMFS Circ. 417, although it appears to us to be an unnatural group.

Lepophidium brevibarbe. C. R. Robins, 1986, Proc. Biol. Soc. Wash. 99:384, showed that *brevibarbe* is the earliest name for *L. graellsi*.

Lepophidium profundorum. C. R. Robins, 1986, Proc. Biol. Soc. Wash. 99:385, noted that this is the senior synonym of *L. cervinum*.

Ophidion beani. As noted by C. R. Robins, G. C. Ray, and J. Douglass, 1986, A Field Guide to Atlantic Coast Fishes of North America, Houghton Mifflin, p. 99, the name *beani* does not apply to this species. A new name is being proposed by C. R. Robins and R. N. Lea.

Petrotyx sanguineus. In the 4th edition of this list (p. 31), this species was inadvertently placed in the Bythitidae.

Echiodon dawsoni. This new species was described by J. T. Williams and R. L. Shipp, 1982, Copeia (4):845, from the eastern Gulf of Mexico off western Florida and in the Straits of Florida at depths of 22–173 m.

Page 32

Lophiodes caulinaris. R. N. Lea, T. Keating, G. Van Dykhuizen, and P. B. Lehtonen, 1984, Calif. Fish Game 70:250, reported the capture of a specimen of this species off Morro Bay, California, at a depth of 146 m.

Antennarius striatus. T. W. Pietsch, 1986, *in* M. M. Smith and P. C. Heemstra, eds., Smiths' Sea Fishes, Springer-Verlag, p. 368, noted that *A. scaber*, splitlure frogfish, was a synonym of this wide-ranging species. The name striated frogfish is adopted for the combined species.

Dibranchus atlanticus. W. B. Scott and M. G. Scott, 1988, Can. Bull. Fish. Aquat. Sci. 213: 240, reported the capture of this species from the Laurentian Channel, southeastern Canada, at a depth of 182 m.

Ogcocephalus corniger. This species, described by M. G. Bradbury, 1980, Proc. Calif. Acad. Sci. 42(7):274, was called *O. vespertilio* in previous editions of this list; *O. vespertilio* is a

South American species. The name longnose batfish is retained for *corniger*.

Ogcocephalus declivirostris. M. G. Bradbury, 1980, Proc. Calif. Acad. Sci. 42(7):269, described this new species from many localities in the northwestern Gulf of Mexico.

Ogcocephalus pantostictus. M. G. Bradbury, 1980, Proc. Calif. Acad. Sci. 42(7):264, described this new species, which ranges widely in coastal waters of the Gulf of Mexico. Also see *Zalieutes elater*, below.

Ogcocephalus radiatus. M. G. Bradbury, 1980, Proc. Calif. Acad. Sci. 42(7):258, regarded this name as unidentifiable and used *O. cubifrons* for it. In our view, *radiatus* is properly applied to this species.

Ogcocephalus rostellum. M. G. Bradbury, 1980, Proc. Calif. Acad. Sci. 42(7):267, described this new species from coastal waters from North Carolina to southern Florida.

Zalieutes elater. The common name roundel batfish is adopted for this species because spotted batfish is used for, and is more appropriately applied to, *O. pantostictus*.

Page 33

Cryptopsaras couesi. We follow W. B. Scott and M. G. Scott, 1988, Can. Bull. Fish. Aquat. Sci. 219:251, and change the name of this species to triplewart seadevil. An "A" is added to the occurrence column because of these Canadian records.

Rimicola dimorpha. The occurrence of this species in southern California was noted by D. J. Miller and R. N. Lea, 1972, Calif. Fish Bull. 157:74, and was inadvertently omitted from the 1980 edition.

Euleptorhamphus viridis. The authority's name was not properly capitalized in the 1980 edition of this list.

Hemiramphus balao. The authority should have been in parentheses as the species was described in *Hemirhamphus*.

Hyporhamphus unifasciatus. We follow recent literature in adding silverstripe to the common name because all fishes of this type are called halfbeaks and some authors recognize a halfbeak family.

Page 34

Aplocheilidae. We follow J. S. Nelson, 1984, Fishes of the World, 2nd ed., Wiley & Sons, p. 218 in recognizing this family, formerly in the Cyprinodontidae. It is equivalent to the Aplocheilidae and Rivulidae of L. R. Parenti, 1981, Bull. Am. Mus. Nat. Hist. 168(4):545.

Rivulus harti. This species, sometimes known as the Trinidad rivulus, is established in southern California. See Appendix 2 (p. 97).

Rivulus marmoratus. *Rivulus ocellatus* Hensel, 1868, is a senior synonym but K. J. Lazara and M. L. Smith have petitioned the International Commission on Zoological Nomenclature to conserve the name *marmoratus*. We continue to employ *marmoratus* pending a decision by the Commission.

Our only native species of *Rivulus* is closely associated with mangroves in south Florida. We adopt the modifier mangrove in the common name in line with the suggestion by W. F. Davis, D. S. Taylor, and B. J. Turner, 1990, Ichthyological Exploration of Freshwaters 1(2): 126.

Cyprinodontidae. In 1981, L. R. Parenti, Bull. Am. Mus. Nat. Hist. 168(4):335–557, published her phylogenetic and biogeographic analysis of the cyprinodontoid fishes, incorporating many proposed changes from previous classifications, notably involving the Cyprinodontidae of this list. We accept the splitting off of a family Aplocheilidae (including Parenti's Rivulidae), but otherwise retain conventional limits of North American groups pending confirmation based on other character suites.

The species of *Crenichthys* and *Empetrichthys* were transferred by Parenti (p. 545) from the Cyprinodontidae to the Mexican livebearing family Goodeidae. These two genera were assigned to a separate family, the Empetrichthyidae, by R. R. Miller and M. L. Smith (1986, *in* C. H. Hocutt and E. O. Wiley, eds., The Zoogeography of North American Freshwater Fishes, Wiley & Sons, p. 495). R. R. Miller calls our attention to the presence in these two genera of nuptial tubercles on the body and dorsal and anal fins, essentially as in several species of *Fundulus*. No species of Goodeidae ever develops nuptial tubercles. In the absence of confirmatory evidence for change, we retain the customary assignment of *Crenichthys* and *Empetrichthys* to the Cyprinodontidae.

Crenichthys baileyi. See Cyprinodontidae.

Crenichthys nevadae. See Cyprinodontidae.

Empetrichthys latos. We follow the advice of J. E. Williams (pers. comm.) in changing the common names of this and the following species to poolfish. See Cyprinodontidae.

Empetrichthys merriami. This species is believed to be extinct (Am. Fish. Soc. Spec. Publ. 12: 101). See *E. latos*.

Fundulus bifax. This new species from the Tallapoosa and lower Coosa river systems of Alabama and Georgia was described by R. C. Cashner and J. S. Rogers, in R. C. Cashner, J. S. Rogers, and J. M. Grady, 1988, Copeia (3):674.

Fundulus dispar. We follow E. O. Wiley III, 1977, Occas. Pap. Mus. Nat. Hist. Univ. Kans. 66:1–31, in recognizing this and *F. escambiae* as distinct species in the *F. notti* species complex (starhead topminnows). New information indicates that members of the group are not entirely allopatric as we formerly believed. The name starhead topminnow is assigned to this wide-ranging species, which lives from the southern Great Lakes to eastern Texas and souhern Alabama.

Fundulus blairae Wiley and Hall, 1975, another form in the complex, however, appears to differ only slightly in color pattern from *F. dispar*, and we retain these two as subspecies of *dispar*, between which there is evidence of intergradation in northeastern Louisiana. R. C. Cashner is studying the group employing biochemical as well as morphological characteristics, and he has generously shared his provisional findings with us. The modifiers northern and southern may be used for *dispar* and *blairae*, respectively, if subspecific common names are used, or if further analysis points to their recognition as species.

Fundulus escambiae. See *F. dispar*. R. C. Cashner suggests the name russetfin topminnow for this species, which ranges from southern Alabama to northcentral Florida.

Fundulus euryzonus. R. D. Suttkus and R. C. Cashner, 1981, Bull. Ala. Mus. Nat. Hist. 6:19, described this new species from fresh waters of Mississippi and Louisiana.

Fundulus julisia. This new species was described by J. D. Williams and D. A. Etnier, 1982, Occas. Pap. Mus. Nat. Hist. Univ. Kans. 102: 11, from springs and spring runs in the Tennessee and Cumberland river systems, Tennessee.

Page 35

Fundulus luciae. D. S. Lee, 1980, in Atlas of North American Freshwater Fishes, N. C. State Mus. Nat. Hist., p. 520, recorded this species from permanent fresh water. An "F" is therefore added to the column of occurrence.

Fundulus majalis. See *F. similis*, below.

Fundulus notti. As a result of division of the *F. notti* complex (see *F. dispar*), we adopt R. C. Cashner's proposal of bayou topminnow for this species, which is of restricted distribution from southeast Louisiana to southwest Alabama.

Fundulus similis. K. G. Relyea, 1983, Bull. Fla. State Mus. Biol. Sci. 29(1):27, synonymized *F. similis* with *F. majalis*, but earlier (1967, Doctoral disser., Tulane Univ.) had recommended recognition of the populations from southeastern Florida and the Florida Keys as an undescribed species. Pending resolution of this problem, we continue to recognize *F. similis* for the southeastern Florida population with the realization that a new scientific name may be needed. In this action we follow C. R. Robins, G. C. Ray, and J. Douglass, 1986, A Field Guide to Atlantic Coast Fishes of North America, Houghton Mifflin, p. 110.

Lucania parva. In Am. Fish. Soc. Spec. Publ. 6, 1970, the authorship of this name was incorrectly changed to Baird from Baird & Girard. This error is corrected.

Gambusia affinis. The mosquitofish of previous editions of this list was regarded as a single species with two well-defined subspecies. Biochemical and chromosome studies have added to the morphological evidence suggesting that populations east and west of the Mobile River system, Alabama, should be regarded as separate species, *G. holbrooki*, eastern mosquitofish, and *G. affinis*, western mosquitofish. See M. C. Wooten, K. T. Scribner, and M. H. Smith, 1988, Copeia (2):283. Also various contributors *in* G. K. Meffe and F. F. Snelson, eds., 1989, Ecology and Evolution of Livebearing Fishes, Prentice-Hall. Some southwestern populations of *G. affinis* are regarded as a distinct species, *G. speciosa*, by M. Rauchenberger, 1989, Am. Mus. Novit. 2951:3, but we view them as, at most, a subspecies of *affinis* (see also J. E. Johnson and C. Hubbs *in* G. K. Meffe and F. F. Snelson, eds., 1989, Ecology and Evolution of Livebearing Fishes (Poeciliidae), Prentice-Hall, p. 302).

Gambusia amistadensis. This species is now believed to be extinct (1980, Am. Fish. Soc. Spec. Publ. 12:101).

Gambusia georgei. This species is now presumed to be extinct (R. R. Miller, J. D. Williams, and J. E. Williams, 1989, Fisheries (Bethesda) 14(6):33).

Gambusia holbrooki. See *G. affinis*, above.

Page 36

Menidia clarkhubbsi. A. A. Echelle and D. T. Mosier, 1982, Copeia (3):533, described this new, all-female, "species" from coastal lagoons in Texas.

Lophotus lacepede. See *Galeocerdo cuvier* (p. 13).

Trachichthyidae. This family is added because of the discovery of the following species in our region.

Gephyroberyx darwini. L. P. Woods and P. M. Sonoda, 1973, Memoir Sears Found. Mar. Res., no. 1, part 6:301 recorded this species from off Virginia in water as shallow as 146 m, a record overlooked in the 1980 edition of this list.

Berycidae. This family is added because of the occurrence in our region of the following species.

Beryx decadactylus. This species occurs along most of the east coast of the United States, but in waters deeper than 200 m. W. B. Scott and M. G. Scott, 1988, Can. Bull. Fish. Aquat. Sci. 219:325, cited a record of this species in 155 m, off the Maine coast.

Holocentrus adscensionis. The species name is emended to conform with the original spelling.

Page 37

Cyttopsis rosea. W. B. Scott and M. G. Scott, 1988, Can. Bull. Fish. Aquat. Sci. 219:328, reported this species at depths shallower than 200 m, off southeastern Canada.

Grammicolepis brachiusculus. *Daramattus americanus* was shown to be a junior synonym of this species by C. Karrer and P. C. Heemstra, 1986, *in* M. M. Smith and P. C. Heemstra, eds., Smiths' Sea Fishes, Springer-Verlag, p. 440.

Acentronura dendritica. C. E. Dawson, 1985, Indo-Pacific Pipefishes, Gulf Coast Research Laboratory, p. 15, synonymized the genus *Amphelikturus* with *Acentronura*. The species name is emended to agree with the feminine generic name.

Anarchopterus criniger. C. E. Dawson, 1982, Memoir Sears Found. Mar. Res., no. 1, part 8:34, recognized *Anarchopterus* and referred *Micrognathus criniger* and *M. tectus* to it.

Anarchopterus tectus. See *A. criniger*.

Bryx dunckeri. C. E. Dawson, 1982, Memoir. Sears Found. Mar. Res., no. 1, part 8:112, recognized *Bryx* and referred *Syngnathus dunckeri* to it.

Cosmocampus albirostris. The authority was incorrectly given as Heckel in the 1980 edition of this list.

Cosmocampus arctus. C. E. Dawson, 1985, Indo-Pacific Pipefishes, Gulf Coast Research Laboratory, p. 48, placed *Syngnathus arctus* in the genus *Cosmocampus*.

Cosmocampus elucens. C. E. Dawson, 1982, Memoir, Sears Found. Mar. Res., no. 1, part 8:132, placed *Syngnathus elucens* in the genus *Cosmocampus*.

Cosmocampus hildebrandi. C. E. Dawson, 1982, Memoir, Sears Found. Mar. Res., no. 1, part 8:139, placed *Syngnathus hildebrandi* in the genus *Cosmocampus*.

Page 38

Micrognathus ensenadae. We follow C. R. Robins, G. C. Ray, and J. Douglass, 1986, A Field Guide to Atlantic Coast Fishes of North America, Houghton Mifflin, p. 127, in continuing to recognize this as a species distinct from *M. crinitus*.

Microphis brachyurus. C. E. Dawson, 1985, Indo-Pacific Pipefishes, Gulf Coast Research Laboratory, p. 126, referred *Oostethus* to the synonymy of *Microphis*.

Dactylopteriformes. The Dactylopteridae are of uncertain position. We follow recent authors in provisionally recognizing this order.

Scorpaeniformes. We follow J. S. Nelson, 1984, Fishes of the World, 2nd ed., Wiley & Sons, p. 255, and most other recent authors in recognizing this order.

Scorpaena mystes. C. Swift, 1986, Calif. Fish Game 72:176, reported the occurrence of *S. plumieri* from Los Angeles, California. Many workers distinguish the Atlantic and Pacific populations and recognize the Pacific form as *S. mystes*, an action we follow.

Page 39

Sebastes fasciatus. The authors of this list (1986, Fisheries (Bethesda) 11(1):28) reviewed the common names of the Atlantic redfishes and emended the common name, Labrador redfish, to Acadian redfish. The market names redfish and ocean perch apply to all Atlantic species of *Sebastes* including the three in our region. The name beaked redfish applies both to this species and to *S. mentella*.

Sebastes levis. The authorities' names are placed in parentheses, correcting an oversight in the 1980 edition of this list.

Sebastes mentella. See *S. fasciatus*.

Sebastes norvegicus. See *S. fasciatus*. The name golden redfish is adopted. The name ocean perch is dropped because it is applied as a market name to all Atlantic species, including the three in our region, and not solely to *S. norvegicus*. It has been shown by B. Fernholm and A. Wheeler, 1983, Zool. J. Linn. Soc. 78:238–240, that the basis of Linnaeus's 1758 account of the taxon *Perca marina*, long-believed to be a scorpaenid "*Sebastes marinus*," is, in fact, referrable to the family Serranidae and to the species generally known as *Serranus scriba* Linnaeus, 1758. The proper name for the golden redfish is *Sebastes norvegicus* (Ascanius, 1772), and a partial synonymy and listing of usage is given by M. Blanc and J. C. Hureau, 1973, Check-List of the Fishes of the North-eastern Atlantic and of the Mediterranean, UNESCO, Paris, pp. 583–584. This change of name was also adopted by D. E. McAllister, 1990, Syllogeus 64:188.

Sebastes polyspinis. The authorities' names are placed in parentheses, correcting an oversight in the 1980 edition of this list.

Page 40

Sebastolobus macrochir. J. J. Long (pers. comm.) informs us that this species has been captured on occasion in the Aleutian Islands.

Prionotus longispinosus. We are assured by G. C. Miller (pers. comm.) that *P. rubio* Jordan is a senior synonym of the blackwing searobin, *P. salmonicolor* (Fowler, 1903), and that *P. longispinosus* is the correct name for what was formerly called blackfin searobin. He further urges that the name bigeye searobin be used, an action we follow. These changes were also adopted by C. R. Robins, G. C. Ray, and J. Douglass, 1986, A Field Guide to Atlantic Coast Fishes of North America, Houghton Mifflin, p. 280.

Prionotus rubio. See *P. longispinosus*. The name blackwing searobin is adopted for the combined species.

Page 41

Cottidae. J. S. Nelson, 1982, Can. J. Zool. 60: 1470, separated the Psychrolutidae from the Cottidae, an action that has been widely followed. However, he noted (p. 1472) "I have neither strong evidence that the family Psychrolutidae is monophyletic nor strong evidence that it should not be combined with the Cottidae . . . I regard the question as to whether or not they should be combined with the Cottidae to be a purely subjective matter at present." We continue to place the "psychrolutids" in the family Cottidae. The six species on our list which could be in the "Psychrolutidae" are *Dasycottus setiger*, *Eurymen gyrinus*, *Malacocottus kincaidi*, *M. zonurus*, *Psychrolutes paradoxus*, and *P. sigalutes*.

Artediellus pacificus. D. W. Kessler, 1985, Alaska's Saltwater Fishes and Other Sea Life, Alaska Northwest Publishing, p. 68, recorded this species from nearshore waters of Alaska north of the Alaska Peninsula.

Cottus hypselurus. C. R. Robins and H. W. Robison, 1985. Am. Mid. Nat. 114(2):360, described this new species from the Ozark uplands of Arkansas and Missouri.

Page 42

Dasycottus setiger. See Cottidae (p. 41).

Eurymen gyrinus. D. W. Kessler, 1985, Alaska's Saltwater Fishes and Other Sea Life, Alaska Northwest Publishing, p. 50, recorded this species from nearshore waters of western Alaska. See Cottidae (p. 41).

Gymnocanthus galeatus. Parentheses were inadvertently omitted from the authorities' names in previous editions of this list.

Gymnocanthus pistilliger. M. J. Allen and G. B. Smith, 1988, NOAA Tech. Rep. NMFS 66:82, recorded this species from numerous localities in western Alaska.

Hemilepidotus papilio. A. E. Peden, 1978, Syesis 11:39, synonymized *Melletes* with *Hemilepidotus*, an action overlooked in the 1980 edition of this list.

Icelus canaliculatus. D. W. Nelson, 1984, Occas. Pap. Calif. Acad. Sci. 138:34, recorded this species from depths of 20–730 m from the Bering Sea, including the Alaskan coast.

Icelus euryops. D. W. Nelson, 1984, Occas. Pap. Calif. Acad. Sci. 138:30, recorded this species from the Bering Sea and northern Gulf of Alaska in depths of 200–740 m.

Icelus uncinalis. D. W. Nelson, 1984, Occas. Pap. Calif. Acad. Sci. 138:32, recorded this species from the western Aleutian Islands in depths of 79–247 m.

Malacocottus kincaidi. See Cottidae (p. 41).

Malacocottus zonurus. D. W. Kessler, 1985, Alaska's Saltwater Fishes and Other Sea Life, Alaska Northwest Publishing, p. 50, recorded this species from western Alaska. See Cottidae (p. 41).

Page 43

Myoxocephalus verrucosus. This sculpin, previously combined with *M. scorpius*, is recognized as a separate species, for reasons cited by M. J. Allen and G. B. Smith, 1988, NOAA Tech. Rep. NMFS 66:92. According to D. W. Kessler, 1985, Alaska's Saltwater Fishes and Other Sea Life, Alaska Northwest Publishing, p. 66, both species occur in western Alaska.

Psychrolutes paradoxus. See Cottidae (p. 41).

Psychrolutes sigalutes. J. S. Nelson, 1982, Can. J. Zool. 60:1487, synonymized *Gilbertidia* with *Psychrolutes*. See Cottidae (p. 41).

Rastrinus scutiger. D. W. Nelson, 1984, Occas. Pap. Calif. Acad. Sci. 138:18, recorded this species from the Gulf of Alaska in depths of 120–512 m.

Ruscarius creaseri. D. P. Begle, 1989, Copeia (4):642, transferred this species and *meanyi* from the genus *Artedius* to *Ruscarius*.

Ruscarius meanyi. See *R. creaseri*.

Scorpaenichthys marmoratus. Opinion 1583 (1990, Bull. Zool. Nomencl. 47(1):79) of the International Commission on Zoological Nomenclature fixed the authorship of this species as Ayres, 1854.

Thyriscus anoplus. J. J. Long informs us that this species is taken along with mass quantities of sponges in waters shallower than 200 m along the coast of Alaska.

Triglops forficatus. The ending of the species name is modified to agree with the masculine gender of *Triglops*.

Triglops nybelini. We follow W. B. Scott and M. G. Scott, 1988, Can. Bull. Fish. Aquat. Sci. 219:510, in using the more distinctive name bigeye sculpin for this species. See *Arctogadus borisovi* (p. 30).

Page 44

Leptagonus decagonus. This species is transferred from *Agonus* to *Leptagonus* on the advice of R. M. Bailey; see A. P. Andriashev, 1954, Acad Sci. USSR, 53:426. See *Arctogadus borisovi* (p. 30).

Percis japonica. D. W. Kessler, 1985, Alaska's Saltwater Fishes and Other Sea Life, Alaska Northwest Publishing, p. 82, recorded this species along the edge of the continental shelf northwest of the Pribilof Islands.

Podothecus acipenserinus. M. B. Ilina, 1978, Akad. Nauk SSSR Zool. Inst., p. 13, placed this species, formerly in *Agonus*, in *Podothecus*.

Cyclopteridae. The pimpled lumpsucker, *Eumicrotremus andriashevi* Perminov, 1936, is an extralimital North Pacific species whose sole basis of inclusion on previous editions of this list was a misidentified specimen from Newfoundland; see *E. spinosus*, below.

Careproctus candidus. J. C. Quast and E. L. Hall, 1972, NOAA Tech. Rep. NMFS SSRF-658, p. 32, recorded this species, as *Temnocara candida*, from Cook Inlet, Alaska. R. Baxter, 1990, Annotated Key to the Fishes of Alaska (manuscript), p. 508A, lists depths of capture from 64–247 m. K. Kido, 1988, Mem. Fac. Fish. Hokkaido Univ. 35(2):193, synonymized *Temnocara* with *Careproctus*.

Careproctus furcellus. M. J. Allen and G. B. Smith, 1988, NOAA Tech. Rep. NMFS 66:66, recorded this species from the Bering Sea in depths as shallow as 98 m. Emarginate snailfish is used for this species because "forktail," used by some authors, more aptly applies to an extralimital species. *Careproctus furcellus* does not have a forked caudal fin.

Careproctus gilberti. D. L. Stein, 1978, Occas. Pap. Calif. Acad. Sci. 127:17, recorded this species from the southeastern Bering Sea to Oregon in waters as shallow as 187 m.

Careproctus phasma. M. J. Allen and G. B. Smith, 1988, NOAA Tech. Rep. NMFS 66:67, recorded this species from the Aleutian Islands in depths as shallow as 84 m.

Careproctus rastrinus. M. J. Allen and G. B. Smith, 1988, NOAA Tech. Rep. NMFS 66:67, recorded this species from the Bering Sea to southeastern Alaska in depths as shallow as 116 m.

Careproctus scottae. M. J. Allen and G. B. Smith, 1988, NOAA Tech. Rep. NMFS 66:67, recorded this species from the Bering Sea to southeastern Alaska in depths as shallow as 183 m.

Careproctus spectrum. J. C. Quast and E. L. Hall, 1972, NOAA Tech. Rep. NMFS SSRF-658:29, recorded this species from Shelikov Strait, Alaska, and R. Baxter, 1990, Annotated Key to the Fishes of Alaska (manuscript), p. 542, listed its depth of capture as 160–210 m.

Cyclopteropsis phrynoides. J. C. Quast and E. L. Hall, 1972, NOAA Tech. Rep. NMFS SSRF-658:29, listed this species as occurring in Cook Inlet and Montague Strait, Alaska.

Eumicrotremus barbatus. T. Ueno, 1970, Cyclopteridae, in Fauna Japonica, Academic Press of Japan, p. 102, recorded this species from the shore of Igitkin Island, Aleutian Islands.

Eumicrotremus birulai. This species was reported from off Kodiak Island, Alaska, by K. Hamada, 1982, Bull. Fac. Fish. Hokkaido Univ. 33(4): 201, at a depth of 140 m.

Eumicrotremus gyrinops. T. Ueno, 1970, Cyclopteridae, in Fauna Japonica, Academic Press of Japan, p. 108, noted that this species is known only from St. Paul and Unalaska islands, Aleutian Islands.

Eumicrotremus spinosus. In the 1960 edition of this list we listed *E. terraenovae* Myers & Böhlke, Newfoundland spiny lumpsucker, and in 1970 and 1980 we referred it to *E. andriashevi* Perminov, pimpled lumpsucker, following Lindberg and Legeza who placed it in the synonymy of that northwestern Pacific species. We now follow W. B. Scott and M. G. Scott, 1988, Can. Bull. Fish. Aquat. Sci. 219:522, in referring the single known specimen of *terraenovae* to *E. spinosus*. See *Arctogadus borisovi* (p. 30).

Lethotremus muticus. T. Ueno, 1970, Cyclopteridae, *in* Fauna Japonica, Academic Press of Japan, p. 127, noted that this species is known only from Unimak Pass, Alaska, and from the Petrel Bank, Bering Sea, in about 100 m.

Liparis atlanticus. Most recent authors have treated *Liparis*, *Nectoliparis*, *Paraliparis*, and other genera ending in *-liparis* as masculine. Some early workers, however, regarded *Liparis* as feminine (e.g., Reinhardt described *L. tunicata* in 1837) and some classical dictionaries give the gender as feminine. We have sought the advice of Dr. H. D. Cameron, Professor of Greek and Latin, University of Michigan, who has painstakingly investigated the philological evidence. He assures us that such classical dictionaries are in error, and it is clear from Rondelet and earlier authors that *Liparis* is properly masculine.

We add the modifier "Atlantic" to the common name of this species.

Liparis beringianus. We follow the merger of *Polypera* Burke, 1912, with *Liparis* by K. Kido, 1988, Mem. Fac. Fish. Hokkaido Univ. 35(2): 165. See *L. atlanticus*.

Liparis bristolensis. C. V. Burke, 1912, Proc. U.S. Natl. Mus. 43:568, described this species from the vicinity of Bristol Bay, Alaska, in depths less than 200 m. This species was excluded previously from our list for lack of information.

Liparis catharus. K. D. Vogt, 1973, Biol. Pap. Univ. Alsk. 13:22–27, described this species from Bradfield Canal, Alaska, at a depth of 127 m.

Page 45

Liparis gibbus. This name, together with the common name variegated snailfish, is adopted for a species that ranges from Kamchatka through the northeast Pacific, Arctic, and northwestern Atlantic oceans and follows conclusions reached by K. W. Able and D. E. McAllister, 1980, Can. Bull. Fish. Aquat. Sci. 208:25–32. It replaces the junior name *L. cyclostigma*, polka-dot snailfish, of prior lists.

Liparis greeni. See *L. beringianus*.

Liparis inquilinus. *Liparis liparis*, striped seasnail, is believed by K. W. Able, 1973, Copeia (4):787, to be restricted to the eastern Atlantic; western Atlantic records apply to *L. inquilinus* or *L. atlanticus*, hence *L. liparis* is removed from this list.

Liparis megacephalus. C. V. Burke, 1912, Proc. U.S. Natl. Mus. 43:569, described this species from the southeastern Bering Sea. R. Baxter, 1990, Annotated Key to the Fishes of Alaska (manuscript), p. 498, lists its depth of capture as 64–247 m.

Liparis micraspidophorus. K. D. Vogt, 1973, Biol. Pap. Univ. Alsk. 13:22–27 recorded this species from the intertidal zone at Cold Bay, Alaska.

Liparis ochotensis. This species, which occurs as shallow as 88 m, has been reported from Kodiak Island, Alaska, by J. C. Quast and E. L.

Hall, 1972, NOAA Tech. Rep. NMFS SSRF-658:31.

Liparis tunicatus. The occurrence is corrected to "A-P" in view of the Arctic distribution from Bering Strait to Labrador (K. W. Able and D. E. McAllister, 1980, Can. Bull. Fish. Aquat. Sci. 208:37). We also use the name kelp snailfish in place of the inappropriate Greenland seasnail.

Lipariscus nanus. The occurrence of this pelagic species in waters as shallow as 60 m in Monterey Bay, California, was noted in the original description and was previously overlooked.

Paraliparis calidus. This deepwater species has been reported from a depth of 150 m by W. B. Scott and M. G. Scott, 1988, Can. Bull. Fish. Aquat. Sci. 219:530, and is therefore added to this list.

Centropomus undecimalis. Because the name "snook" is used for the family, the modifier "common" is added to the name of this species even though this violates Principle 3 (see Introduction, p. 6). The species is known by anglers as the common snook and it is so treated in courts of law.

Percichthyidae. We retain this family for convenience even though it may be polyphyletic. The definitions of many basal perciform families are unclear.

Synagrops spinosus. F. C. Rohde informs us (pers. comm.) that this is a rather common species in the northern Gulf of Mexico and along the southeastern coast of the United States, often in waters less than 200 m.

Serranidae. The limits of the family Serranidae are not very clear. However, the Grammistidae (soapfishes), separated in prior lists, clearly belong within the family as currently defined. *Rypticus* and *Pseudogramma* are therefore returned to the Serranidae and the entry Grammistidae is deleted.

Bathyanthias mexicanus. J. E. Randall and L. Taylor, 1988, Indo-Pac. Fish. 16:4, synonymized *Pikea* with *Liopropoma* and noted that *Bathyanthias* is available for *mexicanus* and its allies.

Epinephelus acanthistius. This species is added on the advice of R. N. Lea and L. Fukuhara. A note documenting the occurrence of this species from California is being prepared by them for Bull. South. Calif. Acad. Sci.

Epinephelus dermatolepis. This species is added based on information provided by R. H. Moore and M. J. Allen. Details regarding the capture of this species off southern California will be published in Calif. Fish Game.

Page 46

Hemanthias signifer. J. E. Fitch, 1982, Contrib. Sci. Nat. Hist. Mus. Los Angeles Co. 339:3, reported on the occurrence of this species in California waters. *Hemanthias peruanus* (Steindachner, 1874), included in previous editions of this list, is deleted because the record of that species in California, dating from 1931, was based on a misidentified specimen of *H. signifer*. *Hemanthias peruanus* is a valid species, but is extralimital to our area of coverage. The name splittail bass is retained for *H. signifer*.

Liopropoma carmabi. C. R. Robins, G. C. Ray, and J. Douglass, 1986, A Field Guide to Atlantic Coast Fishes of North America, Houghton Mifflin, p. 143, noted that this species occurs in the Florida Keys.

Paranthias furcifer. A record of this species collected off San Diego, California, was provided by R. H. Rosenblatt. A "P" is therefore added to the column of occurrence.

Pronotogrammus multifasciatus. This senior synonym replaces *Anthias gordensis* Wade, 1946, as discussed by J. E. Fitch, 1982, Contrib. Sci. Nat. Hist. Mus. Los Angeles Co. 339:2. Additional synonyms are *Holanthias sechurae* Barton, 1947, and *Pacificogramma stepanenkoi* Kharin, 1983, as shown by M. E. Anderson and R. H. Rosenblatt, 1989, Calif. Fish Game 75:124.

Pseudogramma gregoryi. See Serranidae.

Rypticus bistrispinus. See Serranidae.

Rypticus maculatus. See Serranidae.

Rypticus saponaceus. See Serranidae.

Rypticus subbifrenatus. See Serranidae.

Page 47

Grammatidae. The spelling of the family name is corrected to Grammatidae from Grammidae.

Gramma loreto. J. Farrar and W. Becker have collected this species in the Florida Keys (between Maryland and Pelican shoals) and deposited a specimen in the University of Miami collection.

Lipogramma anabantoides. R. G. Gilmore and R. S. Jones, 1987, Bull. Mar. Sci. 42(3):443, recorded this species on the southwestern Florida shelf in 67 m.

Lipogramma trilineatum. Because *Lipogramma* is neuter, the species name is corrected.

Elassoma boehlkei. This new species from North Carolina and South Carolina was described by F. C. Rohde and R. G. Arndt, 1987, Proc. Acad. Nat. Sci. Phila. 139:66.

Elassoma okatie. This new species from South Carolina was described by F. C. Rohde and R. G. Arndt, 1987, Proc. Acad. Nat. Sci. Phila. 139:77.

Lepomis auritus. R. M. Bailey and C. R. Robins, 1988, Bull. Zool. Nomencl. 45(2):100, noted that the gender of *Lepomis* is feminine, and entered corrections in the spelling of names of various species. This matter is the subject of a petition to the International Commission on Zoological Nomenclature, by D. A. Etnier and M. Warren, to declare *Lepomis* to be masculine for nomenclatural purposes. Pending a vote by the Commission, we retain the masculine endings for *auritus*, *cyanellus*, *gibbosus*, *gulosus*, *macrochirus*, *marginatus*, *punctatus*, and *symmetricus*.

Lepomis cyanellus. See *L. auritus*.

Lepomis gibbosus. See *L. auritus*.

Lepomis gulosus. See *L. auritus*.

Lepomis macrochirus. See *L. auritus*.

Lepomis marginatus. See *L. auritus*.

Lepomis punctatus. See *L. auritus*.

Lepomis symmetricus. See *L. auritus*.

Micropterus dolomieu. See *Galeocerdo cuvier*. (p. 13).

Page 48

Etheostoma baileyi. This new species, subgenus *Ulocentra*, was described by L. M. Page and B. M. Burr, 1982, Occas. Pap. Mus. Nat. Hist. Univ. Kans. 101:2, from the upper Kentucky and upper Cumberland river systems, Kentucky and Tennessee.

Etheostoma barrenense. This new species, subgenus *Ulocentra*, was described by Burr and Page *in* L. M. Page and B. M. Burr, 1982, Occas. Pap. Mus. Nat. Hist. Univ. Kans. 101: 15, from the upper Barren River system, Kentucky and Tennessee.

Etheostoma collis. R. E. Jenkins and N. Burkhead, in press, synonymized *E. saludae*, Saluda darter, with *E. collis*, an action followed here.

Etheostoma crossopterum. M. E. Braasch and R. L. Mayden, 1985, Occas. Pap. Mus. Nat. Hist. Univ. Kans. 119:15, described this new species (subgenus *Catonotus*) from localities in Alabama, Kentucky, and Tennessee.

Etheostoma duryi. The common name is changed to black darter from blackside snubnose darter. This frees the name snubnose for *E. simoterum*, here used for the combined *atripinne* and *simoterum* of prior lists. Blackside is in use for *Percina maculata*.

Etheostoma flavum. This new species (subgenus *Ulocentra*) was described from the lower Cumberland and lower Tennessee river drainages of Kentucky and Tennessee by D. A. Etnier and R. M. Bailey, 1989, Occas. Pap. Mus. Zool. Univ. Mich. 717:3.

Etheostoma jessiae. The publication date for this species was given as 1877 in Jordan and Evermann (1896, Fishes of North and Middle America, part 1, p. 1085). It was described in the 2nd edition of Jordan's Manual of the Vertebrates published in 1878 (Jordan, 1884, preface to the 4th edition, p. 4) and confirmed by A. N. Hays (1952, Stanford Univ. Publ., Library Studies, volume 1, Stanford University Press, p. 72).

Etheostoma jordani. Parentheses are removed from the author's name because *jordani* was originally proposed in *Etheostoma*.

Etheostoma lynceum. D. A. Etnier, and W. C. Starnes, 1986, Copeia (3):832, raised this form from subspecific status in *E. zonale* to the rank of full species and proposed the common name.

Page 49

Etheostoma nigripinne. This new species (subgenus *Catonotus*) was described from the Tennessee River system in Alabama, Mississippi, and Tennessee by M. E. Braasch and R. L. Mayden, 1985, Occas. Pap. Mus. Nat. Hist. Univ. Kans. 119:28.

Etheostoma osburni. The common name is changed to candy darter, which is deemed more appropriate than finescale saddled darter.

Etheostoma pyrrhogaster. This new species (subgenus *Ulocentra*) was described from the coastal plain of the Forked Deer and Obion river drainages of western Kentucky and western Tennessee by R. M. Bailey and D. A. Etnier, 1988, Misc. Publ. Mus. Zool. Univ. Mich. 175:31.

Etheostoma rafinesquei. This new species (subgenus *Ulocentra*) was described by Burr and Page *in* L. M. Page and B. M. Burr, 1982, Occas. Pap. Mus. Nat. Hist. Univ. Kans. 101:9, from the upper Green River system and lower Barren River system in Kentucky.

Etheostoma sanguifluum. Formerly regarded as a subspecies of *E. maculatum*, L. M. Page, 1985, Ill. Nat. Hist. Surv. Bull. 33:282, recognized this as a full species in the subgenus *Nothonotus*. It occurs in the middle Cumberland River basin in Kentucky and Tennessee (D. A. Etnier and J. D. Williams, 1989, Proc. Biol. Soc. Wash. 102:987).

Etheostoma serrifer. C. L. Hubbs and M. D. Cannon, 1935, Misc. Publ. Mus. Zool. Univ. Mich. 30:31, 47, described *Hololepis serrifer* and *H. zonifer* without explaining whether the species names were to be treated as gerunds or adjectives. Article 31b (i) of the International Code of Zoological Nomenclature, 3rd ed., 1985, specifically addresses the "-ifer" and "-iger" words stating that where "the evidence of usage is not decisive, it is to be treated as a noun in apposition to the name of its genus; its spelling is not changed if it is combined with a generic name of a different gender." The neuter "-iferum" endings given these names in our prior lists are unjustified emendations. We restore the original spelling.

Etheostoma simoterum. *Etheostoma atripinne* (Jordan, 1877), Cumberland snubnose darter, was reduced to subspecific rank in *E. simoterum*, Tennessee snubnose darter, by R. M. Bailey and D. A. Etnier, 1988, Misc. Publ. Mus. Zool. Univ. Mich 175:13,17. Tennessee was dropped from the common name. See *E. duryi*.

Etheostoma vulneratum. Now recognized as a full species that occurs in the Tennessee River system (D. A. Etnier and J. D. Williams, 1989, Proc. Biol. Soc. Wash. 102:987), the wounded darter has been treated previously as a subspecies of *E. maculatum* and of *E. sanguifluum* in the subgenus *Nothonotus*.

Etheostoma wapiti. This new species in the subgenus *Nothonotus* was described from the Tennessee River system in Alabama and Tennessee by D. A. Etnier and J. D. Williams, 1989, Proc. Biol. Soc. Wash. 102:987.

Page 50

Etheostoma zonifer. See *E. serrifer*.

Etheostoma zonistium. This new species (subgenus *Ulocentra*) was described from the lower Tennessee and Mississippi river drainages of Alabama, Kentucky, Mississippi, and Tennessee by R. M. Bailey and D. A. Etnier, 1988, Misc. Publ. Mus. Zool. Univ. Mich. 175:39.

Gymnocephalus cernuus. The ruffe has been introduced into western Lake Superior, apparently by the discharge of ballast water in ships from Europe (A. Tibbetts, ed., 1989, Seiche (February), Minnesota Sea Grant).

Percina carbonaria. Long submerged in the synonymy of *P. caprodes*, the Texas logperch—chiefly an inhabitant of the Edwards Plateau, Texas—is now accorded full species status (L. M. Page, 1983, Handbook of Darters, TFH Publications; B. A. Thompson, 1985, Occas. Pap. Mus. Zool. La. State Univ. 61:14).

Percina jenkinsi. This new species (subgenus *Percina*) was described from a restricted area of the Conasauga River, Georgia and Tennessee, by B. A. Thompson, 1985, Occas. Pap. Mus. Zool. La. State Univ. 61:4.

Percina oxyrhynchus. This species name is to be treated as a noun in apposition under Article 31b (i) of the International Code of Zoological Nomenclature and is corrected from *P. oxyrhyncha* of the 1980 list.

Percina vigil. This name replaces *P. ouachitae* (Jordan & Gilbert, 1887) as shown by R. D. Suttkus, 1985, Copeia (1):225.

Stizostedion vitreum. This species entry includes also the blue pike, variously regarded as a full species (*S. glaucum*), a subspecies of *S. vitreum*, or a color phase of *vitreum*. Known formerly from Lakes Erie and Ontario, it is now believed to be extinct. *Stizostedion vitreum glaucum* of the previous editions of this list (see 1980 edition, p. 41) is dropped.

Cookeolus japonicus. W. C. Starnes, 1988, Bull. Mar. Sci. 43(2):144, showed that *Anthias boops* Schneider, 1801 (*Cookeolus boops* in the 4th edition of this list), does not apply to this species but is instead a junior synonym of *Priacanthus cruentatus*, and that *C. japonicus* is the correct name for the bulleye.

Priacanthus cruentatus. W. C. Starnes, 1988, Bull. Mar. Sci. 43(2):149, placed this species in the monotypic genus *Heteropriacanthus*, which he regarded as the sister group to *Priacanthus*. We prefer to recognize this distinction at the subgeneric level.

Page 51

Pomatomus saltatrix. The name *saltatrix* is based on M. Catesby's 1743 *Saltatrix* (Linnaeus, 1766, Syst. Nat., 12th ed., p. 491) as *Gasterosteus saltatrix*, not *Perca saltatrix* Linnaeus 1758, p. 293, as contended by some authors. See *Kyphosus sectatrix*, p. 55, the name for Linnaeus' *Perca saltatrix* of 1758, emended under Article 19(a)(i) of the International Code of Zoological Nomenclature.

Echeneis naucrates. C. L. Hubbs, W. I. Follett, and L. J. Dempster, 1979, Occas. Pap. Calif. Acad. Sci. 133:22, recorded this species and *Phtheirichthys lineatus* from California. Accordingly, we emend the occurrence column to "A-P."

Phtheirichthys lineatus. See *Echeneis naucrates*.

Caranx bartholomaei. This species and *C. ruber* are frequently referred to the genus *Carangoides* by ichthyologists who divide *Caranx*.

Caranx dentex. This species, sometimes placed in the genus *Pseudocaranx*, is recorded from North Carolina by F. C. Rohde, S. P. Epperly, and S. W. Ross, in press.

Page 52

Caranx ruber. See *C. bartholomaei*.

Decapterus punctatus. This species is correctly attributed to Cuvier, not Agassiz.

Oligoplites saurus. The common name is shortened to leatherjack on the urging of W. F. Smith-Vaniz, who notes that this name is commonly used and avoids confusion with the use of leatherjackets for fishes of the family Balistidae.

Seriola lalandi. R. M. Bailey and C. R. Robins, 1988, Bull. Zool. Nomencl. 45(2):95, noted that this is the proper spelling of the species name.

Seriola rivoliana. In the 1980 edition of this list (p. 43), we had provisionally retained *S. colburni*, Pacific amberjack, as distinct from *S. rivoliana*. W. F. Smith-Vaniz assures us that the two are synonyms and so we drop *colburni* and add a "P" to the occurrence column of *rivoliana*.

Nematistiidae. W. F. Smith-Vaniz, 1984, Am. Soc. Ichthyol. Herpetol., Spec. Publ. 1:523, and R. H. Rosenblatt and M. A. Bell, 1976, Contrib. Sci. Nat. Hist. Mus. Los Angeles Co. 279:1, demonstrated that the roosterfish is to be removed from the Carangidae and placed in its own family, which is most closely related to the Echeneidae, Rachycentridae, and Coryphaenidae.

Page 53

Lutjanus peru. R. H. Rosenblatt (pers. comm.) notes that a specimen from southern California is in the Scripps Institution of Oceanography collection and that a note on its occurrence is in preparation.

Lutjanus purpureus. W. C. Rohde (pers. comm.) notes that this species has been taken rather frequently in commercial catches from North Carolina and South Carolina, all from depths less than 200 m.

Pristipomoides freemani. F. C. Rohde, S. P. Epperly, and S. W. Ross, in press, record this species from off the southeastern United States, in depths as shallow as 100 m.

Symphysanodon berryi. F. C. Rohde, S. P. Epperly, and S. W. Ross, in press, record this species from off the southeastern United States in depths as shallow as 101 m. There is no current agreement as to the systematic placement of *Symphysanodon*. We assign it to the Lutjanidae, where it has been placed by others in the past, for convenience only.

Eucinostomus argenteus. The authorship of this species was incorrectly changed from Baird & Girard to Baird in the 4th edition of this list (p. 84). This error is corrected.

Eucinostomus harengulus. R. E. Matheson, Jr., and J. D. McEachran, 1984, Copeia (4):893, separated this species from the *E. argenteus* complex. Matheson also suggested (pers. comm.) the name tidewater mojarra.

Haemulidae. The black grunt, *Haemulon bonariense* Cuvier, has been included in previous lists solely on the basis of underwater observations by W. H. Longley at Tortugas, Florida. C. R. Robins, G. C. Ray, and J. Douglass, 1986, A Field Guide to Atlantic Coast Fishes of North America, Houghton Mifflin, p. 180, regarded these records as erroneous. This species is therefore dropped from the list.

Page 54

Haemulon parra. See *Galeocerdo cuvier* (p. 13).

Pagrus pagrus. The parentheses were inadvertently omitted from the author's name in the prior list.

Page 55

Equetus iwamotoi. G. C. Miller and L. P. Woods, 1988, Bull. Mar. Sci. 43(1):88, described this new species, in the genus *Pareques*, from coastal waters from North Carolina to Brazil. We prefer to treat *Pareques* as a subgenus of *Equetus*.

Mulloidichthys dentatus. *Mulloides* Bleeker, 1849, is unavailable for a goatfish genus because the name is preoccupied by *Mulloides* Richardson,

1843. *Mulloidichthys* Whitley, 1929, is the available replacement name. See W. N. Eschmeyer and R. M. Bailey, 1990, *in* W. N. Eschmeyer, Catalogue of the Genera of Recent Fishes. Calif. Acad. Sciences, p. 234.

Mulloidichthys martinicus. See *M. dentatus*.

Page 56

Chaetodon humeralis. This species was included in their list of California fishes by C. L. Hubbs, W. I. Follett, and L. J. Dempster, 1979, Occas. Pap. Calif. Acad. Sci. 133:23.

Pomacanthus zonipectus. This tropical angelfish of the eastern Pacific has been reported as an expatriate off southern California by R. N. Lea, J. M. Duffy, and K. C. Wilson, 1989, Calif. Fish Game 75:45.

Pentaceros pectoralis. The pelagic armorhead, *P. richardsoni*, is extralimital. G. S. Hardy, 1983, N. Z. J. Zool. 10:177, described the species which occurs along our Pacific Coast as *Pseudopentaceros pectoralis*. We regard *Pseudopentaceros* as a synonym of *Pentaceros*.

Cichlidae. *Heros severus* Heckel, 1840, the banded cichlid (termed *Cichlasoma severum* on the 1980 list), briefly established in Rogers Spring, Clark County, Nevada, has been extirpated there (Appendix 2, Table 3). The species is therefore removed from the list.

Cichla ocellaris. The South American peacock cichlid has been extensively planted in Florida and Texas, with at least limited reproduction in Florida. See Appendix 2, Table 1.

Cichlasoma citrinellum. The Central American midas cichlid, also known as red devil, is known to be reproducing in Florida. See Appendix 2, Table 1.

Cichlasoma managuense. The Central American jaguar guapote has been introduced and is reproducing in Utah. See Appendix 2, Table 1.

Cichlasoma meeki. This popular aquarium fish, native to Middle America, has been introduced in Arizona and Florida and is reproducing successfully in Florida. See Appendix 2, Table 1.

Cichlasoma urophthalmus. This Middle American species has been introduced and established in Florida. See Appendix 2, Table 1. W. F. Loftus (pers. comm.) informs us that it also occurs in saline and hypersaline waters of northeastern Florida Bay.

Geophagus surinamensis. This South American mouthbrooder has been introduced and established in Florida. See Appendix 2, Table 1.

Hemichromis bimaculatus. The modifier African has been added to the common name to avoid possible confusion with other "jewelfishes."

Tilapia urolepis. This African species has been established in California. See Appendix 2, Table 1.

Cymatogaster aggregata. As noted by W. N. Eschmeyer, E. S. Herald, and H. Hammann, 1983, A Field Guide to Pacific Coast Fishes of North America, Houghton Mifflin, p. 228, *C. gracilis* is at best a local population of *C. aggregata*. *Cymatogaster gracilis*, island seaperch, is therefore dropped from the list.

Page 57

Chromis cyanea. The International Commission on Zoological Nomenclature, Opinion 1417, 1986, Bull. Zool. Nomencl. 43(3):267, has ruled that *Chromis* is feminine. The species name is accordingly modified to *cyanea*.

Chromis insolata. See *C. cyanea*.

Chromis multilineata. See *C. cyanea*.

Pomacentrus variabilis. The author's name is not in parentheses.

Mugil curema. A "P" is added to the occurrence column based on records from San Diego, California, reported by R. N. Lea, R. J. Lavenberg, and C. C. Swift, 1989, Bull. South. Calif. Acad. Sci. 87(1):31.

Mugil gyrans. L. R. Rivas (pers. comm.) noted that the name *trichodon* is correctly applied to an extralimital species and that *gyrans* is the first available name for the fantail mullet.

Page 58

Clepticus parrae. R. M. Bailey and C. R. Robins, 1988, Bull. Zool. Nomencl. 45(2):93, noted that the original spelling *parrae* should be retained because Parra was treated as a Latin name; see Article 31a (i) of the International Code of Zoological Nomenclature.

Page 59

Rathbunella hypoplecta. W. N. Eschmeyer, E. S. Herald, and H. Hammann, 1983, A Field Guide to Pacific Coast Fishes of North America, Houghton Mifflin, p. 228, noted that *R. alleni*, rough ronquil, is a synonym of *R. hypoplecta*, smooth ronquil, and used the common name stripefin ronquil. We therefore delete the entry for *R. alleni* but use stripedfin because there is more than one stripe in the anal fin.

Bothrocara brunneum. M. J. Allen and G. B. Smith, 1988, NOAA Tech Rep. NMFS 66:100, reported this species from waters as shallow as 199 m (possibly only 25 m) in Alaska.

Eucryphycus californicus. M. E. Anderson, 1988, Proc. Calif. Acad. Sci. 45(5):89, placed *Maynea californica* in his new genus *Eucryphycus*. The ending of the specific trivial name is changed accordingly.

Gymnelus hemifasciatus. M. E. Anderson, 1981, Natl. Mus. Can. Publ. 17, recorded this species from Arctic and Pacific coasts of Canada and Alaska. D. E. McAllister, M. E. Anderson, and J. G. Hunter, 1981, Can. J. Fish. Aquat. Sci. 38:835, showed that the proper spelling of the genus is *Gymnelus*.

Gymnelus popovi. M. E. Anderson, 1982, Natl. Mus. Can. Publ. 17, recorded this species from Aleutian shore waters.

Gymnelus retrodorsalis. M. E. Anderson, 1982, Natl. Mus. Can. Publ. 17, recorded this species from Atlantic and Arctic waters of Canada.

Gymnelus viridis. The spelling of the genus is changed (see *G. hemifasciatus*). A "P" is added to the occurrence column because of records from western Arctic waters by J. C. Quast and E. L. Hall, 1972, NOAA Tech. Rep. NMFS SSRF-658:13.

Lycenchelys paxillus. W. B. Scott and M. G. Scott, 1988, Can. Bull. Fish. Aquat. Sci. 219: 405, recorded this species from waters shallower than 200 m along the southeast coast of Canada. Although *Lycenchelys* is feminine, *paxillus* is a noun in apposition and therefore its ending is not changed.

Lycodapus psarostomatus. This species is added to our list based on a specimen reported from Monterey Bay, California, at a depth of 0–15 m, by M. E. Anderson, 1989, Calif. Fish Game 75:149.

Lycodes concolor. M. J. Allen and G. B. Smith, 1988, NOAA Tech. Rep. NMFS 66:102, recorded this species inside the 200 m isobath along the Aleutian Islands and in the Bering Sea.

Lycodes cortezianus. W. N. Eschmeyer, E. S. Herald, and H. Hammann, 1983, A Field Guide to the Pacific Coast Fishes of North America, Houghton Mifflin, p. 105, synonymized *Aprodon* with *Lycodes* on the advice of M. E. Anderson, an action followed here.

Lycodes esmarki. W. B. Scott and M. G. Scott, 1988, Can. Bull. Fish. Aquat. Sci. 219:407, recorded this species from waters shallower than 200 m along the southeastern coast of Canada.

Lycodes mucosus. D. W. Kessler, 1985, Alaska's Saltwater Fishes and Other Sea Life, Alaska Northwest Publishing, p. 95, listed this Arctic species from Alaskan waters.

Lycodes polaris. An "A" is added to occurrence because this species lives also in the eastern Arctic, J. G. Hunter, S. T. Leach, D. E. McAllister, and M. B. Steigerwald, 1984, Syllogeus 52:22.

Lycodes raridens. M. J. Allen and G. B. Smith, 1988, NOAA Tech. Rep. NMFS 66:100, reported this species from mid-shelf waters of the Bering Sea.

Lycodes reticulatus. See *Arctogadus borisovi* (p. 30).

Lycodes vahli. W. B. Scott and M. G. Scott, 1988, Can. Bull. Fish. Aquat. Sci. 219:411, reported this species from shelf waters of southeastern Canada.

Page 60

Ernogrammus walkeri. W. I. Follett and D. C. Powell, 1988, Copeia (1):137, described this new prickleback from off central California.

Esselenia carli. W. I. Follett and M. E. Anderson, 1990, Copeia (1):147, described this species and *E. laurae* from coastal waters of central and southern California.

Esselenia laurae. See *E. carli*.

Lumpenus medius. Parentheses were omitted in previous editions of this list. The species was described in *Clinus*.

Cryptacanthodes aleutensis. D. E. McAllister, 1990, Syllogeus 64:171, followed Makushok (1981) in synonymizing *Delolepis* and *Lyconectes* with *Cryptacanthodes*, an action followed here.

Cryptacanthodes giganteus. See *C. aleutensis*.

Pholidae. This family has been reviewed by A. Yatsu, 1981, Bull. Natl. Sci. Mus. (Tokyo) Ser. A (Zool.) 7(4):165–190, and 1985, Jpn. J. Ichthyol. 32(3):273–282. We have adopted several of his nomenclatural recommendations, but his placement of three species of *Pholis* (*clemensi*, *laeta*, and *schultzi*) into a new genus (*Allopholis*) has been challenged by A. E. Peden and G. W. Hughes, 1984, Can. J. Zool. 62(2):291, who view this move as needless generic splitting. In particular, they emphasize the intimate relationship of *laeta* and *ornata*, assigned to different genera by Yatsu. We retain the above species in *Pholis*.

Apodichthys fucorum. This species was transferred from *Xererpes* to *Apodichthys* by Yatsu, 1981 and 1985 (see Pholidae).

Pholis fasciata. See *Arctogadus borisovi* (p. 30).

Rhodymenichthys dolichogaster. The stippled gunnel was shifted from *Pholis* to the monotypic genus *Rhodymenichthys* by Yatsu, 1981 and 1985 (see Pholidae).

Anarhichas denticulatus. See *Arctogadus borisovi* (p. 30).

Page 61

Opistognathus macrognathus. The author's name is placed in parentheses because the species was described in *Opisthognathus*.

Opistognathus maxillosus. See *O. macrognathus*.

Opistognathus sp. See the 4th edition of this list (p. 87).

Tripterygiidae. We follow J. S. Nelson, 1984, Fishes of the World, 2nd ed., Wiley & Sons, p. 344, and many others, in recognizing the Tripterygiidae as a distinct family.

Dactyloscopus moorei. C. E. Dawson, 1982, Bull. Mar. Sci. 32(1):37, recognized this as a valid species, occurring along the Atlantic and Gulf coasts from North Carolina to Texas.

Gillellus healae. C. E. Dawson, 1982, Bull. Mar. Sci. 32(1):56, described this new species from South Carolina to southwestern Florida, and Aruba.

Platygillellus rubrocinctus. C. E. Dawson, 1982, Bull. Mar. Sci. 32(1):62, referred this species, previously assigned to *Gillellus*, to *Platygillellus*.

Page 62

Coralliozetus bahamensis. We follow A. Acero P., 1984, An. Inst. Invest. Mar. Punta Betin, 14:29, in recognizing the genus *Coralliozetus*, and we move *Emblemaria bahamensis* and *E. diaphana* to it.

Coralliozetus diaphanus. See *C. bahamensis*.

Gibbonsia montereyensis. C. A. Stepien and R. H. Rosenblatt, in press, Copeia, showed that *G. erythra* Hubbs, 1952, is a synonym of *G. montereyensis*. Accordingly, the entry for *G. erythra*, scarlet kelpfish, is omitted.

Page 63

Hypsoblennius hentz. See *Galeocerdo cuvier* (p. 13).

Hypsoblennius invemar. W. F. Smith-Vaniz and A. Acero P., in W. F. Smith-Vaniz, 1980, Proc. Acad. Nat. Sci. Phila. 132:289, described this new species from Louisiana and Colombia.

Hypsoblennius jenkinsi. Parentheses are added to the authors' names because this species was described in *Chasmodes*.

Ammodytes americanus. See *A. hexapterus*.

Ammodytes hexapterus. Populations of sand lances from the eastern Arctic, previously identified with *hexapterus*, were assigned to *americanus* by S. W. Richards, 1982, J. Northwest Atl. Fish. Sci. 3:93–104.

Diplogrammus pauciradiatus. We follow T. Nakabo, 1982, Publ. Seto Mar. Biol. Lab. 27(4/6): 77, in transferring the three western Atlantic species from *Callionymus* to *Diplogrammus*, *Foetorepus*, and *Paradiplogrammus*.

Foetorepus agassizi. See *Diplogrammus pauciradiatus*.

Paradiplogrammus bairdi. See *Diplogrammus pauciradiatus*.

Bollmannia eigenmanni. J. T. Williams and R. L. Shipp, 1980, Northeast Gulf Sci. 4:23, reported this species from depths of 90–180 m off western Florida in the Gulf of Mexico.

Page 64

Coryphopterus tortugae. J. Garzon-Ferreira and A. Acero P., in press, Northeast Gulf Sci., recognize this as a valid species distinct from *C. glaucofraenum*. Both species are common in Florida shore waters.

Gobionellus oceanicus. F. Pezold and J. M. Grady, 1990, Bull. Mar. Sci. 45(3):648, synonymized *G. gracillimus*, slim goby and *G. hastatus*, sharptail goby, with *G. oceanicus*, highfin goby, an action adopted here.

Gobionellus pseudofasciatus. The note explaining the addition of this species to the list (1980 edition, p. 88) erred in reporting this species from the northeast Gulf of Mexico instead of the east coast of Florida and in neglecting to note the occurrence of this species in fresh water. An "F" is added to the occurrence column.

Gobionellus sagittula. This species was listed as *G. longicaudus* (Jenkins & Evermann) in the 1980 edition of this list (p. 54). C. L. Hubbs, W.

I. Follett, and L. J. Dempster, 1979, Occas. Pap. Calif. Acad. Sci. 133:26, included this species with *sagittula* in their list of California fishes.

Gobiosoma bosc. See *Galeocerdo cuvier* (p. 13).

Ioglossus helenae. C. R. Robins, G. C. Ray, and J. Douglass, 1986, A Field Guide to Atlantic Coast Fishes of North America, Houghton Mifflin, p. 248, noted the occurrence of this species in southeastern Florida.

Lythrypnus elasson. This goby was reported from the northeastern Gulf of Mexico off Florida in depths of 27–36 m by J. T. Williams and R. L. Shipp, 1980, Northeast Gulf Sci. 4:24.

Page 65

Priolepis hipoliti. *Quisquilius* is a junior synonym of *Priolepis* and this species, formerly in *Quisquilius*, was transferred to *Priolepis* by D. W. Greenfield, 1989, Copeia, (2):397, on the advice of D. F. Hoese.

Trichiuridae. We follow those ichthyologists who combine the Gempylidae (snake mackerels) and Trichiuridae (cutlassfishes). Various included genera have been assigned differently by ichthyologists or placed in their own family.

Benthodesmus elongatus. An "A" is added to the occurrence column because of records of this species off southeastern Canada reported by W. B. Scott and M. G. Scott, 1988, Can. Bull. Fish. Aquat. Sci. 219:447.

Lepidopus fitchi. This eastern Pacific scabbardfish was named as a new species by R. H. Rosenblatt and R. R. Wilson, Jr., 1987, Jpn. J. Ichthyol. 33(4):342. It was formerly listed as *L. xantusi* Goode & Bean, scabbardfish, which now is regarded as a synonym of *L. caudatus* (Euphrasen, 1788), a widely distributed species that does not occur within our limits.

Nesiarchus nasutus. N. A. Voss, 1957, Copeia (4):304, recorded juveniles of this species from shelf waters along the eastern coast of Florida, a fact overlooked in previous editions of this list and brought to our attention by P. C. Heemstra.

Scombridae. Atlantic records of the striped bonito, *Sarda orientalis*, are erroneous. B. B. Collette and C. E. Nauen, 1983, FAO Fish. Synop. 125 (vol. 2):52, showed that this is a wide-ranging Indo-Pacific species which does not occur within our limits. The entry for this species is dropped.

Acanthocybium solandri. R. M. Bailey and C. R. Robins, 1988, Bull. Zool. Nomencl. 45(2):93, showed that this is the correct spelling of the species name under the International Rules.

Auxis rochei. Species of the genus *Auxis* are closely allied to the tunas, *Thynnus*, and the bonitos, *Euthynnus*, and share with them many edibility characteristics. Despite this, the long history of use of the name mackerel supports retention of current common names.

Auxis thazard. See *A. rochei*.

Page 66

Katsuwonus pelamis. We follow B. B. Collette and C. E. Nauen, 1983, FAO Fish. Synop. 125 (vol. 2):42, and many other ichthyologists in placing *Euthynnus pelamis* in the monotypic genus *Katsuwonus*.

Cubiceps pauciradiatus. J. L. Baxter, 1979, Bull. Mar. Sci. 29(2):236, synonymized *C. athenae* Haedrich with *C. pauciradiatus*, an action overlooked in the 1980 edition of this list.

Psenes maculatus. The author of this species as given in the 1980 edition (p. 57) was incorrect.

Page 67

Trichopsis vittata. This introduced aquarium fish from southeastern Asia is established in Florida. See Appendix 2, Table 1.

Bothidae. This family has been variously divided in studies recently published and in progress. We believe that it is premature to adopt such changes at this time.

Citharichthys fragilis. In the 1980 edition of this list (p. 64), this Pacific species was inadvertently listed as "A," an error we now correct.

Etropus cyclosquamus This new flatfish was described from continental shelf waters of North Carolina to Mississippi at depths of 28–36 m by A. J. Leslie, Jr., and D. J. Stewart, 1986, Copeia (1):143.

Page 68

Eopsetta exilis. K. Sakamoto, 1984, Mem. Fac. Fish. Hokkaido Univ. 31:95, revised the genera of Pleuronectidae. The following changes, all adopted here, affect our list: *Lyopsetta exilis* is transferred to the genus *Eopsetta*; *Glyptocephalus zachirus* is in *Errex*; *Limanda aspera*, *Limanda ferruginea*, and *Limanda proboscidea* become *Pleuronectes asper*, *Pleuronectes ferrugineus*, and *Pleuronectes proboscideus*; *Liopsetta glacialis*, *Liopsetta putnami*, and

Pseudopleuronectes americanus are also moved to *Pleuronectes*; *Lepidopsetta bilineata* becomes *Pleuronectes bilineatus*; and *Isopsetta isolepis* and *Parophrys vetulus* are transferred to *Pleuronectes*.

Errex zachirus. See *Eopsetta exilis*.

Pleuronectes americanus. See *Eopsetta exilis*.

Pleuronectes asper. See *Eopsetta exilis*.

Pleuronectes bilineatus. See *Eopsetta exilis*.

Pleuronectes ferrugineus. See *Eopsetta exilis*.

Pleuronectes glacialis. See *Eopsetta exilis*.

Pleuronectes isolepis. See *Eopsetta exilis*.

Pleuronectes proboscideus. See *Eopsetta exilis*.

Pleuronectes putnami. See *Eopsetta exilis*.

Pleuronectes vetulus. See *Eopsetta exilis*.

Soleidae. Most recent authors (e.g., E. H. Ahlstrom, K. Amaoka, D. A. Hensley, H. G. Moser, and B. Y. Sumida, 1984, Am. Soc. Ichthyol. Herpetol., Spec. Publ. 1:640) have treated the soles (suborder Soleoidei) as consisting of two families, the Soleidae with two subfamilies (the Old World Soleinae and the New World Achirinae) and the cosmopolitan Cynoglossidae or tonguefishes. It has been contended recently by F. Chapleau and A. Keast, 1988, Can. J. Zool. 66:2797–2810, that the Soleidae so defined are polyphyletic, because the Soleinae are interpreted as the sister group of the Cynoglossidae, these two in turn being sister to the Achirinae. These authors proposed elevation of each group to family level and also tentatively suggested that several subfamilies of Pleuronectidae be raised to family status. We adopt an alternative classification, a single expanded monophyletic Soleidae with three subfamilies (Achirinae—American soles, Cynoglossinae—tonguefishes, and Soleinae—Old World soles) that emphasizes the monophyly of the group but avoids the proliferation of families.

Gymnachirus melas. The parentheses were inadvertently omitted from the author's name in the 1980 edition of this list.

Gymnachirus texae. The parentheses were inadvertently omitted from the author's name in the 1980 edition of this list.

Page 69

Canthidermis maculata. The generic name is feminine so the adjectival specific name is emended to *maculata*.

Tetraodontidae. The relationships of the Diodontidae, the porcupinefishes, lie within those of the Tetraodontidae and the two families are here combined following the phylogenetic arrangement of R. Arai, 1983, Bull. Natl. Sci. Mus. (Tokyo) Ser. A (Zool.) 9(4):207.

Appendix 2
Exotic Fishes[1]

WALTER R. COURTENAY, JR.
Department of Biological Sciences, Florida Atlantic University
Boca Raton, Florida 33431–0991, USA

DAWN P. JENNINGS AND JAMES D. WILLIAMS
U.S. Fish and Wildlife Service, National Fisheries Research Center
7920 Northwest 71st Street, Gainesville, Florida 32606, USA

Established Exotic Fishes

The fourth edition of this list reported 35 exotic species that had become established in the United States and Canada (Robins et al. 1980: Appendix 2 and Appendix 3, footnote 1). Since 1980, stable, reproducing populations of 13 additional species have been found in open waters. The bighead carp, *Hypophthalmichthys nobilis*, is the most recent species to have become established. It apparently was released or escaped from aquaculture facilities. Three species of loricariid catfishes and four of cichlids were released or escaped from aquaria or zoos. Two additional cichlids were introduced by governmental agencies, one for biological control in California and one for sport fishing in Florida. The ruffe, *Gymnocephalus cernuus*, apparently was introduced into the Great Lakes with ballast water of European origin released from cargo ships. The giant rivulus, *Rivulus harti*, previously thought to have become extirpated in southern California, remains established there (J. A. St. Amant, California Department of Fish and Game, personal communication, 1990). The croaking gourami, *Trichopsis vittata*, is established in Florida, and doubtless represents the release of aquarium fish. Conversely, the banded cichlid, *Heros severus* (given in the 1980 list as *Cichlasoma severum*), was eradicated before 1980 from the only locality where it was known to occur in the wild, Rogers Spring, Clark County, Nevada. As a result of these 13 additions and 1 extirpation, the current number of established exotic species in the region is 47 (Table 1). In addition, the silver carp, *Hypophthalmichthys molitrix*, is so widespread in the central United States that its establishment seems assured; only confirmation of a feral breeding population is needed before this species is added to the list of established exotics.

Nine of the species on the 1980 list expanded their distributions across state or provincial boundaries, either by themselves or with human assistance. Complete distributional studies are not available for the other 26 species, but several are known to have increased their ranges within states or provinces.

To the exotic cyprinids included in the 1980 list, we add the bighead carp, whose recent establishment in Missouri is based on collections of larvae and juveniles in the Missouri River drainage (Pflieger 1989). The grass carp, *Ctenopharyngodon idella*, reported as occurring in "many states" in 1980, is now known to have been distributed to at least 36 states and provinces, and is considered as established in 7. Most states now permit stocking only of triploid grass carp, but illegal stocking of diploid fish has apparently occurred and probably continues. Recent reports of larval grass carp in the

[1] The U.S. Fish and Wildlife Service is developing a data base to document the current and historical distributions of exotic fishes in the United States and Canada. Anyone with information on the occurrence of exotic fishes is urged to contact James D. Williams or Dawn P. Jennings at the U.S. Fish and Wildlife Service, National Fisheries Research Center, 7920 Northwest 71st Street, Gainesville, Florida 32606, USA.

Missouri and Ohio river drainages and in the Trinity River of Texas, suggest that this species continues to expand its range. Rudd, *Scardinius erythrophthalmus*, too, is becoming more widespread. Listed only from New York in the 1980 list, it is now established in Maine (Courtenay et al. 1984, 1986). During the past 5 years, the rudd has been cultured extensively in Arkansas and widely distributed in the central and eastern United States as a baitfish and, to a lesser degree, as an outdoor ornamental fish. It has been reported from bait shops in 16 states and from open waters in 11 states. It is probably more widespread than current reports indicate and probably will become established in states from which it has not yet been reported.

The oriental weatherfish, *Misgurnus anguillicaudatus*, remains the only cobitid on our list, but it is now established in Idaho (Courtenay et al. 1988) as well as in California and Michigan. It also has been collected in Florida and Oregon.

The Loricariidae were represented by one species of suckermouth catfish, *Hypostomus plecostomus*, in the 1980 list, which was reported as established in Florida and Texas; however, a member of this genus has been known from Nevada waters for many years (Minckley 1973). Morphological examination of specimens from the three states revealed that they represent three distinct species of *Hypostomus* (Courtenay and Deacon 1982). In addition, a fourth species, the sailfin catfish, *Pterygoplichthys multiradiatus*, is well established in Florida (Ludlow and Walsh, in press).

Although no species were added to the list of established Poeciliidae, three species have extended their distributions. The shortfin molly, *Poecilia mexicana*, now is established in five additional states, the guppy, *Poecilia reticulata*, in two more states (but breeding populations have not been confirmed for Florida), and the green swordtail, *Xiphophorus helleri*, in four new states (but the Alberta population has been extirpated). All these introductions represent released or escaped aquarium fishes.

The Cichlidae have more established exotic species in North America (17) than any other family. Of the 12 cichlids on the 1980 list (Appendices 2 and 3), *Heros severus* was eradicated, but *Astronotus ocellatus*, *Cichlasoma nigrofasciatum*, *Tilapia aurea*, *T. mariae*, *T. mossambica*, and *T. zilli* were reported from additional states; all were released or stocked. Most of the 11 species have expanded their ranges within states where they are established. Six more species have become established since 1980, 4 in Florida and 1 each in California and Utah.

No additional established exotics have been reported for the Cobitidae, Clariidae, Osmeridae, Salmonidae, Sciaenidae, or Gobiidae. Based on unpublished records, only the walking catfish, *Clarias batrachus*, among these species, has substantially increased its intrastate range during the past 10 years.

Nonestablished, Collected Exotic Fishes

Table 2 lists exotic fish species that have been collected from open waters in the continental United States and Canada, none of which is known to have established a reproducing population. The 1980 list did not include most of these species, primarily because records were not easily accessible. Although this list was compiled from reports in the literature, from museum records, and from personal contacts with other biologists, it is doubtless incomplete. Specific dates of collections are not given; however, the list provides an indication of the kinds of exotic fishes that are imported into the United States and Canada and subsequently released into open waters. Most species listed were imported for use in the aquarium trade or for aquaculture and represent accidental releases or escapes. Others, however, were intentionally released as sport fishes; these include species of the families Esocidae, Salmonidae, Centropomidae, Percidae, and Cichlidae.

Formerly Established Populations of Exotic Fishes

Listed in Table 3 are 13 exotic fish species that formerly had established breeding populations in open waters of the United States and Canada. Each of these populations listed, however, was extirpated, either through purposeful eradication or by natural causes.

Exotic Fishes Established in Hawaii

Although the 1980 list contained only species exotic to the continental United States and Canada, many exotic fishes have become established in Hawaii (Maciolek 1984; Randall 1987). Hawaii, with 33 species, now has the dubious distinction of having more established exotic fishes than any other state or province. These are listed in Table 4. Of these, eight are established in marine waters and the remainder in fresh water.

References

Courtenay, W. R., Jr., and J. E. Deacon. 1982. The status of introduced fishes in certain spring systems in southern Nevada. Great Basin Naturalist 42:361–366.

Courtenay, W. R., Jr., D. A. Hensley, J. N. Taylor, and J. A. McCann. 1984. Distribution of exotic fishes in the continental United States. Pages 41–77 *in* W. R. Courtenay, Jr. and J. R. Stauffer, Jr., editors. Distribution, biology, and management of exotic fishes. Johns Hopkins University Press, Baltimore, Maryland.

Courtenay, W. R., Jr., D. A. Hensley, J. N. Taylor, and J. A. McCann. 1986. Distribution of exotic fishes in North America. Pages 675–698 *in* C. H. Hocutt and E. O. Wiley, editors. Zoogeography of North American freshwater fishes. Wiley & Sons, New York.

Courtenay, W. R., Jr., C. R. Robins, R. M. Bailey, and J. E. Deacon. 1988. Records of exotic fishes from Idaho and Wyoming. Great Basin Naturalist 47:523–526.

Ludlow, M. E., and S. J. Walsh. In press. Occurrence of a South American armored catfish in the Hillsborough River, Florida. Florida Scientist.

Maciolek, J. A. 1984. Exotic fishes in Hawaii and other islands of Oceania. Pages 131–161 *in* W. R. Courtenay, Jr. and J. R. Stauffer, Jr., editors. Distribution, biology, and management of exotic fishes. Johns Hopkins University Press, Baltimore, Maryland.

Minckley, W. L. 1973. The fishes of Arizona. Arizona Game and Fish Department, Phoenix.

Nelson, J. S. 1984. The tropical fish fauna in Cave and Basin Hotsprings drainage, Banff National Park. Canadian Field Naturalist 97:255–261.

Pflieger, W. L. 1989. Natural reproduction of bighead carp (*Hypophthalmichthys nobilis*) in Missouri. American Fisheries Society, Introduced Fish Section Newsletter 9(4):9–10. (Bethesda, Maryland.)

Randall, J. E. 1987. Introductions of marine fishes to the Hawaiian Islands. Bulletin of Marine Science 41:490–502.

Robins, C. R., R. M. Bailey, C. E. Bond, J. R. Brooker, E. A. Lachner, R. N. Lea, and W. B. Scott. 1980. A list of common and scientific names of fishes from the United States and Canada. American Fisheries Society Special Publication 12.

Zuckerman, L. D., and R. J. Behnke. 1986. Introduced fishes in the San Luis Valley, Colorado. Pages 435–453 *in* R. H. Stroud, editor. Fish culture in fisheries management. American Fisheries Society, Bethesda, Maryland.

TABLE 1.—Exotic fishes established in the continental United States and Canada.

SCIENTIFIC NAME	COMMON NAME	WHERE ESTABLISHED[a]
	Cyprinidae—carps and minnows	
Carassius auratus	goldfish	Widespread
Ctenopharyngodon idella	grass carp	Arkansas, Louisiana, Minnesota, Mississippi, Missouri, Tennessee, Texas (Alabama, Alberta, Arizona, California, Colorado, Delaware, Florida, Idaho, Illinois, Indiana, Iowa, Kansas, Kentucky, Maryland, Massachusetts, Nebraska, New Mexico, New York, Nevada, North Carolina, Ohio, Oklahoma, Ontario, South Carolina, Utah, Virginia, West Virginia, Wisconsin, Wyoming)
Cyprinus carpio	common carp	Widespread
Hypophthalmichthys nobilis	bighead carp	Missouri (Alabama, Arkansas, Florida, Illinois, Indiana, Kansas, Kentucky)
Leuciscus idus	ide	Maine (Connecticut, New York, Pennsylvania, Tennessee)
Rhodeus sericeus	bitterling	New York
Scardinius erythrophthalmus	rudd	Maine, New York (Arkansas, Illinois, Kansas, Missouri, New Jersey, Oklahoma, Texas, Virginia, Wisconsin)
Tinca tinca	tench	British Columbia, California, Colorado, Connecticut, Idaho, Washington (Alberta,[b] Arizona, Maryland, Missouri, New Mexico, New York, Oregon, Virginia)
	Cobitidae—loaches	
Misgurnus anguillicaudatus	oriental weatherfish	California, Idaho, Michigan (Florida, Oregon)
	Clariidae—labyrinth catfishes	
Clarias batrachus	walking catfish	Florida (California, Georgia, Massachusetts, Nevada)
	Loricariidae—suckermouth catfishes	
Hypostomus sp.	suckermouth catfish	Florida
Hypostomus sp.	suckermouth catfish	Texas
Hypostomus sp.	suckermouth catfish	Nevada
Pterygoplichthys multiradiatus	sailfin catfish	Florida

TABLE 1.—Continued.

SCIENTIFIC NAME	COMMON NAME	WHERE ESTABLISHED[a]
	Osmeridae—smelts	
Hypomesus nipponensis	wakasagi	California
	Salmonidae—trouts	
Salmo trutta	brown trout	Widespread
	Aplocheilidae—rivulins	
Rivulus harti	giant rivulus	California
	Poeciliidae—livebearers	
Belonesox belizanus	pike killifish	Florida (Texas)
Poecilia mexicana	shortfin molly	California, Colorado, Idaho, Montana, Nevada, Texas
Poecilia reticulata	guppy	Alberta, Arizona, Idaho, Nevada, Texas, Wyoming (California, Florida)
Poeciliopsis gracilis	porthole livebearer	California
Xiphophorus helleri	green swordtail	Colorado, Florida, Idaho, Montana, Nevada (hybrid), Wyoming (Alberta,[b] Arizona, California)
Xiphophorus maculatus	southern platyfish	Colorado, Florida, Nevada (hybrid) (California, Texas)
Xiphophorus variatus	variable platyfish	Florida, Montana (Arizona, California)
	Percidae—perches	
Gymnocephalus cernuus	ruffe	Minnesota, Wisconsin
	Sciaenidae—drums	
Bairdiella icistia	bairdiella	California
Cynoscion xanthulus	orangemouth corvina	California
	Cichlidae—cichlids	
Astronotus ocellatus	oscar	Florida (Massachusetts, Mississippi, Ontario, Pennsylvania, Rhode Island)
Cichla ocellaris	peacock cichlid	Florida (Texas)
Cichlasoma bimaculatum	black acara	Florida
Cichlasoma citrinellum	midas cichlid	Florida
Cichlasoma managuense	jaguar guapote	Utah (Ontario)
Cichlasoma meeki	firemouth cichlid	Florida (Arizona)
Cichlasoma nigrofasciatum	convict cichlid	Idaho, Nevada (Alberta,[b] Arizona, Florida)
Cichlasoma octofasciatum	Jack Dempsey	Florida
Cichlasoma urophthalmus	Mayan cichlid	Florida
Geophagus surinamensis	redstriped eartheater	Florida

TABLE 1.—Continued.

SCIENTIFIC NAME	COMMON NAME	WHERE ESTABLISHED[a]
Hemichromis bimaculatus	African jewelfish	Florida
Tilapia aurea	blue tilapia	Arizona, California, Florida, Georgia, North Carolina, Oklahoma, Texas (Alabama, Colorado, Idaho, Pennsylvania)
Tilapia mariae	spotted tilapia	Florida, Nevada
Tilapia melanotheron	blackchin tilapia	Florida
Tilapia mossambica	Mozambique tilapia	Arizona, California, Florida, Idaho, Texas (Alabama, Colorado, Georgia, Illinois, Montana, Nevada, New York, North Carolina)
Tilapia urolepis[c]	Wami tilapia	California
Tilapia zilli	redbelly tilapia	Arizona, California, North Carolina, South Carolina, Texas (Florida, Nevada)
	Gobiidae—gobies	
Acanthogobius flavimanus	yellowfin goby	California
Tridentiger trigonocephalus	chameleon goby	California
	Anabantidae—gouramies	
Trichopsis vittata	croaking gourami	Florida

[a]Jurisdictions in parentheses identify states and provinces where a species has been collected but is not known to be presently established. See Courtenay et al. (1984, 1986) for further information on some of these species.

[b]According to Nelson (1984) this species has been extirpated from Alberta where it was formerly established.

[c]Refers to *T. urolepis hornorum* (Trewavas), usually but not always introduced in southern California as a hybrid with *T. mossambica*.

TABLE 2.—Exotic fishes collected but not known to be established in waters of the continental United States and Canada (in part, after Courtenay et al. 1984, 1986).

SCIENTIFIC NAME	COMMON NAME	WHERE COLLECTED
	Osteoglossidae—bonytongues	
Osteoglossum bicirrhosum Vandelli, 1829	arawana	California, Nevada
	Anguillidae—freshwater eels	
Anguilla anguilla (Linnaeus, 1758)	European eel	California
Anguilla australis Richardson, 1841	shortfin eel	California
	Cyprinidae—carps and minnows	
Barbodes schwanefeldi (Bleeker, 1853)	tinfoil barb	Florida
Danio malabaricus (Jerdon, 1849)	Malabar danio	Florida, Nevada
Danio rerio (Hamilton, 1822)	zebra danio	California, Florida, New Mexico
Hypophthalmichthys molitrix (Valenciennes, 1844)	silver carp	Alabama, Arkansas, Illinois, Indiana, Kansas, Louisiana, Missouri
Labeo chrysophekadion (Bleeker, 1850)	black sharkminnow	Florida
Puntius conchonius (Hamilton, 1822)	rosy barb	Florida
Puntius gelius (Hamilton, 1822)	dwarf barb	Florida
Puntius tetrazona (Bleeker, 1855)	tiger barb	California, Florida
	Characidae—characins	
Colossoma spp.	pacu	Arizona, California, Florida, Missouri, Ohio, Ontario,[a] Texas
Colossoma macropomum (Cuvier, 1818)	tambaquí	Florida
Gymnocorymbus ternetzi (Boulenger, 1895)	black tetra	Colorado,[b] Florida
Hemigrammus ocellifer (Steindachner, 1882)	head-and-taillight tetra	Colorado[b]
Leporinus fasciatus (Bloch, 1794)	banded leporinus	Florida
Metynnis sp.		Florida, Kentucky
Paracheirodon innesi (Myers, 1936)	neon tetra	Colorado[b]
unidentified piranhas		Idaho, Illinois, Kentucky, Missouri, New York, Oklahoma, Pennsylvania, Utah, Washington
Piaractus brachypomus (Cuvier, 1818)	pirapatinga	Florida, Georgia
Pygocentrus nattereri (Kner, 1860)	red piranha	Florida, Massachusetts, Michigan, Pennsylvania
Serrasalmus rhombeus (Linnaeus, 1766)	redeye piranha	Florida

TABLE 2.—Continued.

SCIENTIFIC NAME	COMMON NAME	WHERE COLLECTED
	Doradidae—thorny catfishes	
Platydoras costatus (Linnaeus, 1766)	Raphael catfish	Florida
Pseudodoras niger (Valenciennes, 1817)	ripsaw catfish	Florida
Pterodoras granulosus (Valenciennes, 1833)	granulated catfish	Florida
	Pimelodidae—longwhiskered catfishes	
Phractocephalus hemioliopterus (Bloch & Schneider, 1801)	redtail catfish	Florida
	Callichthyidae—plated catfishes	
Callichthys callichthys (Linnaeus, 1758)	cascarudo	Florida, New York
Corydoras sp.	corydoras	Colorado,[b] Florida
	Loricariidae—suckermouth catfishes	
Hypostomus spp.		Colorado,[b] Pennsylvania
Otocinclus sp.		Colorado[b]
Panaque nigrolineatus (Peters, 1877)	royal panaque	Ontario[a]
	Esocidae—pikes	
Esox reicherti Dybowski, 1869	Amur pike	Pennsylvania
	Plecoglossidae—ayus	
Plecoglossus altivelis Temminck & Schlegel, 1846	ayu	California
	Salmonidae—trouts	
Hucho hucho (Linnaeus, 1758)	huchen	Quebec
Oncorhynchus masou (Brevoort, 1856)	cherry salmon	Washington
Salmo letnica (Karaman, 1924)	Ohrid trout	Colorado, Montana, Tennessee, Wyoming
	Aplocheilidae—rivulins	
Cynolebias nigripinnis Regan, 1912	blackfin pearlfish	California
Cynolebias whitei Myers, 1942	Rio pearlfish	California
	Goodeidae—splitfins	
Ameca splendens Miller & Fitzsimons, 1971	butterfly splitfin	Nevada
	Poeciliidae—livebearers	
Poecilia hybrids[c]		Florida, Nevada
	Atherinidae—silversides	
Chirostoma jordani Woolman, 1894	charal	Texas

TABLE 2.—Continued.

SCIENTIFIC NAME	COMMON NAME	WHERE COLLECTED
	Centropomidae—snooks	
Lates mariae Steindachner, 1909	bigeye lates	Texas
Lates niloticus (Linnaeus, 1758)	Nile perch	Texas
	Percidae—perches	
Stizostedion lucioperca (Linnaeus, 1758)	zander	North Dakota
	Cichlidae—cichlids	
Cichla temensis Humboldt, 1833	speckled pavon	Florida, Texas
Geophagus brasiliensis (Quoy & Gaimard, 1824)	pearl eartheater	Florida
Labeotropheus sp.		Florida
Melanochromis johanni (Eccles, 1973)	blue mbuna	Nevada
Pseudotropheus auratus (Boulenger, 1897)	golden mbuna	Nevada
Pseudotropheus zebra (Boulenger, 1899)	zebra mbuna	Nevada
Pterophyllum scalare (Lichtenstein, 1823)	freshwater angelfish	Florida, Kentucky, Ontario (?)[a,d]
Tilapia nilotica (Linnaeus, 1758)	Nile tilapia	Alabama
Tilapia sparrmani Smith, 1840	banded tilapia	Florida
	Gobiidae—gobies	
Proterorhinus marmoratus (Pallas, 1814)	tubenose goby	Michigan, Ontario
	Anabantidae—gouramies	
Betta splendens Regan, 1909	Siamese fightingfish	Alberta[a]
Colisa fasciata (Schneider, 1801)	banded gourami	Pennsylvania
Colisa labiosa (Day, 1877)	thicklip gourami	Florida
Colisa lalia (Hamilton, 1822)	dwarf gourami	Florida
Helostoma temmincki Cuvier, 1831	kissing gourami	Florida
Macropodus opercularis (Linnaeus, 1758)	paradisefish	Florida
Trichogaster leeri (Bleeker, 1852)	pearl gourami	Florida
Trichogaster trichopterus (Pallas, 1770)	threespot gourami	Alberta,[a] Florida
	Channidae—snakeheads	
Channa micropeltes (Cuvier, 1831)	giant snakehead	Maine, Rhode Island
	Pleuronectidae—righteye flounders	
Platichthys flesus (Linnaeus, 1758)	European flounder	Michigan, Ohio, Ontario

[a]E. J. Crossman (Royal Ontario Museum, personal communication, 1990).
[b]Zuckerman and Behnke (1986).
[c]Includes mostly "black mollies" from the aquarium fish trade.
[d](?) = unverified report or questionable identification.

TABLE 3.—Extirpated populations of exotic species formerly established in the continental United States and Canada (after Courtenay et al. 1986).

SCIENTIFIC NAME	COMMON NAME	FORMER OCCURRENCE
Characidae—characins		
Hoplias malabaricus (Bloch, 1794)	trahira	Florida
Serrasalmus humeralis Valenciennes, 1849	pirambeba	Florida
Adrianichthyidae—ricefishes		
Oryzias latipes (Temminck & Schlegel, 1846)	Japanese medaka	California, New York
Aplocheilidae—rivulins		
Cynolebias bellottii Steindachner, 1881	Argentine pearlfish	California
Cichlidae—cichlids		
Aequidens pulcher (Gill, 1858)	blue acara	Florida
Cichlasoma beani (Jordan, 1889)	green guapote	California
Cichlasoma salvini (Günther, 1862)	yellowbelly cichlid	Florida
Cichlasoma trimaculatum (Günther, 1868)	threespot cichlid	Florida
Heros severus Heckel, 1840	banded cichlid	Nevada
Anabantidae—gouramies		
Anabas testudineus (Bloch, 1795)	climbing perch	Florida
Betta splendens Regan, 1909	Siamese fightingfish	Florida
Ctenopoma nigropannosum Reichenow, 1875	twospot ctenopoma	Florida
Macropodus opercularis (Linnaeus, 1758)	paradisefish	Florida

TABLE 4.—Exotic fishes established in Hawaiian fresh (F) and marine (M) waters.

SCIENTIFIC NAME	COMMON NAME	OCCURRENCE
Clupeidae—herrings		
Herklotsichthys quadrimaculatus (Rüppell, 1837)	goldspot herring	M
Sardinella marquesensis Berry & Whitehead, 1968	Marquesan sardine	M
Cyprinidae—carps and minnows		
Carassius auratus (Linnaeus, 1758)	goldfish	F
Cyprinus carpio Linnaeus, 1758	common carp	F
Puntius semifasciolatus (Günther, 1868)	green barb	F
Cobitidae—loaches		
Misgurnus anguillicaudatus (Cantor, 1842)	oriental weatherfish	F
Clariidae—labyrinth catfishes		
Clarias fuscus (Lacepède, 1803)	whitespotted clarias	F

TABLE 4.—Continued.

SCIENTIFIC NAME	COMMON NAME	OCCURRENCE
Loricariidae—suckermouth catfishes		
Ancistrus sp.		F
Pterygoplichthys multiradiatus (Hancock, 1828)	sailfin catfish	F
Belonidae—needlefishes		
Strongylura krefftii (Günther, 1866)	long tom	F-M
Poeciliidae—livebearers		
Poecilia mexicana Steindachner, 1863	shortfin molly	F
Poecilia reticulata Peters, 1859	guppy	F
Poecilia vittata Guichenot, 1853	Cuban limia	F
Xiphophorus helleri Heckel, 1848	green swordtail	F
Xiphophorus maculatus (Günther, 1866)	southern platyfish	F
Xiphophorus variatus (Meek, 1904)	variable platyfish	F
Synbranchidae—swamp eels		
Monopterus albus (Zuiew, 1793)	swamp eel	F
Serranidae—sea basses		
Epinephelus argus (Schneider, 1801)	bluespotted grouper	M
Lutjanidae—snappers		
Lutjanus fulvus (Schneider, 1801)	blacktail snapper	M
Lutjanus kasmira (Forsskål, 1775)	bluestriped snapper	M
Cichlidae—cichlids		
Astronotus ocellatus (Agassiz, 1831)	oscar	F
Cichla ocellaris Bloch & Schneider, 1801	peacock cichlid	F
Cichlasoma meeki (Brind, 1918)	firemouth cichlid	F
Cichlasoma nigrofasciatum (Günther, 1867)	convict cichlid	F
Cichlasoma spilurum (Günther, 1862)	blue-eye cichlid	F
Pelvicachromis pulcher (Boulenger, 1901)	rainbow krib	F
Tilapia macrochir Boulenger, 1912	longfin tilapia	F
Tilapia melanotheron (Rüppell, 1852)	blackchin tilapia	F-M
Tilapia mossambica (Peters, 1852)	Mozambique tilapia	F
Tilapia rendalli (Boulenger, 1896)	redbreast tilapia	F
Tilapia zilli (Gervais, 1848)	redbelly tilapia	F
Mugilidae—mullets		
Valamugil engeli (Bleeker, 1858)	kanda	M
Channidae—snakeheads		
Channa striata (Bloch, 1793)	chevron snakehead	F

Appendix 3
Names Applied to Hybrid Fishes

Many fish species hybridize in nature and others have been crossed in the laboratory or in fish hatcheries. Scientists routinely refer to hybrids by the names of both parental species, as for example, *Luxilus cornutus* (formerly *Notropis cornutus*) × *Notropis rubellus*, a fairly commonly occurring natural cyprinid hybrid. This hybrid combination when first collected was not recognized as such and was described as a new species, *Notropis macdonaldi* Jordan and Jenkins, 1888. Scientific names based on hybrids have no nomenclatural validity under Article 23(h) of the International Code of Zoological Nomenclature, 3rd ed., 1985, and *Notropis macdonaldi* is, therefore, an unavailable name.

Hybrid fishes generally are not given common names. In a few instances, hybrids have been recognized and named by anglers, and several are listed in the "Tables of World Record Fishes" prepared by the International Game Fish Association. Others have become imporant in fish management or are marketed from aquaculture fisheries and have been accorded common names. The U.S. Food and Drug Administration has required specific labeling of such cultured fishes being sold in consumer markets.

In the table below, we list the parental species (arranged by family) and common name applied to the hybrid fish for those that are established in fishery literature.

PARENTAL SPECIES	COMMON NAME
Salmonidae—trouts	
Salmo trutta × *Salvelinus fontinalis*	tiger trout
Salvelinus fontinalis × *S. namaycush*	splake
Esocidae—pikes	
Esox lucius × *E. masquinongy*	tiger muskellunge
Percichthyidae[a]—temperate basses	
Morone americana ♂ × *M. saxatilis* ♀	Virginia bass
Morone americana ♀ × *M. saxatilis* ♂	Maryland bass
Morone chrysops ♀ × *M. saxatilis* ♂	sunshine bass
Morone chrysops ♂ × *M. saxatilis* ♀	palmetto bass
Morone mississippiensis ♂ × *M. saxatilis* ♀	paradise bass
Centrarchidae—sunfishes	
Lepomis macrochirus × *Micropterus salmoides*	blue bass
Cichlidae—cichlids	
Tilapia mossambica × *T. urolepis*	red tilapia
Pleuronectidae—righteye flounders	
Platichthys stellatus × *Pleuronectes vetulus*	forkline sole

[a]The common names of these crosses between species of *Morone* have been approved by the Striped Bass Committee of the Southern Division of the American Fisheries Society in response to requests from the U.S. Food and Drug Administration. Although various authors give the male or the female first when parental sexes are known, we follow the systematists' practice of listing parental species alphabetically.

Appendix 4
Important References for Determining Publication Dates of Certain Works on Fishes

It is difficult to determine the actual dates on which some early taxonomic publications were issued. Commonly, individual titles in a multititle work were printed and distributed prior to issue of the entire volume, or a volume for a given year was not issued until a later date; thus the attributed date on a title page may be in error. Search for proper dates to ascribe to fish names used in this work has been tedious, often frustrating, and has led to results that sometimes are at variance with customary citations. External sources of information on actual dates of publication exist for certain journal series, authors, or major serial works. Those known to us and used as we assembled this list include the following.

Academy of Natural Sciences of Philadelphia. Edward J. Nolan, 1913, "An Index to the Scientific Contents of the Journal and Proceedings of the Academy of Natural Sciences of Philadelphia, 1812–1912," published in commemoration of the Centenary of the Academy, March 21, 1912, by the Academy. This bulky tome (1,419 pp.) includes publication dates for many works appearing in the *Journal* and the *Proceedings*. Although actual issue dates are not available for many early publications, acknowledged dates of receipt are provided; these are often helpful, though they lag behind true dates of issue.

Cuvier, Georges. 1816 [1817]. "Le Règne Animal Distribue d'après son Organisation . . .," Deterville, Paris, volume 2, 532 pp. This classic work is customarily cited as 1817, but we follow C. Roux, 1976, J. Soc. Bibliogr. Nat. Hist. 8(1):31, who determined that it appeared in November 1816, or perhaps earlier.

Cuvier, G., and A. Valenciennes. 1828–1850. "Histoire Naturelle des Poissons," regular and Strasbourg editions (different pagination). The 22 volumes were written partly by Cuvier and partly by Valenciennes. New names are to be attributed to Cuvier *in* Cuvier and Valenciennes, or, as the case may be, to Valenciennes *in* Cuvier and Valenciennes according to particulars set out in tables published in "Official Lists and Indexes of Names and Works in Zoology," International Commission on Zoological Nomenclature, 1987, p. 314. The pagination, authorship, and dates of publication are there set forth. In four volumes (8, 14, 19, 22), the date on the title page is one year earlier than the actual publication date, as determined from C. D. Sherborn, 1925, Ann. Mag. Nat. Hist. (9) 15:600.

Girard, Charles. "Researches upon the Cyprinoid Fishes Inhabiting the Fresh Waters of the United States of America, West of the Mississippi Valley . . .," Proc. Acad. Nat. Sci. Phila., 1856 (1857), 8(5):165–213. One hundred thirty-four nominal species of cyprinoid fishes were originally described in this paper. Its publication usually is cited as 1856, but some authors cite it as 1857 because of the acknowledged date, April 25, 1857, *in* E. J. Nolan, 1913, xi (see Acad. Nat. Sci. Phila., above). Volume 8 was issued in 1857, but part 5 (pp. 161–258) was distributed on or before December 27, 1856, as shown by R. M. Bailey and R. D. Suttkus (in preparation). Furthermore, a preprint of Girard's article, with different pagination (1–49, with supplementary pages 51–54) and slightly changed title, was published in September 1856.

Günther, A. 1859–1870. "Catalogue of the Fishes in the British Museum." Each of the eight volumes was published in the year indicated on its title page. Precise dates of issue may be found in the minutes of meetings of the Trustees of the British Museum.

Jenyns, Leonard. 1842. The "Zoology of the 'Beagle,' " was published in five parts from 1839 to 1843, of which Part 4, Pisces, appeared in 1842. Confusion on the dating of some included taxa stems from a note by C. D. Sherborn, 1897, Ann. Mag. Nat. Hist., series 6, 20:483. Sherborn listed 19 parts (not equivalent to the five parts mentioned above), of which numbers 12 (January 1840), 14 (June 1840), 16 (April 1841), and 17 (April 1842) treated Pisces. Some workers have adopted these as publication dates. However, Sherborn obtained his information from the printing firm, more than 50 years later. There is no claim that the 19 "parts" were issued separately, and we can find no evidence for their existence. Rather, they appear to represent a shop production schedule. The pagination of the 19 "parts" is mostly in multiples of 16 page signatures, and some parts end in mid-sentence. The introduction to the Pisces part was dated January 8, 1842, and precedes all of the text and plates as issued. It is apparent that Sherborn and his followers have accepted the production schedule uncritically as dates of publication.

Jordan, D. S. Publication dates of his numerous works are given in "David Starr Jordan, a Bibliography of His Writings, 1871–1931," by Alice N. Hays, 1952, Stanford University Publications, University Series, Library Studies, volume 1.

Lacepède, B. "Histoire Naturelle des Poissons," Paris. According to C. Roux, 1973, Bull. Liaison Mus. Hist. Nat. 14:33–35, the five text volumes were published as follows: volume 1, 1798; volume 2, 20 July 1800; volume 3, 16 October 1801 (not 1802 as sometimes cited); volume 4, 6 April 1802; volume 5, 11 July 1803.

Pallas, P. S. "Zoographica Rosso-asiatica." Under Opinion 212 of the International Commission on Zoological Nomenclature, the dates to be assigned to new names published in the three volumes are the following: volumes 1 and 2, 1811; volume 3, 1814.

Poey, Felipe. The prolific Cuban ichthyologist published extensively on Cuban and other West Indian fishes in the period 1851–1883. Some of his works were serialized, making determination of proper dates of issue of individual fascicles difficult. We have relied chiefly on Luis Howell Rivero's compilation, "Bibliografia de los Trabajos sobre Peces Publicados por Felipe Poey," 1936, Mem. Soc. Cubana Hist. Nat. 10(1):43–50, to establish dates.

Proceedings of the Zoological Society of London. The publication by F. Martin Duncan, "On the Dates of Publication of the Society's 'Proceedings,' 1859–1926," 1937, Proc. Zool. Soc. Lond. 107 (part 1, series A):71–84, is most helpful. In addition to giving particulars on publications as listed in the title, this work includes dates of issue for the 'Proceedings,' 1830–1859, compiled earlier by F. H. Waterhouse, and for the 'Transactions' of the Society, 1833–1869, compiled by H. Peavot.

United States National Museum. "A List and Index of the Publications of the United States National Museum (1875–1946)," 1947, U.S. Nat. Mus. Bull. 193, has proved indispensable to the determination of issue dates for papers in the bulletins and proceedings of the museum.

PART III

Index

B

D

F

H

I

L

M

N

P

Q

R

S

T

W